Narrative of a Voyage to New Zealand

Performed in the Years 1814 and 1815, in Company with the Rev. Samuel Marsden

VOLUME 2

JOHN LIDDIARD NICHOLAS

CAMBRIDGE
UNIVERSITY PRESS

CAMBRIDGE UNIVERSITY PRESS

Cambridge, New York, Melbourne, Madrid, Cape Town, Singapore,
São Paolo, Delhi, Dubai, Tokyo

Published in the United States of America by Cambridge University Press, New York

www.cambridge.org
Information on this title: www.cambridge.org/9781108008358

© in this compilation Cambridge University Press 2009

This edition first published 1817
This digitally printed version 2009

ISBN 978-1-108-00835-8 Paperback

CAMBRIDGE LIBRARY COLLECTION
Books of enduring scholarly value

Religion

For centuries, scripture and theology were the focus of prodigious amounts of scholarship and publishing, dominated in the English-speaking world by the work of Protestant Christians. Enlightenment philosophy and science, anthropology, ethnology and the colonial experience all brought new perspectives, lively debates and heated controversies to the study of religion and its role in the world, many of which continue to this day. This series explores the editing and interpretation of religious texts, the history of religious ideas and institutions, and not least the encounter between religion and science.

Narrative of a Voyage to New Zealand

John Liddiard Nicholas (1784-1868), a London iron-founder, arrived in New South Wales in 1813 but rather than develop his business, he accompanied Samuel Marsden on a journey to New Zealand from November 1814 to March 1815 that established the first Christian mission to the Maoris. This two-volume book, first published in 1817 after Nicholas had returned to England, was widely successful, and was translated into Dutch and German in 1819. Based on Nicholas's journal, kept throughout his voyage, it tells the story of the missionaries' efforts but focuses particularly on Nicholas's observations of the Maoris and reflects his desire to share knowledge of a 'people so little known to Europeans, and at the same time so … interesting'. Nicholas pays careful attention to the customs, personalities, and relationships unique to different communities. Volume 2 includes the memoir of a Maori chief, and a Maori vocabulary.

Cambridge University Press has long been a pioneer in the reissuing of out-of-print titles from its own backlist, producing digital reprints of books that are still sought after by scholars and students but could not be reprinted economically using traditional technology. The Cambridge Library Collection extends this activity to a wider range of books which are still of importance to researchers and professionals, either for the source material they contain, or as landmarks in the history of their academic discipline.

Drawing from the world-renowned collections in the Cambridge University Library, and guided by the advice of experts in each subject area, Cambridge University Press is using state-of-the-art scanning machines in its own Printing House to capture the content of each book selected for inclusion. The files are processed to give a consistently clear, crisp image, and the books finished to the high quality standard for which the Press is recognised around the world. The latest print-on-demand technology ensures that the books will remain available indefinitely, and that orders for single or multiple copies can quickly be supplied.

The Cambridge Library Collection will bring back to life books of enduring scholarly value (including out-of-copyright works originally issued by other publishers) across a wide range of disciplines in the humanities and social sciences and in science and technology.

Publisbed Sept. 1. 1817. by James Black & Son Tavistock Street Covent Garden London.

Neele sculp.

North Cape of New Zealand.

NARRATIVE

OF A

VOYAGE

TO

NEW ZEALAND,

Performed in the Years 1814 and 1815,

IN COMPANY WITH THE REV. SAMUEL MARSDEN,

Principal Chaplain of New South Wales.

BY

JOHN LIDDIARD NICHOLAS, ESQ.

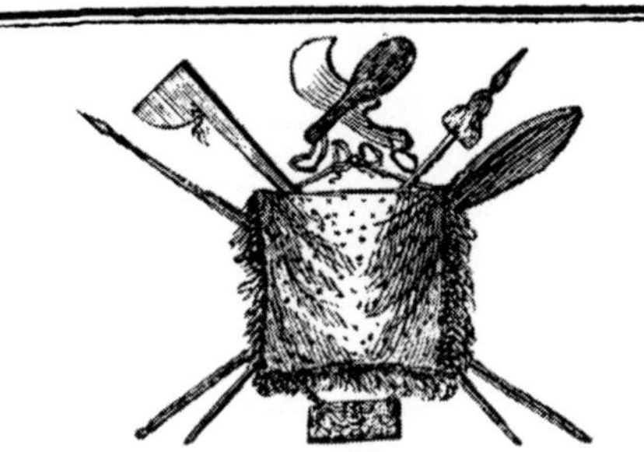

—— utilitati consulens hominum et ei quam sæpe commemoro, humanæ societati.
Cicero de Offic. lib. iii. cap. 5.

IN TWO VOLUMES.

VOL. II.

London:

PRINTED FOR JAMES BLACK AND SON,

TAVISTOCK-STREET, COVENT-GARDEN.

M.DCCC.XVII.

CONTENTS

OF

THE SECOND VOLUME.

CHAP. I.

CHAP. IV.

CHAP. V.

CHAP. VI.

CHAP. VII.

Duaterra still lingers under his illness—Affecting situation of his head wife and the rest of his family

Supplementary Observations.

CHAP. VIII.

CHAP. IX.

CHAP. X.

APPENDIX.

NARRATIVE

OF A

VOYAGE TO NEW ZEALAND.

CHAP. I.

Visit made to the chief of Bream Head—Friendly behaviou
of the natives there—The Author and Mr. Marsden introduced by Moyhanger to the superior chief—Their
friendly reception—Kookoopa, an inferior chief—His
military fame—Further particulars of Moyhanger—Curiosity excited among the natives—Provisions supplied by
the chief—Departure from Bream Head—Danger while
leaving the harbour—Return to the vessel—Arrival of
canoes from the shore—Curious rock near Cape Brett—
Return to Rangehoo—Visit to the Missionaries—Progress made at the settlement—Divine service performed
on shore—Absence of Duaterra with most of the natives
on this occasion, and the reason of it—Formidable demonstrations of approaching hostility between two parties
of the natives—Conference between Duaterra and another chief, and the subject of it—Hostile appearances
removed—The parties in amity with each other—Excursion to procure fish—Parro, the residence of Korra-korra,
visited—His head wife—Character of his people—A fishing party, and their proceedings—The Author and Mr.
Marsden sleep at Parro—Alarmed suddenly in the night
—The cause of it groundless—Tui disgusted with the
state of New Zealand.

Had the wind continued fair, it was our
intention to have proceeded directly to the

Bay of Islands, without depending upon any casual supply of provisions that we might meet with along the coast; but as it blew against us the whole way, and had settled in a contrary direction for some days, while our warriors complained that their stock of fern-root could not possibly last much longer, Mr. Marsden and myself got into the boat about six o'clock in the evening; and though the ship was lying seven or eight miles from the shore, we were determined to land, and get from Moyhanger and his friends whatever could be obtained. The New Zealanders are a people who of all others are the least capable of bearing hunger with patience; and though they will readily submit to other privations, the denial of food, even in a partial degree, discomposes them so much, that they can do nothing until their cravings are satisfied; and should this be rendered impracticable at the time, they never cease to murmur with turbulent impatience. We took a party of them with us in the boat, headed by Korra-korra, who assumed on the occasion a great share of importance, displaying with various ludicrous airs, his characteristic vanity; and after paddling with much exertion, reached the shore about half-past seven.

On our way, we passed some curious-shaped rocks that projected some distance from the land, and had a very singular appearance. The natives perceiving our approach, came out in two canoes to meet us; and Moyhanger, who was in one of them, seemed highly pleased that we had come according to promise; and as there was a heavy surf beating upon the shore, he directed us with much solicitous attention to the part where we could best effect a landing. Here we had scarcely left the boat, when the friendly people of the district came down in crowds to welcome us; and thronging round us with kind but officious civility, were anxious to shew us, by all the manifestations they could display, that we had made them happy by our visit. Moyhanger, putting our arms under his, which he said was " *Europee* fashion," and others linking theirs in the same manner, we proceeded in a line from the beach; and both my friend and myself were highly gratified at the social good-humour and jovial vivacity of our new companions. We had about a mile to walk before we could get to the residence of the chief; and this, though an inconsiderable distance, was rendered both tedious and disagreeable, from

the continued obstructions it offered : being
obliged to climb over rocks that were almost
impervious, and in one place, to cross a small
channel that nearly encompassed the spot
where the village was built. When we had
crossed this channel, and were entering the
little capital, the ladies, always attentive to
the friendly signal, held up their *kackahows*,
and waving them in the air, shouted forth
their salutation according to custom.

Moyhanger now introduced us to the
superior chief Kiwacha, who was sitting on
the ground as we approached him ; and receiving us with a peculiar degree of amenity
and composure, he ordered a clean mat to be
spread for us, and desired us to sit down ;
which we did, with Moyhanger beside us,
who acted as interpreter. As soon as we
were seated, Mr. Marsden explained our
wants to the chief, making him, at the same
time, a present of three tokees, which he
accepted with the same pleasure as the rest
of his countrymen ; and looking at them for
some moments with heartfelt satisfaction, he
seemed impressed with a sense of obligation
for a favour so unexpected. He informed us
that he had plenty of pigs, but that they were
running wild in the woods ; that, however, he

would send his people the following day to catch as many as would supply the vessel, if she remained off the coast; and that we might take any other provisions his district afforded. Of this offer, which was both generous and friendly, we resolved to avail ourselves, if circumstances should permit; and told him, that if the wind did not prove favourable to our getting round to the Bay of Islands, we would hoist our colours and stand in for the shore. This chief was a man very far advanced in years; and the strong lines of his countenance, which bespoke both reflection and gravity, no less than his venerable age, secured to him the reverence of his people, who paid the most submissive regard to his commands, and from strangers claimed the tribute of attention and respect.

Besides the superior chief, we saw a subordinate one, the man whom Moyhanger had accompanied on board in the morning; and whom he described as the commander-in-chief, or fighting man, as he expressed it, of Kiwacha. The name of this chief was Kookoopa, so called from a bird of that name which is very common in New Zealand, and somewhat larger than our pigeon, but of the same species. This man, according to the accounts of our warriors, had repeatedly signalized himself in several desperate actions with the surrounding tribes, and was considered one of the bravest combatants in the island; so that Kiwacha had made a judicious choice of a military commander, his prowess having spread terror through all the parts adjacent, while it secured the district of his superior chief from predatory incursions. Poor Moyhanger was extremely loquacious the whole time, talking with an astonishing volubility, and wishing to engross the whole conversation to himself; but he had nearly forgotten his English, though he did not relax in his attempts to express himself in that language; and jabbering away at random, it was with much difficulty we could comprehend any part of what he said. He attached himself a good deal to me, but in many instances I could have well dispensed with this predilection, for he annoyed me exceedingly with his continual importunities; asking me for every thing he saw in my possession, though I had nothing about me that I could part with but a few nails, which far from satisfying, only served to increase his cupidity. Having changed his mind since he was on board in the morning, he now expressed a desire to go to England again; but I did not encourage this inclination, well knowing that he would be happier in his own country than in any other part of the world, and that he would very soon wish to return to it. He asked after Governor Bligh and General Foveaux, and remembered the Duke of York and Lord Fitzwilliam. We desired him to collect all the flax he could procure, and take it to the Bay of Islands, where the missionaries would always purchase it of him; and this he promised to do, appearing well pleased with the proposal. I again mentioned the name of Mr. Savage to him, but he evinced the same indifference as before; and I knew not whether to ascribe it to insensibility or ingratitude, but the former I should think the most likely.

When we had been here about an hour, we heard the report of the ship's guns, which we had requested the master to fire, the moment a fair breeze should spring up; and we now became very anxious to return on board. But in this desire we could not be speedily indulged; for our party having brought the boat up the channel, there was not sufficient water to float her until the return of the tide, for which we were obliged to wait upwards of three hours. When this time had elapsed it was quite dark ; and the natives being dispersed in groups, sitting round their fires, I was invited by one, and then by another to take my seat among them ; and each group wished to get me within their own circle, while they all appeared very social, though detached from each other. In order to divide my company among them while I remained, I visited them all round alternately ; and derived no small share of amusement from the curiosity which my presence excited through the whole assemblage. As I went up to each separate party, they would instantly place me in the middle of the circle, and examine with minute attention my great coat, my hat, my boots, and, in short, every article of raiment about me ; and the indications of their surprise were as diverting as they were singular. One old man brought me for a wife a girl about twelve years of age, and whom I supposed to be his daughter : presenting her to me with many commendations, and urging the alliance in a copious strain of native oratory. But I, however, thought proper to decline it, notwithstanding all the advantages so eloquently promised, telling him as an excuse that I was *tabooed*, while he replied, in a tone of disappointment, *ittee ittee taboo taboo;** but upon my gravely assuring him that I was *nuee nuee taboo taboo,*† he desisted from pressing me any further. Wherever I mixed among them, I always found the strongest proofs of their friendliness and hospitality; they all presented me with something to eat, and no where did I meet with any thing like selfishness in this respect. Kiwacha himself offered us some pork, which we did not hesitate to accept; and our party had five baskets of dried fish, together with a quantity of fern-root given to them: so that we were secure against their impatient growlings, till we reached the Bay of Islands.

The tide at length affording us sufficient depth of water, we took our leave of Kiwacha and his friendly people; resolving to stand out on our course on getting to the vessel, without waiting for the pigs which were promised to us the ensuing day: as the supply we had received was quite enough to last us till we returned to Rangehoo. Getting, therefore, into the boat, we were proceeding to the ship with all the expedition we could

* Very little tabooed. † Very much tabooed,

make, when we found the opening of this channel into the sea so very dangerous, that had we been previously aware of it, we would by no means have suffered the boat to have been brought into it; but would have gone to some other part of the coast, where we might have put off with safety, and not been subject to the alarming apprehensions we now experienced. The channel, which was very narrow, was formed by two ledges of sharp-pointed rocks, which confined it on each side; and between which the surf rushed with incredible violence, while the danger was still more imminent, from some rocks that were concealed : and had not the natives come down to shew us where these lay scattered about in different parts, the boat must inevitably have been swamped. But it was the admirable coolness and address of Korra-korra in avoiding these rocks when they were pointed out, and in directing his men when to exert all their strength, and when to proceed at a slow rate, that served particularly to rescue us from our critical situation; and he it was to whom the safety of the boat, and very probably of our lives, might be mainly attributed. Before we had been yet relieved from our fears, Mr. Marsden and myself expecting every moment that the boat would be either upset or dashed to pieces against the rocks, prepared for the worst that could happen; and took off our coats, that they might not encumber us, in case we should have occasion to swim; for which, however, there was happily no necessity, as we escaped the danger, and reached the ship about one o'clock in the morning.

Upon getting on board, we found that all those we had left behind us had entertained very serious alarms for our safety; for, not knowing the cause of our delay, they imagined that we had fallen victims to the treachery of the natives, when our presence removed their anxiety, and made them think better of these poor people. Duaterra gave us the European salute of a hearty shake of the hand as soon as we got upon deck, and told us very plainly, that he had concluded his countrymen had killed every one of us, and made a meal of our bodies; but the honest natives we had visited never contemplated so atrocious a deed, and our safe return did justice to their good faith. Our party now distributed the baskets of dried fish and the fern-root they had brought off with them among their friends on board, reserving an ample supply for themselves ; and the master of the vessel getting her under weigh, we shaped our course once more for the district of Duaterra.

While running down the coast with a favourable wind, on the morning of the 21st, we had six canoes alongside; the people in which offered for sale their flax and fishing-lines, and were very anxious to meet with customers. Duaterra and his party having still by them a store of old iron and fish-hooks which they had not disposed of at the River Thames, purchased all the fishing-lines; but for the flax they shewed no desire to bargain, preferring the manufactured article to the raw material, on which they set comparatively very little value. Since our departure from the river above-mentioned, our warriors discontinued their alarming salutes to the canoes that approached us ; and with this we were very well pleased, as it relieved our ears from the torment of listening to their horrible vociferations. The reason of their omitting this furious exhibition was, because they considered that the motive they had first assigned for it, that of terrifying the hostile tribes, was now superseded by our return.

At noon we passed Cape Brett, sailing between the main and a large rock that runs out about a quarter of a mile from it. This rock is a natural curiosity. Rising to a considerable height, it has upon its summit three peaked rocks of a singularly grotesque appearance; and in its centre a perforated arch similar to the one I have described before, and which the imagination might take for the portal of some old castle: while to our eyes the effect was rendered doubly picturesque, by two canoes that we could discern through the arch, with the natives in them, arrayed in the rude apparel of their country, and fishing on the opposite side. To this part of the coast the natives repair in great numbers during the fishing season, to lay in their winter's stock; and their industry is always sure to be requited, for the quantity of fish to be found here is incredible, and would, in the event of the island being colonized, form a most valuable branch of commerce. Our warriors got some fish on board that was dried the season before; but it was filled with maggots, which, though it rendered it disgusting to our palates, was probably rather a recommendation than otherwise with these unsophisticated natives, who on that account partook of it with a more exquisite relish; just as our epicures prefer cheese in the same state to that which is not corrupted. The taste of this fish was not unpleasant, and I could have liked it very well, had it not been for the maggots. When we had got round the point, the canoes came alongside, bringing us an abundant supply, consisting of various descriptions of fish ; among which were snappers, bream, parrot-fish, benecootoos, and some excellent cray-fish.

Continuing our course to the Bay of Islands, without visiting any other part of the coast, we came at four **A. M.** to our former anchorage off Rangehoo; where we could observe Duaterra's colours flying on the top of his *hippah;* and anxious to know how our friends the missionaries had fared in our absence, we lost no time in paying them a visit. Upon going on shore, they welcomed our return with the most lively satisfaction, and informed us that nothing particular had occurred while we were away: they seemed, with their families, in as good health and spirits as when we had left them ; and were all actively employed in making their building secure and comfortable. The sawyers were busy in cutting timber, and the smith had be-gun to work in the forge which Mr. Hall had erected by this time, as also an additional room to his own dwelling; and we were no less pleased than surprised at the progress made at the settlement during the short time we were absent from it. Mr. Hall had got two of the natives in his employ, whom he described as tractable and intelligent, executing his orders with the most attentive promptitude, and readily apprehending them when given: he also said that they were unremitting in their attention, and extremely honest, never stealing a single article from the premises. I saw them at their work, and they appeared both cheerful and diligent; they were employed in grinding some wheat at a steel mill which he had put up, and the remuneration he made them for their labour was their regular meals, as much as they could eat, which was no inconsiderable quantity, and a fish-hook on their return home every evening; with which they were perfectly satisfied. Mr. Kendall had already got two scholars under his care, both fine boys, quick and docile, and who promised in some time to make great improvement. He applied himself to the instruction of these, with a zealous ardour that plainly shewed he was not influenced by mercenary motives in engaging himself for the situation he held.

The twenty-second being the Sabbath, Mr. Marsden performed divine service in the morning, under the shade of a fine spreading tree close to the sea-shore, when we all were present; but, contrary to their usual custom, there were comparatively but very few of the natives in attendance. It surprised us very much that Duaterra, whom we had never before found remiss on these solemn occasions, and who always punctually made his appearance, together with his people, since our arrival at the island, was now absent; and we could not surmise what could have been the cause of it. Korra-korra and Shunghi attended as usual, and behaved with their wonted propriety; but the chief whose presence was more particularly expected, was still missing, nor did he shew himself during the service. However, it was not very long before we ascertained the cause of this chief's absence; for while we were at dinner at Mr. Hall's, we heard a great deal of confusion and tumult among the natives, some of them shouting out with their usual clamour, and others running about the place in a state of the wildest disorder, while a party of them

rushing in to us, informed us there was a
" *nuee nuee fight*," and seemed surprised that
we had not been aware of it before. We
received this information with indifference,
imagining they were only going to amuse
themselves with a sham-fight, which having
witnessed already, our curiosity was satisfied; but others running in and telling us
that several preparations were made which
to us appeared of a formidable nature, and
that a great many men - were coming in
canoes from distant parts of the island, we
became suddenly alarmed lest some of the
hostile tribes had come to make an attack
upon us, in which case the issue might be
doubtful; for though the people here should
do all in their power to protect us, still it was
probable they might be overpowered by superior numbers. We were now in a state of
anxious suspense, not knowing what might
be the event of the contest which we had
reason to suppose was fast approaching; when
going out together, we saw several of the natives running about in different directions, and
exhibiting all the preludes of ferocious hostility. Duaterra and Shunghi we observed
coming down a hill that overlooked some
part of the harbour; and on their coming

up to us we were told by the former, that a great body of people were advancing from the North Cape, and would soon arrive; but with their intentions he was not yet acquainted, nor could he tell for what object they had set out, whether hostile or otherwise. Unwilling to depart without knowing the issue of this affair, we resolved to remain as long as we could with safety before we retired to the ship; and having every thing in readiness for our escape upon any emergency, we waited the meeting of the two parties. Duaterra's warriors having all assembled, *

---

* The chiefs may command the services of their respective tribes at any time they think proper, when they assemble equipped and prepared, without ever questioning for what object they are called together; evincing the most zealous attachment to their rulers, and ready either to be led by them to scenes of blood and ruthless carnage, or to execute for them upon all occasions the gentler offices of peaceful life. It may be here proper to notice that a census, or rather a muster of the whole adult male population, is made at stated periods of the year, when the *rungateedas,* who are all treated with the greatest respect, assist in numbering off the *cookees,* in the same manner as a serjeant does the soldiers of his company. Mr. Marsden, who, among other particulars, received an accurate account of this regulation from Duaterra, thus describes it, in a letter to a friend. "The chiefs muster all their men at particular times of the year. The great muster is taken after the potatoe harvest. The ground from which the potatoes have been lately dug is cleared of the stones and weeds, and

by this time were drawn out round their chief in military array ; and they certainly appeared a formidable band, being all armed with their spears and *pattoo pattoos*, and dressed in their war-mats. Each of these warriors had his hair bound up in the usual manner upon the crown of the head, with the gannet's feathers stuck in it; and his body besmeared with oil and red ochre. Duaterra himself was in his native dress, and painted like the rest of his countrymen ; brandishing a large bill-hook in his right hand, and carrying a spear in his left. Upon second consideration, Mr. Marsden now deemed it most advisable for us to get to the ship as soon as possible, and put the master on his guard against any attack ; conceiving it better that we should be distant spectators from the vessel, than to take a nearer view by remaining

all levelled; upon this ground they all assemble, men, women and children. The men are all drawn up like a regiment or army, and stand in ranks five, six, or seven deep, according to the will of the chief. Then one of the head officers or *runga-teedas* begins to muster them, not by calling over the names, but by passing in front of the ranks, and telling their number. At the head of every hundred men he places a *rungateeda*, and continues in this manner to number the whole, leaving a *rungateeda* with each hundred men : thus ten *rungateedas* answer for a thousand men ; the women and children are never mustered."

on shore, which he thought upon reflection would be much too hazardous at such a conjuncture. We had scarcely got on board, when we observed three large canoes full of people standing in for the shore; and upon inquiring of Tui, who attended us to the ship, if he thought they had come with a hostile intention, he replied in the negative; and said they were his brother's people from the Cavalles, and consequently friends. Our apprehensions being removed by this information, which was very agreeable to us, we hastened back again to observe the meeting between the parties, as we were curious to learn the business of the conference, and what could be the meaning of the formidable demonstrations we beheld on both sides, when neither party meditated an attack.

When the canoes got close enough to the shore for the people in them to land, Duaterra and all his warriors starting up with horrid yells from the place where they were sitting, ran along the shore, making furious gesticulations; and presenting their spears and muskets at the approaching party, as if to intimidate them from landing. In the midst of this tumultuous assemblage I observed the queen, who raved about with as much violent uproar as the wildest of them; carrying in her hand the large horse-pistol that she had in the sham-fight, and having her husband's sword-belt slung over her shoulders. They next danced to the war song, and then sat themselves down opposite to the canoes, apparently exhausted from excessive turbulence, and regarding their seeming opponents with fixed attention: while these were now resting on their paddles, and both parties continued looking at each other, without speaking a word, for at least a quarter of an hour. At length an old chief in one of the canoes was the first to break silence, and rising up with an air of consequential gravity, entered into conversation with some of his people; he then addressed himself to Duaterra, and they talked together for some time, while all the others listened with respectful attention. The subject of their conference was now explained to us. It appeared that some hostile tribes from the North Cape had cut off thirty of the people belonging to Duaterra, in a district near Doubtless Bay, of which he was the owner; and his friend now came to him with an account of the transaction, and to urge him to a prompt retaliation. This was the business that had brought these people; and Duaterra, as soon as he was acquainted with it, invited them all to land, which they did in a very short time, hauling up their canoes upon the beach, out of the reach of the tide.

All symptoms of hostility had now completely vanished, and the cooks being set to work, made fires in different places to dress their provisions; while the party dividing themselves into separate groups, awaited their *kiki* with voracious impatience. Some of these people we had seen before, when we were at the Cavalles; and the whole was, perhaps, as motley a party as could any where be met with. They consisted of men, women and children, who had all something distinctively uncouth and grotesque about them; they were attended by cats and dogs, and had brought with them besides a large stock of fish and fern-root. Korra-korra recognized among the women a relation, with whom he *nosed* very affectionately, and they wept over each other in the usual manner. I observed in one of the canoes a very singular fish, which the natives call *cokiddie*, or the spear-fish. It was about the size of a perch, and shaped very like it, except the head, which was rather oblong, like that of a pig; its skin was quite rough, and behind its head nature had armed it with a sharp bone, about two inches long, which it could extrude and draw in at pleasure. It was from this bone that the natives gave it the name of cokiddie, which signifies *spear* in their language, and therefore appropriate enough. Duaterra was so much engrossed with his new guests, that he gave us very little of his company the whole day; and seemed entirely occupied with the accounts he had received from the chief, nor did we intrude upon him to divide his attention.

As the expenses of the vessel were very heavy, Mr. Marsden conceived it would be a judicious plan to have recourse to such productions as the island afforded, for the means of defraying part of them; and as the fisheries here appeared a valuable source of profit, he resolved to take back with him to the colony as much fish as he could procure; where it would be certain to find a ready market. For this purpose he determined to go to Korra-korra's residence, which, being close to Cape Brett, an excellent fishery, was the most eligible place he could select in the Bay of Islands. We therefore took with us such articles to barter with the natives, as were most likely to attract their attention, and make them anxious to supply us; and got into Korra-korra's canoe, accompanied by five others, in which there were not less than fifty of the inhabitants. We also took with us two casks, one filled with salt, for the purpose of curing the fish, and the other empty, to put it in when salted.

The day, which was January 23d, was uncommonly fine; and a fresh breeze rising just as we were setting off, and the canoes hoisting their sails, the appearance of our little expedition was singularly curious. Our party exerting themselves at the paddle with their usual perseverance, we reached the place of our destination in about two hours and a half; the distance from Rangehoo being somewhat more than fifteen miles. The village was situated on the southern side of the entrance into the bay; and on our landing, the women, who were here quite as hospitable as we found them in the other parts, gave us the customary welcome with no less cordiality. We were now introduced to the queen of Parro, (for so I must designate Korra-korra's head wife,) as also to her sister; and the former was a lady of no very delicate appearance, but, on the contrary,

had all the masculine roughness of the other
sex. She had an infant at her breast, that
looked the picture of rude health.

This place, which was called Parro, and
the capital of the district to which it gave
name, was a very straggling village; and the
houses much inferior to those we had generally met with in our previous excursions.
The inhabitants too, seemed to partake of
the ruder and more impetuous character of
their chief; nor had they by any means the
same tractable simplicity of manner as the
rest of their countrymen; being both obsti-
nate and vehement, though at the same time
friendly and hospitable. Upon an insulated
rock, not far from the village, was built the
hippah, to which they never resorted but
when attacked by their enemies; and in such
cases, from its strength and situation, they
might safely retire to it as a place of security.
In the evening we accompanied Korra-korra
and Tui to an adjoining bay, to see them
draw the nets which the chief had sent round
with men to assist. We walked about two
miles; and passing some lofty hills, came to
two very fine plantations of coomeras, that
appeared to have been cultivated with the
usual exactness of the natives in this branch

of husbandry. The bay, at which we had
now arrived, was but small, and formed by
one of those coves which are so numerous in
all the harbours of this part of the island.
It was, however, beautifully romantic; the
shore being covered with shrubs and trees,
as diversified in their species, and luxuriant
in their growth, as any we had yet seen;
some of which came gently sloping down to
the water's edge, while others, following the
chequered localities of the ground, rose with
rugged ascent to the summit of a hill, or
turned off in a devious direction to some
sequestered valley.　Here were two canoes,
with four men and two boys.　One of the
men standing upon a rock to watch the fish,
soon discovered a large shoal of them rip-
pling the surface of the water, at about a
quarter of a mile from the shore.　Another
of them went in his canoe to drive the fish
into the net, one end of which was held by
the man standing on the rock; while the
other end being held by the man in the
canoe, he let out as much as he thought
necessary to embrace the shoal, hastening
towards the shore at the same time; and the
situation of the net in the water described a
semicircle of considerable extent.　But un-

fortunately their labours proved abortive, for the shoal escaped; we caught, however, from three to four hundred fish, that bore a strong resemblance to the herring, both in shape and appearance. The net employed on this occasion, though to us it appeared of immense size,* Tui said was not near so large as they generally made them, and ascribed the escape of the shoal to this cause; for he thought we could not possibly have missed them, had the net been of a sufficient length to have encompassed them as far as they extended.

The fish we had taken being thrown into the canoes, we went round to Parro, through a communication which the bay has with the entrance of the harbour; and arrived there between ten and eleven o'clock: the moon shining with a mild but vivid light, and enabling us to find our way in safety. We were very much pleased with the activity and steadiness of the two boys who had accompanied us; they shewed considerably more judgment in the management of the

---

* Captain Cook, speaking of one of their nets, srys, " It " was five fathom deep, and by the room it took up it could " not be less than three or four hundred fathom long."— *Hawksworth's edition of Cook's Voyages*, vol. ii. p. 369.

net than we could have expected from lads of so early an age; and they evinced, in other respects, a shrewd intelligence, far beyond the compass of their years. The four men who had been of our party, were all *rungateedas*, as Tui took care to inform us, for these people never forget to acquaint you with their own dignity, and that of their friends; nor do I suppose there is any country in the world where family pride is more predominant than in New Zealand: not excepting even Spain itself, with all its haughty grandees, or Germany with its host of pompous barons. The *Governor* having appropriated one of his houses for us to sleep in, which was not tabooed against the profane, we laid ourselves down to rest with a log of wood for our pillow, and no other covering than our great-coats. But we found no fault with our accommodation, and were enjoying profound repose, when about the hour of midnight we were suddenly awakened by Korra-korra and Tui, who came to inform us that they were obliged to leave us that very instant to go to fight; but more they could not then explain, and immediately departed, telling us they would very soon return. This news was as unexpected as it

was alarming, and for my part I could not
help thinking our situation extremely peri-
lous, though I believe my friend entertained
no serious apprehensions. To escape at that
hour to the ship was utterly impracticable;
and should the chief and his brother be cut
off in any immediate rencounter, the danger
to us might be imminent, as it was more than
probable we should fall into the hands of
the hostile party, who would come with
enraged vengeance to demolish the village,
and from whom we could expect little mercy.
These disquieting reflections occurred to me
frequently through the remainder of the night;
while at the same time I felt tacitly amused
with the confident promise made to us by
our two friends, that they would speedily
return; not appearing to consider that the
issue of the anticipated conflict might be
doubtful, and that the spear or pattoo pattoo
might effectually prevent their ever coming
back.

The morning of the twenty-fourth at
length appeared, and served in a great measure to dispel the gloom that hung over my
mind; though the brothers had not yet returned from their nocturnal expedition, nor
sent us any account of their proceedings.

However, while we were now in some doubt of their safety, they proved as good as their word; and returned about noon, accompanied by their uncle, old Bennee, and a great number of his warriors. Mr. Marsden and myself congratulating them on their safe return, requested they would now inform us what the particular urgency was, that occasioned them to set off to fight at so unseasonable an hour; when Tui told us that it was all a false alarm: that upon receiving information which they then believed to be correct, but which afterwards turned out to be groundless, of a hostile tribe having come from the interior to attack some of their friends, they thought it necessary to proceed against them, without losing a moment; but that on getting to the place they found no enemies to oppose. He moreover assured Mr. Marsden that he was so weary and disgusted with living in such a harassing state of insecurity, that he would go back to Port Jackson, and never more think of revisiting New Zealand. This was not the only instance in which Tui expressed the strongest disapprobation of the lawless practices and barbarous polity of his native land; while he admired our regulations and customs, from the effects he saw them produce at the colony, but where, I am sorry to say, their superiority is but imperfectly exemplified in the propagation of good morals.

CHAP. II.

Covetous disposition of the chief Bennee—The author's project to cure him of it—Preposterous vanity of this chief
—Excursion to a village—The party prepare to leave
Parro—Longevity, and inferences drawn from it—Departure from Korra-korra's district—Tedious and disagreeable passage—Return to the vessel—The author
visits the settlement—Occurrences there, and incidental
remarks—Duaterra's expedition to the North Cape—
Picturesque appearance of his canoe—Further transactions at the settlement—Traffic between the author and
the natives—Their active industry—The ship proceeds
again to the Cowa-cowa—Visited by Tarra and Pomaree
—Detection and punishment of a thief—Mr. Marsden
and the author accompany Pomaree to the timber district.

THE New Zealanders are, of all the people
I ever met with, the most importunate in
their demands upon strangers, and some of
them are of so covetous a disposition, that
give them what you will, they are not to be
satisfied. Old Bennee was a striking instance
of this avaricious spirit, and I would not
hesitate to pronounce him the sturdiest beg-
gar in the whole island. Mr. Marsden gave
him a large fish-hook and some other trifles,

which *he* might consider gifts of immense
value, but these did not prevent him from
annoying us with his teasing solicitations
whenever we approached him, and his constant cry was, " Give it the wow,"* " Give it
the matow,"† " Give it the tokee," which he
kept ringing in our ears, even after he had
obtained them. One day while he was on
board, I was willing, if possible, to cure him
of this propensity, which had now rendered
him perfectly irksome to us; and considering
that ridicule might perhaps be the most
effectual method I could adopt, I resolved
to practise it upon him, and try how far it
might be conducive to my purpose. Walking, therefore, upon the quarter-deck, I
would go up to him and say, " Bennee, homi
wow," (*i. e.* Bennee, give me a nail ;) when he
would stretch out his hand in anxious expectation of receiving one, but instead of giving
it to him, I would look gravely at him, and
make another request, " homi matow," (give
me a fish-hook ;) when he would again hold
out his hand with increased avidity; and dis-
appointing him a second time, I would ask
him again, " homi tokee," at which, unable
to contain himself any longer, he would get

* Nail.   † Fish-hook.

into the wildest transports of delight, expecting every moment this treasure at my
hands. At last, when I had thus raised
his expectation to the highest pitch, and
worked up his impatience to almost convulsive restlessness, I would say to him very
coolly, " Bennee, homi kipoukee," (give
me the ship,) when his features suddenly
changing from the expression of extreme joy
to that of the most dejected hopelessness, he
would shake his head and cry, " Mr. Nicholas *nuee nuee henerecka*," (Mr. Nicholas jokes
too much.) This method had the desired
effect, and the old chief, in his subsequent
interviews with us, took very good care to
restrain his impatience; while desisting from
his troublesome urgency, he left it entirely to
ourselves to give him whatever we thought
proper. I should not, however, have played
so much upon his feelings, had I not known
him to be insatiable in his cupidity; and it
was necessary for our own quiet, to devise
some such means in order to free ourselves
from his constant annoyance. Most of the
members of his family were equally importunate with himself; and the begging conta-
gion seemed to have spread among them
with the same irritating prurience.

The whole of this day Mr. Marsden and myself were busied in salting and curing fish, and the natives rendered us every possible assistance on the occasion. The women and girls were employed in opening them and taking out the entrails, while the men occasionally assisted in these operations; or going in their canoes, supplied the industry of the others by bringing in plenty of bream and snappers, which they caught with the hook and line. It was pleasing to observe with what promptitude and cheerful willingness they all exerted themselves. They worked incessantly, and though they would sometimes jokingly call out to us for a *wow*, and affect to suspend their labours till it was given to them, they never relaxed a single instant; and we certainly were careful to requite them for their perseverance. Old Bennee was extremely amusing, and we were much diverted by his ludicrous behaviour. So very aristocratical was he in his notions, and such was the mean light in which he held all those who employed themselves at any kind of manual labour, that looking at us with a scornful glance, and suddenly averting his eye, as if afraid of being degraded by the very sight of our work, he exclaimed, contemptuously, " Mr. Marsden and Mr. Nicholas *cookee cookee*," and with a smile of self-importance cried out, " Mr. Bennee, nuee nuee rungateeda." But Bennee's ideas of exalted rank were as preposterous as they were laughable; and while he despised us for salting fish, he could bring himself to the humiliating degradation of begging a nail from us, if I had not ridiculed him out of his importunity. In the evening I walked to a small village at a short distance from the *Governor's*, and purchased some thread and fish-hooks from the inhabitants. One of them had the ingenuity to make a very tolerable fish-hook out of a large nail; he had bent it to the proper shape, and had made a barb to it with a degree of skill that reflected no ordinary credit on his talent for imitation. After walking all over this village, I could perceive nothing in it worthy of notice, the huts being of a similar construction with those I had observed in the other parts, but meaner and more uncomfortable in their appearance.

Having, on the morning of the 25th, filled both our casks with fish, we prepared for our return to the vessel; leaving a sailor that we had brought with us, to salt whatever other quantity the natives might bring in. From the sultry state of the weather, it was impossible for us to cure them effectually, and a great part of what had been caught and salted on the preceding night, we found either fly-blown or crawling with maggots in the morning. The meat-fly in this country is similar to the blue-bottle fly in England, and equally destructive to provisions; but is by no means so bad as that in New South Wales, which is there a perfect nuisance, depositing its maggots alive upon the meat as soon as it is killed, and even while at table;* so that it is absolutely necessary for you to examine each morsel carefully before you put it

* A friend of mine, on his first arrival at New South Wales, was not a little astonished, while going to put a piece of hot mutton-chop into his mouth, to find it almost a mass of live maggots; and being at a loss to account for it, he facetiously remarked, that they must be so many young salamanders. But a ludicrous circumstance happened to another gentleman of my acquaintance, and which arose from the same cause, for he found a number of these living maggots deposited in his ear; and as he had a complaint in his head, he began to be seriously alarmed lest the intruders were breeding there; nor could he for a long time divest himself of the apprehension that a crawling progeny would issue forth from his ear at certain intervals.

into your mouth, or you may swallow down a plentiful number of these obnoxious crawlers.

Before we left this place, Korra-korra was visited by a very old man, and Tui, upon seeing him, remarked to us, rather emphatically, that he had been a " *nuee nuee* time out of the belly." This poor man was drooping under the last stage of decrepitude; his emaciated frame presented nothing to the eye but a dry and wrinkled skin adhering to the bones, in frightful decay; and his intellectual faculties were quite as exhausted as his physical powers. From the many instances of similar longevity that we met with in this country since our arrival, I should be inclined to draw two conclusions; the one, that the climate here and manner of living must be particularly favourable towards the prolonging of human existence; and the other, that their wars are not at all so destructive as might be imagined. I observed here a most deplorable looking object, that I believe was a woman, though from the dress and disfigurement the sex appeared doubtful; her face, hands, and indeed her whole body, seemed one mass of running sores and fetid ulcers, the effect, most probably, of the venereal poison, which unfortunately has been communicated to these poor natives by that unfeeling description of characters whose conduct has been so often the subject of my reproach, the crews of European vessels.

Our friends having eaten their usual quantity of *kiki* as a necessary preparation before their departure, we now got into the canoe; and Mr. Marsden gave Korra-korra the *tokees*, and other articles of traffic that we had brought with us, to distribute among his people as he thought proper. The chief, however, did not make this distribution all at once; but intending to apportion rewards at stated times to those he deemed most deserving, he deposited the several articles in his chest, and hung up the key on the outside of his house, which shewed us that he did not distrust the honesty of his people.* Indeed

---

* I am inclined to believe that the New Zealanders very rarely plunder either from the particular tribe to which they belong themselves, or from those tribes with which they are in alliance; but that all their rapacity is directed against those of their countrymen with whom they have not entered into a friendly compact. This rapacity, as it gives rise to frequent lawless incursions, is in my opinion the originating cause of the numberless feuds that distract the island; and avarice, not ambition, may be here considered the predominant prin-

I must do them the justice to say, that while we remained at this place, though we left every thing exposed, and they might without

ciple, while the thirst of fame, though it burns among them, is much easier allayed than the thirst of plunder. In a very interesting communication which I have had from Mr. Kendall since my return to England, I find that Korra-korra and his uncle old Bennee have been committing outrages on their neighbours, not long after our departure; and as this account may give the reader some further insight into the character and disposition of these singular people, I shall subjoin it here in the writer's own words. "Shunghi is a staunch friend; I can depend upon him: Korra-korra is by no means so steady. I must tell you that Korra-korra has been displaying his valour by killing one man of the party of Okeda, the brother-in-law of Shunghi, near one of the Cavalle Islands, where we came to an anchor on our way to the Bay of Islands. Mr. Bennee had been *matowing* (stealing) some potatoes, while upon an expedition along the coast, which the proprietors resenting, recourse was had to arms: one of Okeda's men fell. Soon after this Okeda mustered all his force, and coming to the Bay, he made a descent upon Mr. Korra-korra, and took away all his hogs and the greatest part of his property. The foal was also slaughtered, as a retaliation for the loss of the man. Shunghi approved of this measure: he said Korra-korra had made a solemn promise to his Excellency Governor Macquarie, that 'he would fight no more;' he had broken that engagement, it was therefore perfectly right that the foal should be destroyed. After the affair was over, Korra-korra paid us a visit. He wept bitterly, said 'he was no good,' and was very much afraid lest he had incurred our displeasure. He added, he had been provoked to give battle by the excessive violence of the person who had been slain. He made use of the New Zealand curse, *poke tokke tokke*, or, in English, to hell to be damned."

fear of detection have taken what they pleased, yet we did not lose a single article. This surprised me the more when I reflected on the cupidity of old Bennee and others among them, who I imagined would have disregarded all prohibitions and despised every injunction, to possess themselves of those trifles for which they had so often worried our patience.

We were a long time in reaching the ship, and all the while exposed to a sun that was more intense than usual, and with not a single breath of air. But, besides this oppressive state of the weather, we experienced also the disagreeable effects of our wretched accommodation on the preceding night; and were anxious to obtain as soon as possible some necessary refreshment, but particularly the comfort of clean linen, having good reason to suppose that we were not altogether free from New Zealand *cootoos*. It was not, therefore, without indignant sensations that we beheld Korra-korra, in place of urging his men to be expeditious, amusing them with a long story of his adventures at Port Jackson; while they occasionally rested on their paddles to listen to it. I repeatedly begged of him to use more exertion, else we should lose too much time in getting to the vessel; but

he heard me with the greatest possible indifference, and the more importunate I was in
pressing my request, the more heedless was
he in attending to it, answering me only with
a vacant laugh, and then going on with his
story as before. Mr. Marsden, whose patience
far exceeded mine, bore this irksome delay
with the resignation of a true philosopher;
and finding no other remedy myself, I thought
it better at length to follow his example as
well as I could, though I certainly was ill
prepared to assume the feelings of a Stoic
upon the occasion. It appeared to us, so far
as we could conjecture from his pronouncing
repeatedly the names of several places and
persons at the colony, that our untoward
friend had entered into an ample detail of all
the occurrences he had met with; and could
we have understood his language, I doubt
not but we should have been quite as much
amused as his gaping auditors. The name
of Mr. Cartwright, a clergyman, at whose
house he had been residing for some time,
was frequently in his mouth, as were also the
words Parramatta, Sydney, &c.; and the
looks of amazement which his story excited
among his people, were a sure indication of
the wonders he recounted.

At length we got to the ship, where, having well washed myself, and changed my dress, which I was so impatient for, I found that I had brought away with me from the *Governor's* mansion no small number of its crawling inmates. Being now refreshed, and having the satisfaction to find my person perfectly clear from such disgusting companions, I went on shore to dine with Mr. Kendall. Arriving at the house, I found the door completely beset by a crowd of the natives, whose curiosity to observe all the actions of the *packahá* would induce them to remain there from morning till night, without ever once stirring from it; unless urged by hunger, an impulse they were always unable to resist. The chiefs would generally force their way in, and as surely leave behind them a plentiful stock of *cootoos,* to the great annoyance of poor Mrs. Kendall, who complained to me sadly of their filthy habits. But however obnoxious these must be at present, both she and her husband have too much good sense and strength of principle, not to submit to them with as much patience as can be expected under the circumstances in which they are placed, and for the advancement of that important purpose for which they have

been selected. Their example and instruc-
tions, I should hope, will in some time teach
these people to accommodate themselves to
cleanly habits; and the loathsome nastiness
to which the missionaries are now exposed,
may, by their own exertions, be eventually
removed.

Mr. Kendall having brought from England an excellent barrel organ, tried the
effect of music upon his savage auditors;
and it was highly diverting to see them
thrusting in their grisly visages, and gaping
with astonishment while they listened attentively to the unusual sounds. Two or three
of them seemed particularly delighted, un-
bending their dark and tattooed features into
the liveliest ecstasy; and Mr. Kendall was
here another Orpheus, for though, unlike
that celebrated musician, his notes had not
the magic power to make the woods follow
him with charmed obedience, still their animated natives were attracted by his performance in immense numbers.

Duaterra came alongside in the course of
the day in his war-canoe, accompanied by
two others. He was going to visit his district in Doubtless Bay, in consequence of
the information he had lately received of its

having been-invaded. The canoes were full of warriors, all of them armed with the usual weapons; and they appeared well able and prepared to revenge the injuries of their chief. Any attempt on our part to dissuade Duaterra from this expedition would have been unavailing, his resentment being worked up to the highest pitch from the unprovoked attack made upon his people; and we therefore thought it best to urge no arguments against it, seeing he was resolved to have recourse to arms, and determined on retaliation. His own canoe was a very attractive spectacle, being elegantly decorated with ingenious devices, and containing a group of the most beautiful young women in the island; who seated themselves at the paddle with a peculiar grace and easiness of attitude, while the pliancy of the action displayed their fine forms to the greatest advantage. In this canoe were likewise his wife and her handsome sister; and the whole party were gay and lively as possible. Duaterra told us, that if the account of a descent having been made upon his district should prove correct, he would, after retaliating the injury, bring away his people from that place, and settle them at Rangehoo; but that if he had been misinformed, he would suffer them to remain there, and allot to each of them a portion of land and some wheat to sow it with. This first measure would have been the most judicious he could adopt; for by thus bringing to his principal territory an accession of population to the number of at least two hundred souls, he would concentrate all his people in one formidable body, and his enemies would most probably be deterred from further incursions; whereas by leaving his subjects at such a distance from each other, he would only expose them separately to more frequent attacks.

At parting he gave us a salute with eight muskets, * and requested the loan of a brace of pistols, in addition to his supply of firearms, which was readily granted. But this favour excited the jealousy of Korra-korra, who immediately asked us to let him have a

* So great is the passion of the New Zealanders for military display, that they never take into account any consideration that might dissuade them from indulging it; and scarcity or abundance, safety or danger, are all the same when this favourite propensity is to be gratified. Though gunpowder is an article so very valuable to them, and one with which they are so rarely furnished, yet Duaterra did not hesitate to make this unnecessary waste of it, to indulge his desire for warlike pomp; even at the very moment he was going to oppose his enemies, when he knew not how much he might stand in need of the quantity he thus idly expended.

brace likewise, which we however as promptly refused, not deeming it expedient to gratify him in this instance. He appeared much chagrined at the denial, but it caused only a momentary impression; and he left us immediately after, to return to his district, being accompanied by the mate of the vessel, whom we sent with him with a quantity of salt and some casks for the fish.

After we had dined with Mr. Kendall, who entertained us with the warmest cordiality in his new habitation, we went to drink tea at Mr. Hall's, where we were presented with a lively scene of active industry. He was occupied himself in various departments of useful employment; and Mrs. Hall, while she took the chief part in the domestic concerns, had two of the native women under her instruction as assistants, and who were now very busy in washing our clothes. I went up to the town in the course of the evening, and purchased some thread and a few more curiosities in addition to the stock I had already by me; but I found the place almost deserted, the greater part of the inhabitants having gone with their chief to Doubtless Bay.

The twenty-seventh was a day of more

than usual bustle and activity; the sawyers cutting timber from morning till night without intermission, the smith making axes with the same industry, and the carpenter employed with no less diligence in cutting out two draught holes in the bows of the vessel, to enable her to take in a cargo of timber; and when these were completed, we were to take her round to the Cowa-cowa to receive the freight.   None of the artisans that accompanied us to New Zealand attracted so much attention among the natives as the smith. To watch his various labours, they would seat themselves for hours together in his forge; looking at each other occasionally with significant amazement, whenever any part of his operations appeared more intricate than usual to their rude conceptions. On these operations they made several remarks among each other; and at first all their senses were astonished at the malleability of iron in its ignited state. They always took care to keep at a secure distance from the sparks that were struck out by the hammering, of which they seemed extremely apprehensive; and aware of their fears in this particular, I put one of them into a serious fright, for the sake of a little harmless amusement. He was looking on while the smith was taking what is termed a welding heat; and just as the hammer-man began to strike, and the sparks to fly out, I took hold of his *kackahow*, and giving it a violent shake, I called out with instantaneous alarm, "*carpulo, carpulo, carpulo!*" (fire, fire, fire!) when springing from my hands with an inconceivable agility, he escaped from the forge almost before I could suppose he was frightened.

Upon going into the town on Saturday January 28th, the few inhabitants who had remained there brought me several articles to purchase; some offering me thread and fishing-lines, and others spears, mats, and different sorts of curiosities, some of which were exquisite specimens of original genius. The dealers on this occasion were chiefly women, the men for the most part being all absent; and these ladies appeared to me perfect models of prudent industry and strict application. They were all as busy as they could be; and some of them I saw employed in twisting thread, and several others in making mats, while the same women who sold me thread on the preceding day, were now engaged in preparing more for the market; which proves the activity of their dispositions.* One of the few men who had stayed behind I saw very busy in rubbing a battle-axe·over with oil, and polishing it up with his *kackahow:* when he thought he had made it shine sufficiently, and had rendered it in other respects completely marketable, he brought it to me for sale; and that I might thoroughly comprehend the use of it, he put himself into a fighting attitude, and shewed me by various explanatory evolutions, the manner he dispatched his enemies. He was not however more careful in shewing me the use of the weapon than he was in setting a price upon it, and I found him a complete proficient in the art of dealing. He asked for it considerably more than it was worth; and to enhance its value, turned it over in his hand several times, that I might see what a good state it was in, assuring me all the while that it was " *nuee nuee miti*," and driving his bargain like an experienced trader.

* From all I could see of these people in the different parts I have visited, I am firmly persuaded that no where can be found a race who are more inclined to industrious pursuits; and when supplied with proper means by which they can exercise their native ingenuity to advantage, they will, in my opinion, not only realize to the full the benevolent views of the Missionary Society, but even exceed their most sanguine expectations.

The carpenter having now completed the draught-holes, we repaired on board the vessel, taking our friend Gunnah and another of the natives along with us; and weighing anchor at two P. M. we proceeded to the Cowa-cowa, the wind blowing fresh the whole time. We entered this river about five o'clock, when we made all the necessary preparations for getting the cargo on board as soon as possible. The anchorage here is much more secure than off Rangehoo, and we considered ourselves very fortunate in coming to this place, as well as in having the draught-holes finished at this critical time, for it blew excessively hard during the night; and the following day, Sunday the twenty-ninth, was ushered in with continual rain.

The natives being apprized of our arrival, brought down five spars at an early hour in the morning; and we received visits from several of them, among whom were old Tarra and the bustling Pomaree. While we were sitting at breakfast, we were disturbed by a great clamour upon deck, when leaving the cabin, we found Gunnah in a violent passion with one of the natives who had contrived to secrete a marline spike under his *kackahow*, but was watched by our friend, who suspected his design. The man believing that he had purloined his valuable prize in perfect security, was just in the act of concealing it, as he supposed, when Gunnah rushed upon him with indignant rage, and taking it from him, instantly shouted out for Mr. Marsden to come upon deck. But being now brought into our presence, the culprit denied his having stolen it, insisting that it had been given to him by one of the sailors; Gunnah, however, declared positively that he saw him steal it; "me *tickee, tickee*," said he with much vehemence, addressing himself to Mr. Marsden, "*tungata tihi*, no good;" and he described the way in which he saw him secrete it. This testimony being corroborated by some of our people upon deck, Mr. Marsden had the man put into the hold, and the hatchway fastened down; but before this was done, the offender entreated we would allow him to return in the canoe that had brought him to the vessel: his companion, however, refused to take him, and paddling away to the shore, joined with Gunnah in the cry of "*tungata tihi*, no good." We had no objection to release him, but being thus left behind and despised by his countrymen, Mr. Marsden thought it better to deliver him up to Tarra, whose subject we understood he was, and let that chief punish him as he thought proper. All the natives who were upon deck spoke in terms of warm approbation of our lenity to this delinquent; and they unanimously pronounced us "*nuee nuee miti*" for not flogging him, declaring that had he been guilty of a similar offence on board any other ship, he would have been severely punished. They mentioned to us an instance of extreme severity in this respect, which, as it affects the character of a British subject, it pains me to record. The commander of one of our vessels, they said, had a man shot *

---

* How lost to every sense of feeling and humanity must be the callous and cruel man who could thus devote his fellow-creature to destruction, for an offence of the criminality of which he was perhaps unconscious; and one which in our own country would at most be only visited with temporary exile, but among poor savages ought to be considered excusable! Widely different from this barbarous conduct was that of the excellent and humane Captain Cook, who would neither himself punish petty thefts with death, nor suffer any of his people to do it. It were much to be desired that his countrymen who visit the same regions would follow his example, in place of rendering themselves odious in the sight of every man who has a fellow-feeling for his species. And while he took care to guard the lives of the natives against the wanton cruelty of his people, he also made it his particular business to see that their property was respected, repressing with rigid severity the plundering incursions of his sailors, who considered

for stealing a small axe, during the time he was lying in this cove.   Pomaree, whose heart never seemed to incline towards the side of mercy, and who was in the literal sense of the word a cruel savage, though we never had occasion to complain of his ferocity, advised us to hang him up immediately; and the other natives, while they applauded our humanity, evinced at the same time the

themselves privileged to rob the poor Indians with impunity, but who deemed any fraud committed upon themselves as deserving the most condign punishment.

During the time he was lying at anchor in this bay, he had occasion to punish some of the sailors for their depredations on the natives, which he thus relates. "In the mean time some of our people, who when the Indians were to be punished assumed the inexorable justice of a Lycurgus, thought fit to break into one of their plantations, and dig up some of their potatoes; for this offence I ordered some of them to be punished with twelve lashes, after which two of them were discharged; but the third insisting that it was no crime in an Englishman to plunder an Indian plantation, though it was a crime for an Indian to defraud an Englishman of a nail, I ordered him back into his confinement, from which I would not release him till he had received six lashes more."—*Hawksworth*, vol. ii. p. 366.

And again, where he shews how little the lives of these poor people are regarded by European sailors, he says, "In this skirmish only two of the Indians were hurt with the small shot, and not a single life was lost, which would not have been the case, if I had not restrained the men, who either from fear or the love of mischief, shewed as much impatience to destroy them as a sportsman to kill his game."—*Ibid.* vol. ii. p. 365.

greatest indignation against their guilty countryman. When Tarra came on board we
related the circumstance to him, and the old
chief was so incensed with the offender, who
was now brought before him, trembling with
fear, and hardly able to support himself,
that snatching up a billet of wood, he threw
it at the unfortunate creature with such violence that he laid him prostrate upon the
deck. Here he began to kick him without
mercy; foaming with rage all the while, and
exclaiming against him with furious re-
proaches: nor would he probably have desisted before he had beaten him out of existence, had not Mr. Marsden interfered to beg
him off, while the enraged chief, yielding to
his solicitations, consented to pardon the hapless culprit; ordering him into a canoe, and
charging him, as he valued his life, never more
to appear in his district. But all this indignant vengeance against the wretched creature
was only because we were considered as
friends; the immorality of the offence being
viewed but through the medium of existing
circumstances.

Both Tarra and Pomaree visited us again
on the following day, the 30th, at an early
hour; and the latter, who was as usual, inde-

fatigable in business, would not let us rest till we shewed him what articles we had for trade, when he became extremely urgent for the market to begin, and was all impatience to make new bargains. He told us that he had several of his people working at the timber district, where they had cut down a number of fine spars; but that they would not be contented, unless we went along with him, and distributed some small presents among them, as a partial remuneration for their labour. This, though we were acquainted with the character of the man, Mr. Marsden and myself did not hesitate to do; and getting into his canoe, we took with us a quantity of nails, scissars and plane irons, with other articles of similar value, to reward their industry.

CHAP. III.

The Author suspects the good faith of Pomaree—Is alarmed in consequence—His fears removed—Presents distributed among Pomaree's people—Cannibalism of the New Zealanders—Captain Cook's and Dr. Forster's opinions respecting it—Believed erroneous by the Author, and his reasons for it—Return from Pomaree's district—Interesting document presented by a chief to Mr. Marsden—Part of its contents refuted—Arrival of Korrakorra with war-canoes—Tupee's detraction of the other chiefs—An East Indian found among the natives—Character of the chief Tekokee—False alarm—The Author goes on shore, and on his way visits the island of Motooroa—This island offered for sale to the Missionaries—Remarks with respect to it.

In going up the fresh-water stream we met some of the natives bringing down spars; and stopping at the foot of Tekokee's village, Pomaree requested Mr. Marsden to walk with him through the woods, while I should go round in the canoe, and take charge of the articles we brought with us. To this my friend made no objection; and I was now paddled about a mile further up the river, till we came to a long vista that presented a romantic view through the forest, and where we found assembled a considerable number of the natives, but I could neither observe Pomaree nor Mr. Marsden among them. As we approached the land, three or four men came down to the water's edge with their faces daubed over with a blue paint, and carrying in their hands the long spears they use in battle. This sight was by no means pleasing to me, and I now for the first time began to entertain serious apprehensions of the good faith of Pomaree. My eyes still wandered anxiously in search of Mr. Marsden, but he was not to be seen; and I was particularly uneasy lest the chief had verified the bad character given of him by Duaterra, and decoyed my friend in order to ensure his destruction. The report that we had heard concerning his intention to cut off the ship* now recurred to me with alarming certainty, while I could not help apprehending that he had brought us hither for the sole purpose of realizing his atrocious project, and thus securing to himself and his tribe all the property we possessed. Such were the dreadful suspicions that alarmed my mind, on finding myself separated from my friend, and surrounded by the dependants of a ruthless savage; who, according to all the accounts I

* See Vol. i. p. 384, 385.

had heard of him, had given repeated proofs
of his excessive cruelty; yet I thought it
most prudent to dissemble my fears, and
assume an air of implicit confidence in their
sincerity. I therefore jumped on shore, with
my fowling-piece in my hand, determined to
employ it against the first that should attack
me; and to sell my life as dearly as possible,
if destined by Providence for such an extremity. None of the people, however, who
were assembled here offered me the least
violence, or shewed any disposition to interrupt my progress; and it was in some degree
consoling to me, that what Pomaree had told
us of a number of spars being cut down, was
perfectly correct. This afforded me some
hope that he had meditated no treachery;
but still Mr. Marsden did not present himself to my impatient view, and I looked out
for him in a state of the greatest agitation and
ominous suspense. The assemblage was
composed of men, women and children; and
they had erected for themselves temporary
huts, to serve as a shelter against the rain,
while they were cutting down the timber.
But it was the hideous appearance of the
men with their daubed cheeks and disfigured
eye-brows that contributed most of all to ex-

cite my suspicions; for Duaterra told me,
that when his countrymen prepared themselves for any violent enterprise, either against
congregated bodies or individuals, it was their
invariable practice to make their faces look
as frightful as possible, in order to terrify
their opponents.*   While I thus continued a
prey to the most anxious disquietude, almost
hopeless of the safety of my friend, and expecting every moment some terrible·fatality
to myself, Mr. Marsden and Pomaree, together with another chief, made their appearance through an opening in the wood; and
though I always met my friend with sincere
pleasure, never did I experience the same
happiness at seeing him as on this occasion.

* This practice is not peculiar to New Zealand alone, and
it may be traced to several other nations in a similar state of
barbarism. Tacitus, speaking of one of the German hordes,
describes them as dyeing their bodies and carrying black
shields to frighten their enemies; while to increase the terror
of the effect, they always chose dark nights for their battles.
The following is his description of them:—" Ceterum Arii
super vires, quibus enumeratos paulo ante populos antecedunt,
truces, insitæ feritati arte ac tempore lenocinantur. Nigra
scuta, tincta corpora, atras ad prælia noctes legunt: ipsaque
formidine atque umbra feralis exercitus terrorem inferunt,
nullo hostium sustinente novum ac velut infernum aspectum;
nam primi in omnibus pœliis oculi vincuntur."—*Tacitus de
Moribus Germ.*

I thought we should have never met again; and that I, if allowed to survive, should have to lament the loss of that intimate friendship which I shall never cease to value, and the community that benevolence which they must always admire. But happily this was not the case, so my fears were now dissipated, and my mind set at rest.

Pomaree now calling his people toge- ther, made them sit down in a circle round us, requesting Mr. Marsden at the same time to distribute his presents among them; and to those who are fond of seeing happy faces, this would have been a very gratifying spec- tacle; for every countenance exhibited the most animated demonstrations of joyful satis- faction. Several of them danced through excessive delight at the treasure they had received; and others laughed incessantly, from their immoderate transports. Mr. Marsden gave to Pomaree himself, for his own use, five axes and three hoes; for which that chief agreed to bring down sixteen spars, ap- pearing well pleased with the bargain.

I observed suspended at the breast of one of these people an instrument like a flute, made of bone, in the carving of which a considerable degree of ingenuity was displayed. As they have only two native quadrupeds upon the island that are large enough to supply them with bone for their ornaments ; and as neither of these animals could furnish one of such a size as this instrument was made of, it occurred to me at once, that it must be a human bone; and upon asking the man who wore it, if it was not *evee tungata*, (the bone of a man,) he told me it was, and confirmed my supposition. Though from the respectable testimony of Captain Cook, who is generally accurate in his statement of facts, no doubt had existed in my mind upon the subject of these people being cannibals; still I was resolved, on getting to the island, to obtain the unequivocal acknowledgment of the natives themselves in this particular, and thus satisfy myself completely respecting it. Accordingly I frequently questioned them on this head, and they never denied the fact; but acknowledging it candidly, excused it with their usual apology for all their barbarous customs, that "it was good in New Zealand." Abhorrent, however, as this subject is to the common feelings of mankind, still as it marks so decidedly the character of these people, it deserves to be thoroughly investigated, and the originating principle should, if possible, be ascertained. The reader will therefore indulge me, while I digress somewhat from the narrative, to examine the opinions both of Captain Cook and the ingenious Dr. Forster on this question, neither of whom, as I conceive, attributes the cannibalism of the New Zealanders to the actual cause.

Captain Cook is very brief in accounting for it, ascribing it merely to the want of a sufficiency * of food; a convincing reason enough, if such want existed, but this not being the case, it will of course be found erroneous. It remains for me, however, to shew that this want does not exist; and which I am prepared to do from the experience of my own observation as well as from the acknowledgment of the natives themselves. The island, besides its being abundantly supplied with the fern-root, (which, as has been observed, forms the principal article of diet among the natives,) has also plenty of other esculent roots which are very nutritious, and a profusion of the best fish, so that a scarcity of food is a thing never known in the country. The industry of the natives too in laying up their stores of provisions, is such as to antici-

* Hawksworth, vol. iii. p. 44.

pate all future exigencies; and each district
is furnished with magazines to supply the
inhabitants as occasion requires. It is therefore evident that the reason assigned by Captain Cook for the revolting practice among
them of eating human flesh, cannot be correct; and I shall now proceed to shew that
the opinion of Dr. Forster, though urged
with much philosophical acumen, is equally
without foundation. But I shall first give
this opinion in the learned gentleman's own
words, that the reader may form a more perfect estimate of the propositions he would
maintain.

" If we examine (says he) the whole economy of their societies, we shall find that
their education is the chief cause of their
enormities. The men train up the boys in a
kind of liberty which at last degenerates into
licentiousness: they suffer not the mothers to
strike petulant, unruly and wicked sons, for
fear of breaking that spirit of independency
which they seem to value above all things,
and as the most necessary qualification for
their societies: this naturally brings on an
irascibility which in the men cannot brook
any controul, action, or word, that can be
construed according to their manners and

principles, into an affront or injury; inflamed by passion, they are impatient to wreak their vengeance; wild fancy paints the injury so atrocious, that it must be washed in blood; they know not where to stop, and being more and more incensed by the power of the imagination, they go to battle with a loud and barbarous song: each feature is distorted, each limb is set in a cadenced motion; they brandish their destructive weapons, and stamp upon the ground with their feet, while the whole band join in an awful tremendous groan; the song begins anew, and at last the whole troop is lost in frenzy and rage; they fall to, and every one fights as if animated by furies, and destruction and carnage await the routed party: whosoever falls is murdered without mercy, and the corses of the slain immediately serve to glut the inhuman appetites of the conquerors. When the bounds of humanity are once passed, and the reverence due to the bright image of divinity is conquered by frenzy, the practice soon becomes habitual, especially as it is reckoned among the honours due to the conqueror, to feast upon the wretched victims of savage victory; add to this, that a nation which has no other animal food than a few stupid dogs and fish, will soon reconcile themselves to human flesh, which according to several known instances,* is reputed to be one of the most palatable dishes."

Thus it will be seen that this ingenious writer ascribes the inhuman practice in question, together with their other enormities, to their education exclusively ; a position which no judicious reasoner will dispute, so far as education, taken in the unlimited sense of the term, is concerned; but when he refers these enormities to that particular part of education which includes the management of male children, I must differ with him completely, while at the same time I do not take upon myself to controvert some of the details of his argument, but rather to disprove his hypothesis. Far from being petulant or unruly, I observed on the contrary, all the children in New Zealand, both male and female, remarkably submissive and obedient towards their mothers;

* In the province of Matto-grosso in Brazil, a woman told his excellency Chevalier Pinto, who was the governor, that human flesh was extremely palatable, especially if taken from a young person. And during the last dearth in Germany, a shepherd killed first a young person, to satisfy the cravings of hunger with his flesh ; and afterwards several more, in order to please his luxurious palate.—*Forster's Observations,* p. 328, 329.

and in the whole course of my observation
among them, I never met with a single instance of undutiful behaviour. But, besides
that my own eyes bore testimony to their
docile and tractable dispositions, I found in
answer to several inquiries I made on the
subject, that they were never in the habit of
treating their mothers with disrespect; nor, if
inclined to do so, could I discover that they
would be at all protected by their fathers
against the punishment due to their irreve-
rence. So far has my own observation
and the concurring acknowledgments of the
inhabitants, enabled me to combat the principle laid down by the learned gentleman as
the basis of his argument; and I am persuaded that the evidence I have offered will
be satisfactory to the reader. Now with
respect to the details of Dr. Forster's argument, I have only to oppose that part which
ascribes to the New Zealanders a particular
liking for human flesh, in consequence of their
having " no other animal food than a few
stupid dogs and. fish;" and in doing this I
have to adduce precisely the same testimony
as before: I never observed them myself
evince this liking in the smallest degree;
and many of them told me that they had

no greater relish for this than for any other food.

My opinion on the subject is, that a kind of superstitious revenge is the grand actuating principle that incites them to this horrible practice. Born in the grossest ignorance, and nurtured amidst wild dissensions, they give loose to all the violence of their ungovernable passions; while superstition teaches them to believe that their revenge can reach beyond the grave, and that the future existence of their wretched victims must be totally annihilated, by this unnatural destruction of their mortal remains. With this shocking idea the children are bred up from their infancy; when hearing continually of bloody achievements, and learning from the lips of their fathers the various deeds of carnage in which they have been engaged, they grow up so much habituated to these enormities, that they consider them congenial with their very existence, while they form the favourite topic of their conversations, and the darling theme of their poetical rhapsodies. But there are several circumstances which serve to corroborate, if not to establish the opinion I here offer on the subject in question. While they devour the bodies of their enemies with a furious greediness that instantly tears them reeking from the slaughter, they look with horror on the idea of feeding on the corses of their friends; and burying them with many superstitious obsequies, the place is for ever after held sacred against the intrusion of all persons who are not among the number of the initiated. Hence I should draw the conclusion, that the desire of devouring human flesh is not the motive that leads them to do so; but that the same superstition which disposes them to respect with the most scrupulous veneration the dead bodies of their friends, acting conversely, impels them to gorge themselves upon the mangled remains of their hostile opponents. Such in my mind is the true cause of cannibalism in New Zealand, and I have now to observe that it does not prevail in this island alone, but is also common to some others in the Pacific Ocean. At the Fegees the natives are well known to be cannibals. It was no longer back than the year 1813, since they massacred and devoured fourteen of the people belonging to two vessels that had sailed from Port Jackson, for the purpose of procuring bech-le-mer and sandal-wood for the China market. It cannot be argued that these islanders

could have been instigated to this atrocious
deed by any want of food ; as nature has supplied them with an abundance of provisions
of the most excellent quality ; among which
may be reckoned the bread fruit, the cocoa-
nut, the banana, with yams and esculent roots
of various kinds.   No, they were actuated, I
doubt not, by the same principle with the
New Zealand cannibals ; they were led on
to the massacre by the terrible impulse of
uncontrouled frenzy, and to the devouring of
their victims by the implacable rage of a
vengeful superstition.   Indeed it appears to
me very probable that all the natives of the
South Sea Islands have at one period or
other been equally guilty of this horrible
practice.   At Otaheite, where the very idea
of eating human flesh is now held in the utmost abhorrence, a tradition has obtained
from time immemorial, of men-eaters having
been upon the island at some remote period,
who made great havoc among the inhabitants; but that this cruel* race has been long
since extinct.   Having thus stated what I
conceived necessary towards the elucidation
of a subject which it would have been in-

* Forster's Observations, p. 277.

excusable in me to have omitted, I shall now resume the narrative; trusting at the same time that the digression I have made, will by none of my readers be deemed irrelevant.

On our return from Pomaree's district we passed a fleet of canoes coming to the ship; having spars tied to the sides of them, and other spars were lashed together, forming a raft on which the natives sat and paddled. Arriving at the vessel we found there before us, Tarra and Tupee with Tekokee, and a chief of the name of Tenangha, a robust handsome looking man, who put into our hands a written document given to him by a Captain Pattison of the ship *City of Edinburgh*, and of which the following is a copy.

" The masters of ships frequenting New
" Zealand are directed to be careful in
" admitting many of the natives on board,
" as they may be cut off in a moment by
" surprise.

" These are to certify, that during our stay
" in this harbour we had frequent reports of
" a ship being taken by the natives in the
" neighbouring harbour of Wangeroa, and
" that the ship's crew were killed and eaten.

" In order to ascertain the truth of this
" report, as well as to rescue a few peo-
" ple who were said to be spared in the
" general massacre, Mr. Berry, accompanied
" by Mr. Russel and Metangango, a principal
" chief in the Bay of Islands, who volunteered
" his services, set out for Wangeroa in three
" armed boats, on Sunday the 31st Decem-
" ber 1809, and upon their arrival they found
" the miserable remains of the ship Boyd,
" Captain John Thompson, which the natives,
" after stripping of every thing of value, had
" burnt down to the water's edge. From
" the handsome conduct of Metangango, they
" were able to rescue a boy, a woman and
" two children, the only survivors of this
" shocking event, which according to the
" most satisfactory information, was perpe-
" trated entirely under the direction of that
" old rascal Tippahee, who had been so
" much and so undeservedly caressed at Port
" Jackson.

" This unfortunate vessel intending to load
" with spars, was taken three days after her
" arrival; the natives informed the master
" the second day, that they would show
" the spars the next day; in the morning
" Tippahee arrived from Tippoonah and

" went aboard, he staid only a few minutes,
" and then went into his canoe, but remained
" alongside the vessel, which was surrounded
" by a considerable number of canoes, which
" appeared collected for the purpose of
" trading; and a considerable number of
" the natives gradually intruded into the
" ship, and sat down upon the deck.   After
" breakfast the master left the ship with
" two boats, to look out for spars; Tippa-
" hee, after waiting a convenient time, now
" gave the signal of massacre; in an in-
" stant the savages, who appeared sitting
" peaceable upon deck, rushed upon the un-
" armed crew, who were dispersed about the
" ship at their -various employments; the
" greater part were massacred in a moment,
" and were no sooner knocked down, than
" they were cut up while still alive ; five or
" six of the hands escaped up the rigging.
" Tippahee now having possession of the
" ship, hailed them with a speaking trumpet,
" and ordered them to unbend the sails and
" cut away the rigging, and they should not
" be hurt,—they complied with his com-
" mands, and afterwards came down ; he
" then took them ashore in his canoe, and
" afterwards killed them; the master went

" ashore without arms, and of course was
" easily dispatched.

" The names of the survivors are, Mrs.
" Nanny Morley and child, Betsy Broughton,
" and Thomas Davis, boy. The natives of
" the spar district in this harbour, have be-
" haved well even beyond expectation, and
" seem much concerned on account of this
" unfortunate event ; and dreading the dis-
" pleasure of King George, have requested
" certificates of their good conduct, in order
" to exempt them from his vengeance ; but let
" no man after this trust a New Zealander.

" We further certify, that we have left
" with the bearer Mete-coge, a jolly-boat
" belonging to the Boyd, we brought round
" to Wangeroa, who has always behaved in
" the best manner.

" SIMEON PATTISON.
" ALEX. BERRY, Supercargo.
" JAMES RUSSELL.
" Given on board the ship City of
" Edinburgh, Capt. S. Pattison,
" Bay of Islands, 6th Jan.
" 1810."

This document is curious, as being written almost immediately after the catastrophe
of the Boyd ; but the assertions it contains

respecting Tippahee, are completely falsified, not only by the testimony of George himself, the principal actor in that tragical event, as has been already shown, in the account I have given of the conference we had with him; but also by the declarations of Dua-terra, Korra-korra, and numbers besides, who had an opportunity of knowing the particulars of this shocking transaction, and who assured us in the sincerity of their hearts, that Tippahee* was entirely innocent of the imputed atrocity. Indeed I am fully convinced that this foul stigma was cast upon him from the fortuitous circumstance of his having unhappily come into the harbour of Wangeroa on that fatal morning; but what fur-

* Though it is certain that this chief never contemplated a deed of such enormity as the cutting off of any of our vessels; still the provocation he received from the commander of one of them, might well have suggested even so terrible a retaliation. In No. II. of the Appendix to this work, will be found a detailed account of the provocation alluded to, being an extract from *Turnbull's Voyage round the World;* in which the reader will find that the daughter of this chief, had been torn away, by an unfeeling man, from the society of her father, and the fond embraces of a husband, with whom she had been united in the strictest bonds of mutual attachment, while their union was brought about by a romantic adventure; he being a native of England, the land of culture and of science, and she the child of rude nature, wild as the country of her birth, but still susceptible of the tenderest emotions.

ther served to fix the guilt upon him, was the similarity of sound between his name and that of Tippouie, the brother of George, and next to him the most prominent leader in this dreadful massacre. In addition to this, Tarra and Tupee, being his mortal enemies, spread the vile calumny through the whole island; and their malevolence in the end produced all the effect they desired. To this fatal combination of causes it was owing, that the name of poor Tippahee was branded with an atrocious criminality, his people extirpated, and his little island, once the seat of his fondest hopes, deluged with blood and ravaged with desolation.

In the course of the evening Korra-korra came alongside in his war-canoe, accompanied by four others all full of men, and presenting their usual appearance of martial equipment. He was going to make war upon Wiveeah, the chief of Wycaddie, who it appeared had been seducing the wife of another chief, whose friends were now summoned by him as auxiliaries to assist him in revenging the injurious affront. He had scarcely left us to proceed on this expedition, when I had another opportunity of witnessing the malignant jealousy with which the different chiefs view each other; while in this instance I observed a subtle duplicity that is not I believe common among them, and might be worthy an accomplished practitioner in deceit. Tupee, who upon Korra-korra's coming on deck, *nosed* with him (as our sailors expressed it) in the most affectionate manner, and evinced apparently the most unfeigned pleasure at seeing him, began the moment he had taken his departure to traduce him to us with a virulent calumny that knew no moderation. He told us that we had taken him to Port Jackson, where he had been treated with the most generous hospitality, and had experienced in every instance the friendly attention both of the Governor and of the people, and that we had brought him back loaded with tokees and axes; but yet that he was so *nuee nuee kackeeno* (very bad) as to be unworthy of these or any other favours. He then went on to describe him in the blackest colours, telling us he had murdered and devoured two of our countrymen without any provocation; and in short, so far as his testimony could go, (which however had no weight with us,) making our wayward friend appear a perfect monster. Nor was he more sparing of the reputation of Duaterra, and our steady friend Shunghi was also the object of his rancorous slander; but as to Pomaree, he spoke of him with such envenomed malignity, that the ferocious enormities for which this chief was noted, could not justify the tenth part of the detail. Having it in contemplation himself to accompany us to Port Jackson, he expressed his positive determination not to do so if Pomaree were to go likewise.

On Tuesday, January the 31st, so great was the number of canoes that came to visit us, that the ship was completely invested by them; and had the natives chosen to have broken their good faith with us, and betrayed the confidence we reposed in them, there was nothing that could prevent them from cutting off the vessel, as their numerical strength must have ultimately prevailed over any resistance we could offer. But no tragic event of this kind will, I hope, be ever again repeated in the island; and happy am I to observe, that the people express their unfeigned regret at that which has occurred. In the midst of the motley assemblage who crowded the decks and intruded themselves on us in spite of all our efforts against admitting them, I saw with no small degree of surprise a native of Hindostan, whose small stature and slender make might lead one to imagine him a pigmy among giants. He told me he had made his escape from the *City of Edinburgh*, the vessel I have lately noticed, and had been living among these people ever since; that he was not only reconciled to their habits and mode of living, but found himself happy in the practice of them, and preferred by much residing here, to returning to his own country. He was married, he said, and experienced the kindest treatment from the natives. I offered him some rice, but custom had reconciled him so well to the fern-root, that he gave it a decided preference. Having asked him if the natives obliged him to work hard, he replied in the negative, and said they always supplied him with plenty of food.

The chief Tekokee expressed on this day a particular desire that we should take his son (a fine lad about fourteen) with us to Port Jackson; to which we did not object. This chief particularly recommended himself to us, by the gentleness of his manners, the natural ease of his demeanour, and by an unobtrusive diffidence scarcely ever found in a savage, unless as the consequence of fear, and pleasing in the most civilized individual. While he yielded to none of the other chiefs in activity and intelligence, he did not assume upon any occasion that bustling importance, which rendered many of them troublesome, as well as ridiculous.

Mr. Kendall paid us a visit on Wednesday, February the 1st, accompanied by Themorangha, the chief of Thiomi; and on this day we found that a report, which was afterwards proved to have no foundation in truth, caused some agitation at the settlement. Themorangha had brought to the missionaries a gun, the lock of which wanted repairing, and for this service he presented to them at the same time two pigs, which he offered as payment, and were received accordingly. But as the smith had strict orders from Mr. Marsden to employ himself at no other kind of work but the making of tokees and axes, without a sufficient supply of which we could not purchase the quantity of spars that the natives were hourly bringing down; the gun was necessarily neglected, and Themorangha began to be rather impatient at the delay. This impatience, however, was magnified into a determination on his part, to attack the settlement, and revenge himself upon the missionaries and all their adherents, while the report received additional strength from his having landed a large party there a few days before. But this was only another of those idle alarms which the New Zealanders in many instances are so fond of exciting; and the party landed by the chief evinced the most amicable intentions, nor did Themorangha himself, who ordered them away almost immediately, betray less cordial demonstrations of friendship; so far was he from meditating the design imputed to him. His coming now on board with honest confidence, and placing himself without hesitation in our hands, confirmed our belief that the report was groundless.

That no unnecessary delay should take place with respect to the cargo, and to forward the smith in the execution of his work, I returned with Mr. Kendall to Rangehoo, leaving Themorangha still on board. Getting into the canoe of a neighbouring chief, we proceeded with him to Motooroa,* a large island immediately opposite the opening of the harbour, and which was under his ex-

---

* It is so called from its shape; *motoo* being the name for *island,* and *roa* the term for *long,* so that the union of both words is descriptive of its figure. In the chart laid down by Captain Cook, this island is erroneously called Motuaro.

clusive sovereignty. We landed here, and the chief not choosing to accompany us any farther, took his leave, sending his people with us at the same time, to paddle us on the remainder of the distance. This island, though the only territory he possessed, he offered to dispose of to the missionaries, at the cheap price of two muskets; and said, that in the event of the purchase being made, that part of the land which was tabooed should have the taboo taken off, and made free like the rest. From this I should infer that their laws with respect to the taboo may be abrogated at pleasure, and have not the unchangeable character of those of the Medes and Persians. We walked over part of the island, and found it tolerably level, and the land apparently fertile. Could the missionaries live on it in security, I doubt not but it would make a desirable settlement; it would produce not only grain enough for their own consumption, but leave such a surplus as might supply the shipping that should arrive there. We saw some plantations, in one of which there were about an hundred stalks of Indian corn, but of a very unpromising appearance. We told the chief that he did not understand the cultivation of this grain; that the stalks, instead of being only twelve and eighteen inches asunder, as he had them, should be separated from each other by a distance of four feet, and the intermediate space not planted with potatoes, as was the case. They told us, that the Indian corn in the district of Thiomi was in a very flourishing condition; but at that place they probably adopted a different mode of cultivating it. As these people understand nothing of grinding, nor have any means to perform that process, they roast the ears of corn in the fire, in the same manner as the original natives do at New South Wales. I observed in this island* a great variety of plants and shrubs, but which were not different from those generally found upon the main land.

* While here I purchased from some of the natives the *Syngathus Hippocampas*, or *Sea-horse*, which they dry and hang to their ears by way of ornament.

CHAP. IV.

Duaterra's abhorrence of the chief Themorangha—His slan-
derous report respecting him—Motive of his enmity—
His extreme caution—Axes brought by the Author to
the vessel—Tarra's impatience on seeing them—The
Author proceeds with Themorangha to see a battle at the
Wycaddie—Particulars of the passage, and reception of
the party—Warriors of the chief Henou—His martial
orators—Their conference with the chief Wiveeah and
his party—An interesting speaker—Speeches continued
—Amicable adjustment between the parties—Description of Wiveeah—His adversary Henou—The Author
passes through the warriors—Occurrences among them—
Deformed object—Provisions distributed—Martial appearance of Warree, and his interview with Themorangha—Singular dress of a warrior—The chiefs strangely
attired—War evolutions—Conference renewed—Female
orators—Reconciliation established—Incidental reflections—Return of the Author and his party to the vessel.

ON arriving at the settlement, I found all
our friends perfectly well, and with the exception of two or three who were more timid
and credulous than the rest, quite free from
any apprehension of being attacked. The
report was never believed by the more re-
flective among them, who could not bring
themselves to entertain those suspicions of
Themorangha which they knew were not

warranted either by his conduct or disposition, and must have been maliciously excited
against him, in order to serve some private
purpose. In this I am persuaded they judged
very rightly, and on paying a visit to Duaterra, I had every reason to suspect, from the
manner he vilified the chief in question, that
he wished to provoke our detestation against
him, at the expense of all truth and justice;
though it is but right I should observe, that
this was the first time I had occasion entirely
to disbelieve any statement he made. In-
veighing against Themorangha with the same
malevolence as Tupee did against Korra-
korra; he told us he was one of the most
ferocious and treacherous characters in the
island, that he was fully determined to cut
us off, and only waited for a favourable opportunity. Of this meditated atrocity he said
he had been informed himself by Warrakee,
who happened to hear the people of Thiomi
declare their intention of destroying all the
Europeans, both on board the vessel and at
the settlement; and that Themorangha, on
being asked how many were in the cabin, said
two or three, sometimes none, adding moreover, that from the number of New Zealanders always on board, the ship might be cut

off without the least difficulty.   I now asked
Duaterra, if such was the determination of
the chief, why did he not attempt the execution of it? To which he replied, that certain
reasons prevented him, and among others,
the dread of the areekee Tarra, who would
punish him with death for such an outrage
on hospitality, within the limits of his jurisdiction.   The details of this story appeared
to me not only improbable, but as originating
in complete falsehood; and as we had given
permission to Themorangha to accompany us
to Port Jackson, which he had an anxious
desire to visit, I doubt not but it excited the
jealousy of our friend the chief of Rangehoo;
for such was his wish to monopolize our
friendship, that he could not bear we should
extend it to any individual of a different
tribe from his own.   Urged on by this
jealousy, and probably incited also by some
idle conversation with Warrakee, he did not
hesitate to indulge in the slander so preva-
lent among the other chiefs; though it is my
opinion, that nothing but an impulse of this
kind could lead him to do so, as he was
rather remarkable for his veracity than otherwise.

While I was yet standing in conversation

with Duaterra, some of his people came to inform him that his cow had calved; when anxious to see this increase to his wealth, he set out with one of his warriors, arming himself with a pistol stuck in his breast, and a bill-hook in his hand. Surprised at this precaution, (for the distance he had to go was not more than five hundred yards, and in the midst of his own people,) I asked him what danger he could anticipate, that had made him thus prepare for it; and his reply was, that he was not sure of his life upon any occasion, since he became possessed of so much wealth, and that he made it a rule ever since the hostile chief was going to spear him, when he was returning from his farm, never to go any where without proper means of defence. The circumstances of the case might have justified this precaution, but still Duaterra appeared to me of a very suspicious disposition, ever apt to imagine violence where none was intended, and not feeling himself safe in the midst of security. This was certainly the consequence of that habitual vigilance to which men in the savage state are necessarily accustomed; for danger, however actually remote, is always present in the minds of such people. On going down the hill, we saw his people driving the cow into his stock-yard, followed by a very fine bull calf; so that in a little time, this part of the island may probably be well stocked with a breed of black cattle.

On Thursday, Feb. 2nd, Shunghi and his brother Kangeroa, having come to pay us a visit, Mr. Marsden invited the former to dine with us, and we were glad to shew every possible attention to this chief, for whom we entertained a particular regard.

The following day, Feb. 3rd, passed away without any occurrence worthy of notice. I took my usual rounds through the town, and made a few purchases of thread and other trifling articles, but no circumstance worth recording came under my observation.

The smith having by the 4th, got a number of axes ready, I prepared to take them to the vessel, and applied to Duaterra for a canoe; but he told me it was impossible he could accommodate me, as he had not one of his own convenient, and that his influence over the people* did not extend so far as to

* The people of Rangehoo, besides holding their ground by an independent tenure, have other immunities which are not common to the rest of the natives.

oblige them to take me, though in other respects he might command their services. I prevailed on him, however, to engage three of the natives to go with me, though he was necessitated to use some persuasion before they would consent to it. I was going to have my dinner before I set off, but he told me, if I did not take the men while they were in the humour, it was very doubtful if I could prevail upon them to go at all; so reluctant were they to lend their services on the present occasion. It appeared to me, therefore, much better to forego my dinner, than to run the chance of losing a conveyance to the vessel; and I got into their canoe that very instant. I had a most tedious and disagreeable passage, being no less than seven hours before I reached the ship; the wind blew directly against us the greater part of the way, with a very heavy swell coming in from the heads. On arriving at Motooroa, the men landed, and cut down a large stick for a mast, to which they tied their kackahows, as a substitute for a sail.

It was quite dark when I regained the vessel, where, on going into the cabin, the first spectacle that presented itself to me, was old Tarra and his wife Mrs. Goshore, lying upon the lockers. Here they had chosen to take up their night's lodging, having made on that day a visit on board; but as soon as the old chief heard the rattling of the axes, he could no longer compose himself to rest, and jumping up with an agility unusual in one of his grave deportment and venerable years, he began to examine them all very attentively; and selecting out the largest of them, he tabooed it immediately, and set it apart for his own exclusive use. Pomaree, who was on board, waited my return with anxious impatience, and appeared quite overjoyed at the sight of the supply I had brought with me, fixing his eyes on the axes with his usual avidity. He told us, that he intended returning to his district the following day, for the purpose of providing us with more timber, and said he would take care that no delay should be made in getting as much as would be necessary to complete the cargo. But he observed at the same time, that there were some of his people who had not yet received any presents, and who envied the good fortune of the others so much, that they could not support the idea of it, while they reflected that themselves had 'not an opportunity of an equal participation. This had caused, he said, *nuee nuee tanghee tanghee* (a good deal of crying) among them : he therefore requested Mr. Marsden would give him some nails to distribute among them, which would make them all happy ; and with these, as well as some other trifles, he was immediately furnished.

There was on Sunday morning, Feb. 5th, a report very current among the natives on board, that a great battle was to be fought in the course of the day between Wiveeah, the chief against whom Korra-korra's* expedition was directed, and Henou, the chief whose wife had been seduced.- As Themorangha expressed his intention of being a neutral spectator of this conflict, I felt no hesitation in accompanying him, while he pledged himself that I should be perfectly secure ; and the calumnious report I had heard respecting this chief, had no effect in making me doubt his sincerity. It being the sabbath, Mr. Marsden was prevented from joining us, by that peculiar reverence for the day, which he always observed : so, taking

---

* What the result of this expedition was, I could never ascertain ; but I think it likely that the belligerent parties came to some temporary adjustment, for I believe there was no fighting.

thirteen of the natives with us, we set out together, a strong curiosity urging me to disregard in this instance, the pious example of
my reverend friend. Our party, of whom I
was the only European, anxious to arrive at
the scene of action as soon as possible, plied
their paddles with so much activity, that in
the space of three hours we arrived at the
Wycaddie, where lay the district of the
offending chief, and the general rendezvous
of the contending parties.

The landing place here is about half a
mile from the village, which I have already
described ;* but our approach had been perceived, and two of the natives, running up
and down the beach with long whalebone
pattoo pattoos in their hands, shook them
at us in their usual style of defiance. My
friends, however, who were all armed,
jumped on shore without more delay, and
put them to flight that very instant; the
whole party pursuing them at the same time,
with the exception of Themorangha, whose
friendly attention to me would not suffer him
to leave me behind, seeing that all the speed
I could make would be very soon outstripped

* See vol. i. p. 250,

by the fleetness of his countrymen. We both
walked on together with a moderate pace,
and were met before we entered the village
by a considerable number of warriors, among
whom I observed our people mingle with a
social familiarity. I now entered this little
capital, and found it one scene of bustle and
confusion, being full of armed men, who ran
wildly about through every part of it, with
impatient anticipation of the savage affray.
Here I recognized our friend Tupee, together
with two other chiefs whom I knew, Guy and
Show. They were sitting on the roof of a
house, and Tupee, the moment he observed
me, beckoned to me to come and sit beside
him, which I did, and had an opportunity of
viewing from this dignified elevation (for as
such it was considered) the whole strength
of the combatants on both sides. Directly
opposite to where we were sitting was a large
enclosure separated from us by the Wycaddie, and here Henou and his party were
encamped. This party, amounting to the
number of at least two hundred men, and
composed of different tribes, headed by their
respective chiefs, were sitting on the ground
dispersed in groups, and all attentively
watching an old warrior, who had risen for

the purpose of addressing Wiveeah and his followers. In this old man, who appeared a complete oratorical champion, I beheld a curious sample of the popular eloquence of the country; and from the martial vehemence of the action he employed, I should suppose that "his voice was still for war," nor were his hearers uninfluenced by his harangue. Walking, or rather running up and down behind the paling that was drawn along the verge of the opposite bank, he uttered his words in a tone of violent resentment; and these we could distinctly hear, the distance between the parties not being more than a hundred yards. He occasionally shook his head with the view as it were of confirming his arguments; and brandishing his spear as if he could exterminate Wiveeah and his entire host with a single stroke, the veteran appeared ungovernable in his passion for the conflict. The most profound silence prevailed; and when he had finished his vehement address, two of the warriors on our side rose to reply.

The persons deputed for this purpose by general consent, were Tupee and Themorangha, who answered him with an accent and manner as mild and conciliating as his were obstreperous and turbulent. They appeared, however, to urge their cause with a steady and determined firmness, and the opposite party listened to them all the while with becoming attention. Their speeches were not delivered together; but Tupee rising first, commenced his reply, which occupied only a few minutes, when taking his seat again, he was succeeded by Themorangha, who spoke somewhat more at length, but with the same gentle and persuasive manner as his companion, whose arguments I should suppose he enforced with some cogency. To him also the opposite band were equally attentive; and I was much struck with the coolness and good order observed on both sides during the time these harangues were delivered. Themorangha having concluded, I expected there would be no more speeches, but that the parties would instantly rush upon each other, and employ the *pattoo pattoo* instead of the tongue. This, however, was not the case; for they seemed resolved to decide their quarrel by the latter weapon, a determination that afforded me no small degree of pleasure; preferring by far to witness among them such a conciliatory disposition, than, to have my curiosity gratified by beholding a real New Zealand battle. The speeches of Tupee and Themorangha were answered by another warrior of Henou's party, who rising up from among the group that surrounded him, advanced to the same spot where the veteran had stood, and began his rejoinder in a masterly style of native eloquence. There was an easy dignity in the manner of this man, that peculiarly distinguished him from the other orators. He spoke for a considerable time; and I could not behold without admiration the graceful elegance of his deportment, and the appropriate accordance of his action. Holding his *pattoo pattoo* in his hand, he walked up and down along the margin of the river with a firm and manly step, arrayed in a plain mat, which being tied over his right shoulder, descended with a kind of Roman negligence down to his ancles, and to the mind of the classical beholder, might well represent the *toga;* while his towering stature and perfect symmetry gave even more than Roman dignity to the illusion. His words, though delivered in impassioned accents, seemed by no means expressive of a violent or unaccommodating spirit; and though ignorant of the tenor of them, in consequence of my knowing so little of their language, I have no doubt, from the manner they were uttered, but they were of a conciliating import.

To this orator, (who might well deserve the name, all the necessary requisites being united in his person in an eminent degree,) Tupee and Themorangha, as well as two other chiefs on our side, replied individually; and their rejoinder was answered by a third speaker of the opposite party, who had nothing remarkable in his manner or delivery. The harangue of this man was the last that was delivered on either side; and having now an opportunity of asking Tupee what the result of this oratorical debate was to be, he told me that the parties had already come to an amicable adjustment. Some preliminary ceremonies, it appeared, had taken place between Wiveeah and Henou before my arrival; and though I doubt not but the old warrior urged the necessity of having immediate recourse to arms, his arguments, I am persuaded, were over-ruled by the others, who were not hurried forward by the same impulse of implacable hostility. One man told me, that before I had arrived the parties threw spears at each other; but this, on making further inquiries, I had reason to believe incorrect; and nothing had passed previously to my coming but certain formalities, which, from the want of an interpreter, I could not get explained.

As yet I had not seen Wiveeah, but he now advanced towards me in a very friendly manner, attended by five or six of his warriors; and after shaking me by the hand with much cordiality, returned back again, and mingled with his people. This man, whose lawless intrigue was the cause of all the speeches I had heard and all the demonstrations I had witnessed, was the gallant gay Lothario of this quarter. He appeared about five-and-thirty, of the middle size, but of a graceful figure, and remarkably well proportioned. He had a handsome mat, adorned with feathers, tied round his waist, leaving bare the upper part of his body, which was deeply besmeared with oil and red ochre; his hair was nicely tied up on the crown of his head, and a large comb, as white as ivory, made of the bone of some cetaceous animal, and curiously cut in filigree work, stuck in it. His cheeks were painted red, which giving fire and vivacity to his eyes, formed a curious and not unbecoming contrast to his black and bushy beard. His appearance altogether was such as might attract the attention of the ladies of his country, who looked upon him as the very *acme* of elegant manliness.

Tupee informed me, that the forces both under Wiveeah and Henou belonged to him, though on this occasion they were obliged to follow separate interests, from the circumstances in which they were placed, as deriving immediately under these inferior chiefs who had thus led them out in opposition to each other. But I should suppose he only meant to say, that they acknowledged the authority of his brother Tarra, who was the areekee, and that himself being the fighting-man, he had a control over them in consequence.

All differences being now amicably settled, and no variance existing between the parties, they were willing to consummate their reconciliation by a plentiful banquet; and Tupee conducting me over to Henou's side, one of the natives carried me on his back across the river, while we were followed by others bringing a quantity of potatoes to Henou, as a present from Wiveeah, who sent this supply for the use of his late adversary seeing that he was short of provisions to celebrate the joyous occasion. I found Henou with his son Temoutee, sitting in the middle of the field, surrounded by warriors, who were either of his own tribe or those in alliance with him; and passing through a file of these, I went up to the chief, and touching noses with him in the usual style of ceremonious formality, seated myself beside him at his particular request. There was no similarity either of face or figure between this chief and Wiveeah. Henou, though at an earlier period of life he must have been a well-looking man, had now nothing in his appearance that could secure to him the attachment of a woman, whose fidelity was solely to depend on external impressions. All the vigour of youth was completely wasted in the gradual progress of declining years; and it was not matter of surprise that his wife, who conceived herself bound by no other tie than that of sensual gratification, should have preferred his rival, who was in the prime of life, and remarkable for those personal attractions which are most admired in the country. The son of Henou was quite as old as Wiveeah, and the chief himself could not have been less than seventy, with a beard

as white as snow, and covering his breast
with patriarchal gravity.

After sitting a little time with Henou,
during which he never uttered a word, (but
looking at me steadfastly in the face, seemed
employed in drawing from my countenance
inferences respecting my intentions,) I rose up
and joined the different groups dispersed in
the enclosure. These were all exceedingly
amused at the sight of me, and pressed me
with their usual earnestness to seat myself
among them. They examined my boots and
clothes with minute attention, and no article
of dress about me escaped their notice. I
felt it rather inconvenient to be subjected to
this impatient scrutiny, as they thronged
round me in such a manner as to bring me
in contact with their *cootoos*, from which I
had already but too frequent occasion to
clear myself: they were not, however, to be
denied this freedom, except by absolutely
repelling them, a measure to which I did not
deem it prudent to resort. Some of them
would unbutton my waistcoast, and insist
upon seeing my breast;* and looking at each

* The cause of this I should suppose was for the purpose
of ascertaining my sex, being in doubt, as I thought, whether
they should consider me to be a man or a woman.

other, as if they beheld in me some creature differently organized from themselves, and entirely heterogeneous in the economy of my frame, they uttered a few words occasionally, according as their wonder was excited by each new object of astonishment. While I was shewing them my watch, the ticking of which did not fail to call forth their wonted indications of surprise, the chiefs cried out in their true style of native haughtiness, *ittee ittee tungata*, meaning that the persons whose curiosity I was gratifying were common men, and as such ought not to be noticed. I did not however indulge them in this ungenerous exclusion; nor did their ill-natured pride make me withhold from the poor *cookees* a sight so peculiarly attractive to their superiors. In the midst of one of these groups I observed a man who was born a cripple; he had a hunch-back with crooked legs, and his stature was so very diminutive, that he looked quite dwarfish. This was the only instance of similar deformity that I discovered among these people; for in general all the members of their body were perfect and shapely; nor could any unsightly blemishes be perceived in their persons, except such as they themselves caused, in conformity with their superstitious rites of mourning, or had produced under the preposterous idea of enhancing their native endowments.

During the time that I still continued here, a party of cooks prepared themselves for dressing the baskets of potatoes that were sent over by Wiveeah. These being first brought into the middle of the field, under the direction of a chief belonging to Wiveeah, were all placed there together; and certain ceremonies being gone through, which consisted partly in the repetition of some words which I could not comprehend, and in the interchange of various movements among the assemblage, they were regularly distributed through the different tribes.

Of all the warriors assembled here, I saw none more conspicuous than Warree, the man who had seduced Duaterra's wife, and who now presented himself to us for the second time since he had made his escape from the vessel. Though not habited in the same attire with his countrymen, his appearance was no less formidable and imposing, and none of them betrayed a more martial air or determined countenance. He was dressed in a sailor's jacket and trowsers, and had a musket in his hand, with a cartridge-box hanging by his side ; he offered me his hand, and not deeming it politic to shew on this occasion, any recollection of his offence by repelling the familiarity, I shook it as if completely unmindful that he had ever transgressed in the manner I have recorded. Entering freely into conversation with him, I was asking him some questions respecting the people in this quarter, and the merits of the scene of which I was a spectator ; when Themorangha coming up, shook his head at him with indignant resentment, and reprobated his conduct in the strongest terms of violent reproach. Warree himself explained to me the particulars of this invective ; and the epithets made use of against him were such as betrayed the enraged feelings of the other, and the abhorrence in which he held him, for the crime he had committed. But the chief, now that he saw me inclined to converse familiarly with him, gradually altered his tone ; and asking me if he was *miti*, I replied that he certainly had done wrong, but would, I hoped, do better in future ; upon which he readily became reconciled to him, and touched noses with him in testimony of all resentment having vanished. As I stood in conversation with these, I was accosted by a man of the name of Hereco, who informed me that he had been at Norfolk Island, and also at Port Jackson ; he inquired with an earnest solicitude after Governor King, and Captains Piper and Brabyn, all of whom he recollected perfectly, and was anxious to learn if they were yet at the colony.

The number of fires kindled by the cooks, who were by this time as industrious as possible, raised such a smoke, that to avoid the suffocating volumes which were constantly wafting in my face, I was glad to get out of the field with all the expèdition I could make ; when re-crossing the river, I again joined Wiveeah and his party. Here I found them all regaling themselves with potatoes, which were distributed in baskets among the several detached groups who sat round them, and who enjoyed their kiki with their usual appetite. I offered the chief some biscuit, but he would not touch it, as he happened to be then under the taboo, and consequently precluded from feeding himself ; he ordered, however, some of his people to lay it by for him, till he was released from this mystical quarantine, when he purposed to gratify his palate with the welcome rarity. One of his warriors, a man of commanding stature and expressive countenance, was very singularly dressed. Round his waist he had a mat lined with birds' feathers of various colours, which were carefully connected together in a thick texture, and sewed to the garment with much exactness : over this was another mat, that hung with graceful freedom over his right shoulder, and on the outside of all was a piece of red India print, with another stripe of the same material bound round his forehead. His hair was .gaily, but at the same time most fantastically decorated; in every part of it were stuck long feathers of a snowy whiteness, and these were disposed in such an outlandish style of savage fancy, as to produce an effect that was irresistibly ludicrous. His cheeks were painted red, and in his hand he carried a tremendous iron pike, with a long pattoo pattoo stuck in his belt or girdle. Thus equipped, he paced about with an air of stately importance, holding up his head in as good style as the best disciplined grenadier, and regulating all his movements by a sort of military cadence, intuitively suggested to him, and adopted according to the occasion; being always in practical readiness for any, whether grave, lively, or vehement. Going up to shake hands with him, I was willing to flatter his vanity, by telling him he was *nuee nuee miti*, which I here meant should imply *very fine;* he received the compliment as if he considered it a just tribute to his lofty consequence, regarding me nevertheless with much complacency, and telling me in turn, that I was *nuee nuee miti* Europee—a very good European.

The chiefs upon this occasion were principally distinguished from the inferior warriors, by their dog-skin dresses ; the different coloured furs presenting an uncommonly curious appearance, from the strange devices they had conceived, in joining them together ; some of them being cut in square patches, as white as snow, and others extending in long mottled streaks, while intermingled with these, were several spots all differing from each other in shape, colour and size ; and in these garments there was evidently more regard paid to gaudy show than to taste or uniformity. Perhaps a panther's skin may convey the best idea that can be given of them, but even this must present but an imperfect notion of their grotesque varieties. Indeed I observed on this day a greater display in point of dress and gorgeous decoration, than I had yet met with; and this was also the largest assemblage of warriors I had hitherto seen, being at least double the number of the Wangeroan forces, among whom we had spent the night on our first arrival. The sublime grandeur of the adjacent scenery, gave additional interest to this spectacle ; and while the mind was inspired with a feeling of awe and wonder, at the mysterious dispensations of Providence, in thus leaving man in a state of rude nature, though formed with a genius for intellectual attainments, and placed in a country so much more favoured than many where science has left nothing unexplored; while this sentiment was continually present, the poor barbarian, who was unaided but by his own individual faculties, and could not resort to concentrated talent to furnish his equipment, claimed an involuntary respect for his devices, and a due regard for his astonishing expedients.

When both parties had sufficiently refreshed themselves, they prepared, as a necessary conclusion to the reconciliation that had taken place, to go through their war evolutions. Henou assembling all his people, formed them into two divisions, when the foremost being armed with spears of an immense length, rushed down to the paling; vociferating with their wonted clamour, and followed closely by the other division. Halting here, they collected themselves into one compact phalanx; and the chiefs taking their stations according to their rank, and the number of warriors they respectively commanded, the whole party commenced their military manœuvres; betraying their usual impetuosity, and roaring out with the same tremendous shouts as in the former similar exhibition that we had witnessed. But it was truly terrific to see with what violence of gesture, they feigned to charge upon their supposed enemies; while the chiefs appearing always prominent in every dangerous exploit, incited by their example, the furious courage of their warriors; and worked up their passions to such a pitch, that the scene, though unbloody, seemed fraught with slaughter, and that which was but the semblance, assumed all the horrors of actual reality. Twice did they make this dreadful charge with the same apparent fury, after which they danced and sung the war-song, when the raging vengeance of the scene was softened down by three females, who joining in the dance amidst the plaudits of the assemblage, soon chased away the horrid discord, and held all the warriors in mute attention to their graceful movements. When these females had concluded their performance, the entire party seated themselves down in the midst of the enclosure, and it being Wiveeah's turn now to exhibit a similar display of martial tumult, this chief drew out his men in order of battle; and leading them down to the water's edge, in the same manner as his adversary, he put them through evolutions equally violent, and resembling as nearly as possible, those that had been practised on the opposite side.

This frantic exhibition of their respective strength, being now concluded on both sides, the orators again stood up, and again claimed the same attention from the assemblage. The first of these was the veteran speaker, who now presented himself with renewed vehemence; and whether the display of these warlike movements had called forth all his martial spirit, or whether he thought his countrymen too tame in wasting their military energies in mock encounters, I know not; but from being only vehement at the beginning of his harangue, he became, as he proceeded, quite outrageous, and literally jumped about the field with raving violence. He was answered by Wiveeah in a speech of some length, as were also two other orators who succeeded him ; and at length the injured chief Henou, rising from his seat with venerable gravity, delivered an address with much gentleness of manner, and which was probably an affecting lecture to his rival, though unmarked by any symptoms of indignant re-crimination. Wiveeah replied to this address with equal mildness, and his three wives now deemed it expedient to interpose their oratory, as confirming mediators between the parties, though there was no longer any enmity existing on either side. They spoke with great animation, and the warriors listened to their separate speeches in attentive silence; they assumed, I thought, a very determined tone, employing a great deal of impressive action, and looking towards the opposite chief with an asperity of countenance, not warranted by the mild forbearance of his deportment. The expostulating harangues (as I should suppose they were) of these sturdy ladies, completed the ceremonials of this singular conference ; and the reconciliation being thus consummated, the parties now entertained no sentiments towards each other but those of reciprocal amity. Happy

would it be for the natives of this country,
if all their dissensions were adjusted in this
amicable manner; and I am rather inclined
to believe, that however great is their impatience for war, they are still not insensible
to the dictates of peace, but are often ready,
as in this instance, to compromise their feuds
with a mutual spirit of forbearance. This
disposition to let the force of reason super-
sede the violence of resentment, even in the
very height of their rage, and at the moment
when its ebullitions seem too furious to sub-
side, is a fine proof of the great intellectual
character of these people; and perhaps a
nobler instance cannot be given of the superiority of the human mind over the instinc-
tive faculty of the brute species, than that
the savage is capable of this unexpected
transition.

Henou and his party now left the field,
and went to their respective places of residence; and it was certainly fortunate for
Wiveeah that they had forborne to attack
him, the advantage being evidently on their
side in point of numbers. When these had
departed, the warriors on our side dispersed
likewise; and being much entertained with
the spectacle I had witnessed, I now col-

lected my party together, and got into the canoe, attended by Tupee, who wished to accompany me to the vessel. As we were rowing down the river, the sun was setting behind the distant hills, and as it cast its parting rays upon them, I could discern the Indian warriors winding their devious course over the high lands; and the sight was altogether so imposing and singular, when connected with the romantic localities of the scene, and the associations they induced, that I beheld it with a pleasing admiration while it was yet in view; nor can I at this moment bring the picture to my recollection, without having my mind impressed with a similar feeling.

CHAP. V.

The natives crowd on board the ship, and become an annoyance—Bargain between the Author and one of them—Themorangha's interference—Arrival of a canoe with potatoes—Singular ceremony in the purchase of an article—Mr. Kendall arrives on board from the settlement—His complaint of Duaterra—Excursion on shore, and incidents connected with it—The Author leaves the vessel to sojourn at the settlement—Curious exchange between the Author and one of the natives—Arrival of Tui from his brother's district—Cowittee, a native, visits the settlement—Accompanies the Author and Mr. Kendall on an excursion—The Phormium Tenax, or flax-plant—Death and funeral preparations of a native—Remarks on the mourners—Mr. Kendall's complaint of Duaterra removed—Selfishness of some natives—Character of the people of Tippoonah—Divine service performed at the settlement—Petty thefts on board the vessel—Dangerous quarrel on shore.

THE time was now fast approaching when we were to take our final leave of this island; and as there existed between us and the natives the most amicable intercourse, Mr. Marsden was unwilling to put any of them out of temper by excluding* them

* I would strongly dissuade all commanders of vessels, who may happen to trade in these parts, or in any of the South Sea Islands, from following our example; for by

peremptorily from the vessel, while we yet remained; though they flocked on board in such numbers as to render our situation extremely disagreeable, and most dangerous, if our friendship with them had not been firmly established. We had groups of them continually intruding themselves, and they were always to be found in every part of the ship; the decks were literally covered with them, the cabin was quite full, and even the hold had an assemblage that possessed themselves of all the space it contained. Tupee having spent the night on board, left us early in the morning, February the 6th, to return to his residence, and we were visited in the course of the day by Wiveeah, Tenangha, and some other chiefs from the Cowacowa and the Wycaddie; all of whom were followed by their respective attendants, bringing a fresh increase to the crowds of their countrymen, who were already stowed about the vessel. The chiefs, intruding themselves into the cabin with their customary

permitting an indiscriminate concourse of the natives on board, quarrels between them and the sailors will most commonly ensue; and perhaps the ultimate destruction of the vessel may be the disastrous result. It will therefore be always advisable never to suffer any but the chiefs to come on board.

indifference to our accommodation, engrossed it almost entirely to themselves; while the possession, which they had obtained by their native rudeness, was still maintained by their disgusting habits, which made us rather submit to a temporary exclusion, than remain confined among them to experience the stench emitted from their dirty persons. We were, however, obliged to endure this loathsome annoyance, when the time for taking our meals came round; and on this day, while we were at dinner, Tenangha was so very offensive by his unconscious disregard of all propriety of behaviour, that we were under the necessity of desiring him to quit the cabin instantly; but which he as positively refused to do, and sitting down near the door, seemed fully resolved on maintaining his post, telling Mr. Marsden that he was *nuee nuee kackeeno*, (very bad,) for insisting on his expulsion. But as my friend was a universal favourite among them, Tenangha very soon evinced his impatience to be reconciled to him; and being made sensible of the offence he had committed, which was of the most revolting description, and such as could not be mentioned without offering a violation to decency, he was again re-admitted into favour.

A canoe from the district of Thiomi came alongside in the afternoon, bringing a group of Themorangha's people, among whom were some very pretty women, who, on getting into the cabin, took particular delight in viewing their handsome features in the looking-glass. They remained however but a short time, when taking their leave of us with an air of peculiar complacency and satisfaction at the visit, they set off again for the shore. Wishing to purchase his *pattoo pattoo*, from one of the men who came in this canoe, I offered him a large fish-hook for it; when his chief coming up, snatched it rudely out of his hand, and presented it to me: this was done in so instantaneous a manner, that he had not time to decide whether he should approve of the exchange or not, and he stood gaping at me for some moments in a state of apparent confusion and suspense. The motive of Themorangha for this arbitrary interference, was the wish to make amends for his previous conduct in urging his countrymen to demand considerably more for their various articles than they were worth; which he always did, as

well as most of the other chiefs,* and would
still continue to follow the same practice,
had I not seriously remonstrated with him
on the palpable impropriety of such behaviour. My lecture produced the best
effects, and all my subsequent bargains with
the natives were made without the least
inconvenience; while in this instance the
chief was willing to give an unequivocal
proof of a new mode-of conduct, and one
quite different from that he had previously
adopted.

The morning of the 7th brought us another
canoe from Thiomi, with twenty-four baskets
of potatoes, sent by his people to Themorangha, as his provision during the voyage
to Port Jackson, whither, as I have stated,
he was resolved to accompany us. Ten of
of these baskets he presented to Mr. Marsden
with a friendly generosity, and reserved the

---

* I had frequently occasion to complain of this disposition
in the chiefs; but in none of them so much as in Themorangha. It was absolutely impossible to purchase any article
from the natives while he was present; for he would always
interfere to spoil the bargain, by fixing an arbitrary price on it
himself, of such immoderate extravagance, that no one could
agree to it; and if a fair value was offered, he would instantly
cry out to the owner of the article, *ittee ittee*, (too little,) and
prevail on him to urge his unreasonable demand.

remainder for his own use ; a small store enough, considering the length of the voyage, and the quantity he devoured.

Before breakfast this morning, a ceremony of a curious description took place, of which I was the principal subject, in consequence of a bargain that was to be ratified between myself and Wiveeah. Desirous to purchase of this chief the comb worn by him in his late conference with Henou, I told him on returning from the Wycaddie, to bring it with him to the vessel, and that I would give him the full value for it, which he accordingly did ; and giving him on the preceding day a bill-hook in exchange for it, he was perfectly satisfied, but waited till this morning before he would deliver up the comb in return. The cause of this delay was both serious and solemn. The chief, it would appear, attached to the comb no ordinary degree of sacred importance ; and fearful of incurring the guilt of profanation by parting with it in the same precipitate manner as with any other article of less awful attributes, he deemed it expedient to wait a certain time, and then transmit it to my hands with proper solemnities. This indispensable ceremony being now to be celebrated,

Wiveeah, attended by three chiefs, who officiated as his assistants, requested I would come into the cabin to receive the comb according to agreement. It will be necessary for me here to observe, that Wiveeah was recognized by his countrymen in the twofold character of a priest and a chief, as was the case with old Tarra and some others; and as he was now to act in the former capacity, he assumed a more grave deportment than usual, preparing himself with a serious air for the mystical functions. He began the ceremony by desiring me to hold open the palms of my hands before him; he then put them together, and holding one of my fingers with one hand, he dipped the other into a basin of water, and crossed my right hand with it, repeating all the while, in a quick tone of voice, and with a sudden volubility, some words which I supposed to be a form of prayer; and he appeared as he proceeded to have all his faculties completely inflamed with a glowing enthusiasm, nor could the genius of superstition have ever found in any individual a more ardent votary. After this he applied his spittle to his fingers, and crossed the palms of my hands with it, still talking in the same rapid accents, and seemingly absorbed in the rites he was celebrating. Having gone so far in these momentous formalities, his next step was to take a piece of dried fish, which having slightly touched my hands with, he applied it immediately after to the mouths of the three officiating chiefs, each of whom bit a small piece off; and this part of the ceremony was repeated three times successively. Now came the concluding form which was to put me in possession of this venerated treasure; and one of the chiefs approaching Wiveeah in a solemn pace, took the comb from his head, and delivered it over to me without uttering a word. Thus ended this singular ceremony, without which it would have been impossible for me to obtain the comb, as the chief would never have disposed of it under the ordinary forms. I was now going to deposit the revered curiosity in my sea-chest, but Wiveeah told me I must not put it there by any means, and when I attempted it, would not permit me; but desiring me to wrap it up very carefully in some paper, pointed to a locker that was over my bed-place, and charged me to lay it there and no where else. I felt no reluctance in obeying this peremptory injunction, and my doing so seemed to afford him a peculiar degree of pleasure, his profound respect for the article still remaining, after it had ceased to be his property. This comb was the only one of the kind I could ever observe in the island; but Captain Cook mentions its being worn by the people in the southern parts. It was indeed a curiosity both tasteful and ingenious in its execution; and those persons to whom I afterwards shewed it, could not help admiring the extraordinary inventive talents of the uninstructed maker.

Mr. Kendall, who arrived at the ship in the course of the day from Rangehoo, complained that there was no more iron to work up, excepting what was under the care of Duaterra, who refused to part with it upon any account, claiming it as his own property, and denying our right to take it from him. This chief also, it appeared, insisted that the ground occupied by the missionaries should be paid for, as the people to whom it belonged were dissatisfied respecting it, and wished him to urge their demands with positive earnestness. We were not much surprised at this latter information, as it was but just that the natives should receive some equivalent for their ground; but that Duaterra could have withheld the iron, was more than we had reason to expect, particularly as he had ever before shewn himself ready to promote the object of the mission, and as we always reposed the fullest confidence in his integrity. It was therefore resolved, that we should take the first convenient opportunity to inquire into the matter, and avoid, if possible, any misunderstanding with the chief.

On this day Pomaree fulfilled his contract with us, by bringing down the remainder of the spars, which he did with such a strict punctuality, that, however dishonest he might be viewed by his countrymen, who reprobated him upon all occasions, with us, he completely established his character for fair dealing. I have before stated how much more useful we found this man than any of the other chiefs, in supplying us with timber; and though the reports I continually heard of his character made me suspect his integrity, there was at the same time in his bustling manner an ingenuous openness that did not correspond with the designing knavery for which, among his other vices, he was stigmatized. Cruel he was, beyond a doubt, and perhaps treacherous; but we experienced his friendliness and good faith in our various transactions with him, and it is but right that

I should render this justice even to a savage, who was universally considered as most atrocious and implacable.

In the evening, Mr. Marsden and myself got into the boat, and took Gunnah with us, to cut down some of the small spars that line the sides of the cove. We landed on the eastern side; and our friend immediately setting to work, exerted himself to some purpose, handling the axe with all the dexterity of an expert woodman. It was curious to observe his ingenuity in getting to those trees which, from the nature of the place where they grew, were inaccessible to his labours, unless by some artificial contrivance. Extending a sort of platform from the high banks on one side against the tree on the other, he made it perfectly firm at both ends; and having, in effect, formed a complete scaffolding by this device, he would stand upon it to accomplish his work, removing it occasionally from one tree to another, according to his progress.

Observing a hole at the foot of one of these trees, which evidently appeared to have been burrowed by some quadruped, we inquired of Gunnah what animal he supposed it was; and from his description of it, we had reason to believe that it must be the Guana, though Dr. Forster, in enumerating the quadrupeds* of this island, makes no mention of such a one being found among them. Wishing to know how far our surmise was correct, we desired our friend to thrust a stick into the hole, and endeavour to worry the animal out of it; but this he tried with no effect, for either it was not in the hole at the time, or, if there, not to be dislodged by such means. Gunnah, however, was rather well pleased than otherwise at not meeting with this animal; for his dread of it was so great, that he shrunk back with terror at the time he thought it would come out, nor did he examine the hole but with great reluctance. This we thought very strange, for the Guana (the animal we took it for) is perfectly harmless. It may not be improper to mention here, that from all the inquiries we made among the natives, we could not ascer-

---

* Besides the dog, New Zealand boasts four other quadrupeds: one is, the rat; the other, a small bat, resembling that described in Mr. Pennant's Synopsis of Quadrupeds, No. 283, under the name of New York bat; the third is, the sea bear, or ursine seal, Penn. Syn. Quad. No. 27 (Phoca ursina, Linn.); and the fourth, the animal which Lord Anson calls a sea lion, Phoca leonina, Linn. leonine seal, Penn. Syn. Quad. No. 272.—*Dr. Forster's Observations*, p. 190.

tain that there were any venomous reptiles*
found on the island ; and we did not, in the
progress of our different excursions, meet
with a single noxious animal. On our return
from the place where we cut down the spars,
we met one of the native dogs, running about
in a wild state. It was considerably larger
than any of the dogs that we had seen domes-
ticated among them, and bore a strong resemblance to the shepherd's dog so well
known in England. The moment it came in
sight of us, it set up a terrific howling ; and
never ceased the same baleful discord till we
had left the place. There are numbers of
dogs running wild in this manner through
the different parts of the island ; but I could
not discover that they ever offered any injury
to the inhabitants, who prize them very
highly, as well for the sake of their flesh,

* Duaterra, however, informed us, that a most destructive
animal was found in the interior of the country, which made
great havoc among the children, carrying them off and devouring them, whenever they came in its way. The description he gave of it corresponded exactly with that of the
alligator ; but I should still doubt that either this or any other
predaceous animal of so formidable a description exists in
New Zealand. The chief had never seen the animal himself,
but received his accounts from others ; and hence it appears
to me very probable that his credulity might have been imposed upon.

which serves them for a delicious article of food, as for their hide and bones, which they convert to a variety of purposes, in the way of ornamental devices.

Glad to get away from the vessel, which was still crowded with the natives as usual, and extremely unpleasant in consequence, I accompanied Mr. Kendall back to Rangehoo, on Wednesday, February 8th, intending to remain there till every thing was in readiness for our return to the colony. But I was in this respect much more fastidious than my friend Mr. Marsden; for such was his zeal in the cause he had undertaken, and so ardent an interest did he feel in favour of these poor people, that he never once complained of the inconvenience of being subject to their constant intrusion, which was become perfectly irksome to all in the ship except himself. He could sit among them in the cabin, inhaling their intolerable stench, and beholding their filthy habits, with as much composure as if he had been in the midst of the most elegant circle in Europe; and though I doubt not but his olfactory nerves were quite as acute as mine, still, on these occasions, it would seem that they were utterly incapable of executing their office. Arriving at the settlement, I

found all the people who composed it, both
males and females, in perfect health, and
attending as usual to their respective occupations.　Duaterra, whom I wished to see
respecting the iron, was not at home, having
gone to visit his farm in the interior; so I
was obliged to wait his return before I could
speak to him on the subject.

Passing the night in Mr. Kendall's habitation, who invited me to take up my abode
with him while I remained on shore, and who
endeavoured to render my accommodation as
comfortable as the circumstances he was
placed in would admit, I got up next
morning, February the 9th, at an early hour,
and went into the town, where the inhabitants
having already come forth from their huts,
flocked round the packahâ with their wonted
eagerness.　They shewed me several of their
usual curiosities, as well as some of a novel
description, which they had to dispose of;
and I made them happy by purchasing a few
articles.　But one bargain that I made,
afforded them the highest gratification.　A
sturdy old man who had all the appearance
of a keen dealer, coming up to me with a
large mat, offered to exchange it with me for
my coat, to which I made not the least objec-

tion, seeing I should not lose much by the bargain; while it would afford me no inconsiderable degree of entertainment, by its giving an adventitious consequence to the old man among the other natives. The exchange therefore took place immediately; when the old man putting on the coat, and I the mat, we walked about to the supreme enjoyment of the surrounding crowd; who regarded me with an air that shewed how much their vanity was flattered by my appearing in their native attire, and stared at their countryman as if they doubted his identity, and believed that his person had suffered transformation by being arrayed in this strange habit; bursting at the same time into occasional transports of merriment, and laughing heartily at the appearance he made. He was certainly an admirable subject for their good humour to indulge itself upon; nor was I surprised that they should think him quite another man, from the moment he put on the coat. His manner and movements were entirely altered; his figure, which before seemed bent with age, now became suddenly erect; and his gait, which but lately was grave and circumspect, was now light and frivolous as that of the most idle lounger in the British metropolis; and there were instantaneously so many ludicrous airs of pompous consequence about him, as I never till that moment beheld, and thought it impossible for any individual to affect.

One of the women here came up to tell me, that a relation of Gunnah's, a man who lived in one of the adjacent huts, was so very ill that his life was despaired of; but though I offered to accompany her to the shed where he was lying, in order to render any assistance in my power towards his recovery, she would not permit me; as he was under the *taboo*, and not to be approached till the *Etua* was pleased to deliver him from his sufferings, by putting an end to his existence.

I observed among the women assembled round me this morning, one who was if possible a more hideous martyr to disease than the frightful object I met at Parro. But in this instance the malady I believe proceeded from a different cause; and was the consequence, not of the venereal poison, but of some latent impurity of the blood, produced most probably by inattention to cleanliness, or living too long upon the fern-root, without having recourse to any other kind of sustenance. Either one of these causes, or both of them together, might have operated to produce it; as it appeared to me to be nothing else than an inveterate scurvy. But though the con dition of this creature was such as to render her one of the most deplorable objects that ever laboured under bodily affliction; strange to say, she appeared as happy and cheerful as if she had been in the full vigour of health, and enjoyed all the comforts of civilized affluence. Her hands were all over in a state of livid ulceration, nor could she make the least use of them; her face and the different parts of her body were equally festering in disease; and superstition rendering her situation still more miserable, she was obliged to take off the ground with her mouth, the potatoes thrown to her by her friends, whose commiseration she neither desired, nor in any instance would solicit. Here was such an example, not only of resignation, but of mirthful contentment under excessive sufferings, as the reader will hardly suppose could exist in human nature; yet have I seen this wretched object, and witnessed what I assert. While speaking of this pitiable creature, I must also remark, that in New Zealand sore eyes is a general complaint; in the

cure of which **Mr. Kendall*** has been very
successful, by using goulard; a remedy that
he found to answer invariably, whenever he
applied it.   I had frequent occasion to notice
the prevalence of this complaint among these
people.   Several of them were afflicted with
it, and I should attribute it to their sleeping

* In forming an establishment for the purpose of civilizing
a rude and barbarous people, it were I think highly advise-
able, that one, at least, of the persons belonging to it, should
have some knowledge of medicine. The advantage of this
will appear obvious for two reasons : in the first place, it will
give to the mission a considerable importance among the
natives, who will rejoice in the opportunity of getting a remedy
for their complaints ; while they will look with profound
respect to the source whence it is afforded : and secondly,
the cause of humanity will be served by it ; for that philan-
throphy must be preposterous, which can infuse light into the
mind of the savage, and suffer his wretched body at the same
time to waste away under some pestilential disease or loathsome distemper. For the skill of the physician there is not
(a few cases excepted) much necessity in New Zealand ; yet
it has considerably enhanced Mr. Kendall in the estimation of
his new friends, that he is enabled to cure them of their sore
eyes. There was one case in particular, that raised his fame
among them to a high degree of celebrity : the widow of the
late chief Tippahee, had her eyes for a long time in so bad
a state, that she could not open them except with the most painful difficulty ; when Mr. Kendall happening to see her, undertook to cure her of her complaint, if she would call upon him
every morning for a certain time, which she accordingly did ;
and by washing her eyes with goulard, they soon got quite well ;
while she extolled his skill through all the district, and expressed her grateful acknowledgments for its efficacy.

so frequently in the open air, under the heavy
dews, and always with their heads uncovered.
I have repeatedly seen them get up in the
morning with their hair and beards quite
wet ; and I am only surprised how they can
at all preserve their health, considering the
number of severe privations to which they
are exposed ; but habit is sufficient to reconcile man to any condition, and can prepare
him even for the most deplorable state of
human endurance.

About noon we had a visit at the settlement
from Tui and some of his brother Korra-korra's
people, who came from Parro to get provisions for the men we had left there,.and for some
more salt to cure fish. I inquired of him what
progress they were making, and he informed
me that they were getting on very rapidly, and
would soon have as much cured as we could
conveniently take with us, but that the salt and
provisions must be sent without delay. Not
long after these came Cowittee, a man who
lived on the eastern side of the bay, and to
whom Mr. Hall had given an axe in consideration of his bringing him a canoe, which he engaged to do, but could not perform his promise.
However, as he was not able to procure the
canoe, he now brought with him a large pig,

and presenting it to Mr. Hall, expressed his regret that it was not in his power to fulfil his engagement, in consequence of an unexpected disappointment; hoping at the same time, that what he offered would be accepted as an equivalent for the axe. There was an unequivocal sincerity in his manner that interested me very much in his favour, and such as could leave no doubt of his being honestly disposed.

After dinner we got into this man's canoe, and taking him with us, went to shoot seagulls, which are very numerous in the different parts adjacent to the bay: we had not proceeded very far, when we shot two birds about the size of a duck.* Cowittee was highly gratified at our permitting him to take a gun, and he soon gave evident demonstrations that he could use it to some purpose; for he proved to be an excellent marksman. In the course of this excursion we had occasion to land upon one of the small islands in the bay, where I observed the flax-plant growing in great luxuriance; and the seed being ripe, I collected a quantity of it, which I afterwards brought with me to England; but unfortunately it lost during the voyage all its

* For a description of these birds, see vol. i. p. 426.

vegetative properties. That this plant would, by proper management, come to perfection in our country, I have not the least doubt, and it were much to be desired that so valuable a production were introduced into it. This plant, the botanical name for which is the Phormium Tenax, has been cultivated in some parts of France with much success, as will appear from the note* which I subjoin ; and though England cannot boast a climate

* "We should be glad to see the Phormium Tenax, or New Holland Flax, figured in this work (the Botanical Magazine ;) which we were informed blossomed, though imperfectly, some years ago in the neighbourhood of London. In France, in the department of La Drome, this plant is cultivated in the open air with great success, as appears from a letter from M. Fanjas St. Fond, to M. Thouin, inserted in the Annals du Museum d' Histoire Naturelle; in which he announces that the Phormium Tenax, or New Zealand Flax, had produced flowers in the garden of M. Freycinet, the father of two officers who were in Capt. Baudin's expedition. 'The Phormium Tenax,' M. Faujas St. Fond adds, ' was cultivated in the garden of M. Freycinet, and in my own. We took care to cover it in the winter: but as we were at first anxious to multiply our plants, we cut off shoots every year, which greatly impoverished the principal plants, and of course interrupted their flowering : at length, when we became anxious to see the flower, we reserved about ten, which we left to themselves. These plants soon increased prodigiously; and on the 10th of May 1813, M. Freycinet informed me that a very vigorous flower stalk was shooting out from the centre of one of his strongest plants. Seven days afterward, this stalk was three feet high; on the 31st it was five feet six inches, and on the

equally genial with the mild air of that favoured country, still I think that the flax-plant of New Zealand might be grown in it to considerable advantage.

In the middle of the ensuing night, Mr. Kendall was disturbed as well as myself, by the incessant talking of the natives, and there was a sort of clamorous bustle among them for which we knew not how to account The morning however of the 10th, put us in pos-session of the cause of it; when we discovered that Gunnah's relation had died in the course of the preceding day, and that a number of the people were assembled at Tippoonah for the purpose of attending his interment; while the noisy conversations that had disturbed us, proceeded from their discussing how his obsequies were to be regulated. It would appear from this expedition in providing for the burial of the deceased, that the New

7th of June, six feet ten inches. On the 14th, its term of greatest increase, it was seven feet six lines; the stalk was then three inches and four lines in circumference at the base, and two inches and a half, half way up. The flowers, to the number of a hundred and nine, are borne upon alternate pe-duncles, and have a pleasing effect. The colour of the flower is a greenish yellow, that of the stamina a golden yellow. I have made some very strong ropes with the leaves, from which I obtained the flax by a very simple process.' "—*Monthly Magazine, August* 1814.

Zealanders never suffer their dead to remain longer above ground, after the vital spark is extinguished, than till they can arrange the forms of their inhumation. Being curious to observe their ceremonies upon this occasion, we immediately hastened to the place where the corpse was lying, which was about a mile from Rangehoo. Arriving here, we found several of the natives on the beach before us, and the body of the deceased bundled up in the clothes he wore at the time he expired; the knees and feet being apparently brought close to the body, as in the case of the native who had died on board; and the whole fastened tight round with a belt, and placed upon a bank between two poles, which had served to convey* it thither. — Though the assemblage was large, the number of mourners were few; and of all who were standing beside the corpse, I could see only the widow of Tippahee and another woman, who appeared seriously affected. These wept bitterly, and were particularly

* They make in several parts of the island a kind of carriage or bier for their dead; on which they carve the most indelicate representations, and such as describe the grossest indulgence of sensual pleasures. I have never seen one of these biers myself, but Mr. Kendall informed me that he had met with them; and on his statement I can perfectly rely.

careful that we should not approach too near the body; telling us with anxious precaution, that it was *taboo taboo*, and shewing violent signs of uneasiness, lest we should advance beyond certain prescribed limits. The other natives who were in attendance, though some of them had all the hideous marks of sorrow inscribed on their faces, felt I am persuaded no real concern.   One young man who was probably a near relation of the deceased, had his face lacerated in a frightful manner, and was shedding tears very copiously; but on going up to this mourner, I witnessed in him a most unseemly transition; for he smiled with a degree of vivacious levity, that proved his grief to be only in the revolting semblance. I shook hands with him, and from only smiling at first, he now laughed very heartily, and his behaviour was altogether so inconsistent with the appearance he assumed, that I knew not how to account for it, unless by considering the most doleful testimonies of sorrow among some of these people, as nothing more than common-place forms, prescribed by long established usage. But this opinion will by no means apply to the New Zealanders in the aggregate; for no people in existence can feel grief more acutely than they do as a body; and their mournings, though enjoined by outward custom, are nevertheless sanctioned by the heart. The women, excepting the two first I have mentioned, evinced in the present instance no regret whatsoever. They laughed and talked away without the least reserve, quite heedless of the occasion, being much more inclined to loquacity and mirth, than to silence or dejection. Several of them asked me for nails, and told me they had thread for sale which they wished me to purchase.

We had not been here very long before a canoe, loaded with potatoes, approached the shore, and among the persons who were in it, I observed Gunnah's wife, who seemed as little affected at the loss of her husband's relation, as the most unconcerned of the other ladies. On landing, she laughed and chattered with the same vivacity as they did, nor were any symptoms of grief perceptible in her appearance or behaviour. The whole assembled concourse now began to dress their provisions, and making their fires, prepared to satisfy their appetites before they would proceed with the body to the place of interment. To this place we were prevented from accompanying it by the absolute enact-

ments of the *taboo*, an authority we durst
not venture to impugn, nor did we think it
prudent to question; though we had hoped
on our setting out that we should be allowed
to see all the forms made use of in their
burials. Whether any ceremonies had been
performed over the body before our arrival,
we could not learn; but after we had got
into Cowittee's canoe, and as we were turning
off the point of land that separates this place
from the town, we saw it carried away, sup-
ported upon the poles, and borne on the
shoulders of two men, while three or four
more of the natives composed the whole train
of the funeral. Judging from the small number thus in attendance at the last obsequies,
I should suppose that the majority of the
assemblage were either unwilling to be present on the occasion, or more probably, like
ourselves, were precluded by the superstition
of the country.

Duaterra having returned from his farm
in the course of the day, I lost no time in
seeing him about the iron, which, without
any difficulty, he now consented to deliver,
though he had at first obstinately persisted
in withholding it. He refused to inform me
what his motive was for objecting to give it

up to the missionaries ; but this chief, though of an excellent disposition, was, I am rather inclined to think, somewhat capricious in his temper; and while his heart remained always the same, his head was not equally constant. The demand, however, of payment for the land on which the missionaries had erected their dwellings, was again urged by him ; and as Gunnah and his brother Warree were the proprietors, he suggested the expediency of settling with them for it, which I promised should be done as soon as Mr. Marsden came on shore.

Next day, February 11th, Mr. Hall wanting to go to the ship on particular business, I applied to Duaterra, to provide him with a canoe; but in this instance I was more unsuccessful than before, for the chief, telling me again that he had not one of his own convenient, assured me very candidly, that it was not in his power to command those of his people, whom now even all the force of persuasion would not induce to accommodate us, as they complained of not being paid on the former occasion. The reason assigned by the chief, with regard to himself, was satisfactory enough; for we were convinced that, had he a canoe in readiness, he would not have hesitated to oblige us ; and were also certain that what he said of his circumscribed authority over his subjects was perfectly correct, nor could we blame him for not using that compulsion with them which their established privileges did not recognize, and which might consequently be dangerous to his own safety; but we could not help thinking that the men who had made the complaint were both selfish and ungrateful. The fact was, that Mr. Marsden, who intended to have recompensed them for their services, had not risen at the time I found it necessary to hurry them back with me to the shore; but as they were well fed while they remained on board, and received on their return a present of fish-hooks from Mr. Kendall, their murmurs against us were by no means deserved. But they expected, I should suppose, either a large axe, or something else equally valuable, which, considering the price set upon such articles, and the cheapness of labour in this country, would have been most unreasonable, and quite disproportioned to the service performed. However despotic may be the authority of the rest of the chiefs, on whose systems of government 1 cannot, for want of sufficient information, comment, the power of Duaterra, I have reason to believe, is confined to very narrow limits; and the people of Tippoonah live in a state of stubborn independence, either utterly unknown, or only partially experienced in the other districts. Indeed, the immunities they enjoy have a visible effect on their manners, which assume in consequence rather an unaccommodating tone; nor is the behaviour of these savages characterized by that obliging promptness which marks the demeanour of most of their countrymen.— They are, however, steady in their attachments, and faithful to their obligations, qualities of a very high nature in such a race; and it is only doing justice to the character of these people, that the mission is settled at Rangehoo, and the protection of it intrusted to the inhabitants, above any of the other tribes in the island. Mr. Hall succeeded in getting the canoe by some means or other, though not by the interference of the chief, who still declared that he could do nothing in the affair.

The weather having changed on the 12th, we had continual rain the whole day; and as it was the sabbath, Mr. Kendall went through a suitable form of worship, in place of my reverend friend, who was prevented by the concerns of the vessel from coming on shore on this occasion.   All the settlers were present, with the exception of Mr. Hall, who had not yet returned; and Duaterra did not fail to attend, while he brought with him as many of his people of both sexes as he could collect. The chief was dressed in his European clothes, and I never saw him look to more advantage.   In his appearance there was not the least trace of that slovenly awkwardness which the attire of civilized men might be supposed to give to a person in the savage state, from the circumstance of such an habiliment being strange and unusual; on the contrary, he looked as neat and smart as if he had been accustomed all his life to the apparel he then wore.

Mr. Hall, who had by this time returned from the vessel, informed me that it was still as much crowded by the natives as ever; and that he was glad to get away as well as myself, having found it absolutely impossible to remain on board with the smallest degree of comfort.   This I could readily believe from the disagreeable experience I had of it myself; and I now felt a sort of selfish satisfaction at being exempt from the annoyance, while I enjoyed the freedom of the shore, in company with my European friends. Since I had left the ship, it appeared that some petty thefts had been committed, in which Wiveeah's party were chiefly implicated.— This occasioned Mr. Marsden to remonstrate with the chief, who expressed the greatest concern at such dishonest practices on the part of his people, while he solemnly declared that he had no share in them himself. Being, however, afraid lest he, as well as his tribe, had provoked our vengeance, and that we should follow up the offence with some signal punishment, he was willing to avert the anti-cipated blow, by presenting Mr. Marsden with two very handsome mats as a propitia-tion. He assured my friend, at the same time, that he would use all the means in his power to discover the thieves, whom he would instantly punish in the most exemplary man-ner. But we had very little occasion to com-plain of this species of misconduct on the part of the natives, while we remained among them; and had the vessel been subject to the same influx of Europeans, and had we trusted them as unreservedly as we did, these poor islanders, I am fully persuaded, that not only our losses would have borne no proportion to the few we sustained, but that we should have been stripped of every article we possessed. The chiefs, with all their absurd vanity in point of distinction, have yet a sort of pride about them that is truly noble in its character. This pride, however, does not in many cases proceed so much from innate principle, as from the idea of its being a necessary attribute to their elevation; and though they will often descend to the same meanness as the *cookees*, it must be always under quite different circumstances, and such as lead them to believe that they are not derogating from their consequence in the slightest degree. Valuing themselves as belonging to the highest class of *rungateedas*, they will tell you, with an air of self-gratulation, that "*rungateeda* is no *tungata tihi*, but he asks for things;" and this is certainly correct, so far as the whole body is concerned, but there are some exceptions.

The tranquillity of the settlement was on this day much disturbed, and its ultimate security very near being compromised, by the bad conduct of the convict who had secreted himself on board the vessel when we sailed from Port Jackson. This man, through some unwarrantable provocation on his part, had got into a quarrel with Tenana, when both of them, inflamed with violent rage against each other, rushed out of the missionary house to provide themselves with sticks for the purpose of belabouring each other. Hearing a tumultuous uproar outside, I left Mr. Kendall's dwelling, and found the parties going to decide the affray with a pair of tremendous bludgeons ; Tenana, pale and trembling from the effect of passion, and his adversary with a countenance no less ferocious, while they both stood with arms uplifted, and were just ready to strike, when I rushed in to prevent them. This I effectually did by ordering the convict to go instantly into the house, appeasing the enraged native at the same time, by telling him that I would take care the fellow should be punished. Had the parties been allowed to indulge their mutual vengeance in the manner they proposed, the danger I am certain would not have been confined to themselves, but all the unoffending members of the missionary establishment, would beyond a doubt have been exposed to imminent peril. The natives, without inquiring into the justice of his cause, would have joined their countryman, and acting only under the impulse of ungovernable resentment, their vengeance might have been attended with the most fatal consequences. From all that I have seen of the temper of savages, the necessity cannot be too often urged, of preserving an equability of temper towards them, if it be intended to rescue them from their degraded state; harshness and coercive measures will generally prove abortive, and should only be resorted to in extreme cases. The derelictions of a people sunk in utter darkness, should always be viewed with a spirit of forbearance; and perhaps it is this disposition to excuse their errors, by imputing them to their abject condition, together with a sympathizing tenderness, that makes Mr. Marsden the fittest man of any I have ever seen, to undertake the great work of civilization among such a race. But the worthless individual who rashly provoked the anger of Tenana, was not capable of these sentiments; nor could he make any more allowance for the uncultured mind of such a man, than if the poor savage had been a person who knew how to draw the most logical distinctions between *right* and *wrong*, and had learned how to regulate his conduct by the exact rules of perfect propriety.

CHAP. VI.

Duaterra taken suddenly ill—Visited by the Author and the
Missionaries—Sorrowful appearance of his family—The
Author visits him again and finds him in a dangerous
state—Interview between the Author and the first mate
of the ship Jefferson—The Author and Mr. Kendall
accompany him on board his ship—The Captain complains
of Tarra and Tupee—Improper behaviour of his sailors
towards the natives—Directions about dealing with
savages—The distribution of presents injurious—Tarra
forbids all intercourse with the Jefferson—Stricture on
the conduct of European sailors—Capricious inhuma-
nity—The Author repeats his visits to Duaterra, and is
ultimately denied admittance—Rigorous observance of the
taboo—Singular notion respecting the *Etua*—Mr. Marsden
comes to see Duaterra, and is admitted—The Author
again refused access to him—Delivery of Mrs. King,
the wife of one of the Missionaries, and remarks upon
it by a native—Transfer of three fugitive convicts to the
vessel—Sympathy of Mrs. Goshore—A *tabooed* glutton—
Operation of hair-cutting connected with a religious
superstition—The ship returns with her cargo from the
Cowa-cowa—Mr. Marsden opposed in visiting Duaterra—
Gains admittance by a threat—Gunnah exclaims against
the *taboo*—Hopeless state of Duaterra—Superstitious
scruples.

AFTER a heavy fall of rain during the preceding night, the atmosphere on Monday the
13th, was more than usually dull and cloudy,

and the thermometer at noon was at 63°, temperate enough for the season of the year in these regions. On this day Duaterra, being taken suddenly ill, was not able to visit the settlement; but I could not yet discover what the complaint was with which he was attacked: I resolved, however, to take an early opportunity of ascertaining it, in order to administer any comfort in my power to that excellent chief, for whom I had a sincere regard. Having made my usual visit to the town this morning, I set one of the natives to work to make me six *poes* or balls, such as I have described in a former part of this narrative; and the person I selected, who was one of the most ingenious of their rude artisans, promised to complete them without delay, and seemed quite overjoyed with the order. Some of the inhabitants reported about the district, that a ship had come into the harbour, and was lying off Tarra's village, Corroraddickie; and this we afterwards found to be correct.

As Duaterra still continued seriously indisposed, I went to see him on the following day, February the 14th, and found him labouring under severe illness and very feverish. His complaint appeared to be the consequence of a violent cold, and as it was attended with inflammatory symptoms, I thought that a dose of rheubarb, in the absence of a more efficacious remedy, might do him some service. To procure this I instantly hastened back to the settlement, and the missionaries participating in my solicitude for the poor chief, accompanied me on my return to the shed where he was lying, bringing with them such little necessaries as they supposed could be conducive towards restoring him. He took the rheubarb without the least hesitation, and appeared very grateful for our attention to him; while his head wife and the other members of his family stood round his wretched couch in sorrowful dejection. However insincere might be the grief of some others of the natives, whom I observed under similar visitations; it was evident from the countenances of these poor inmates, that they were deeply afflicted; and they seemed from their looks of doleful anxiety, to have an ominous prescience that the chief whom they loved would soon be no more. The scene was touching to the heart of sympathy; and after administering what relief I could to the poor sufferer, I was glad to withdraw from his presence, as well as from the afflicted group by whom he was surrounded. But it was only as a matter of particular favour, that we were allowed to see him at all, as he was under the *taboo*, and interdicted from any intercourse whatsoever with the profane; and I should suppose that the indulgence in our favour was not granted without some expiatory rites on the part of the family. He was also precluded from all communication with his principal dwelling, nor had he any other exemption from this extraordinary superstition, that was not equally shared by the meanest of his subjects, except that of not being obliged to feed himself, having persons appointed to wait upon him for the purpose.

The anxiety about this friendly chief, who possessed so many excellent qualities, and whose failings were so few, increased at the settlement with the continuance of his complaint; and I went again to see him on the 15th, when I found that no favourable change had taken place since the day before, but that the symptoms had become rather more alarming. I did not stay longer than while I gave some few directions to those who were in attendance, concerning the manner they should treat him in his present state; but either they did not sufficiently understand what I would have them do, or they were prevented by the *taboo* from following the system I proposed to them. The consequence was, the hapless patient became progressively worse, and in a few days his disorder arrived at a crisis which left no hopes of recovery. Returning from this melancholy visit, I met with some of the natives who had in their possession some of the blue pigment with which they paint their faces;* and upon asking them where they found it, they told me they dug it up in the lands bordering on the Cowa-cowa, which were full of it, though in the other parts of the island, scarcely any could be had. But they were obliged, they said, to dig to a great depth before they could get at it, and the labour required upon the occasion, enhanced its value among them considerably.

Having called again on the 16th to inquire after Duaterra, I was told by his family that he was then in a profound sleep; but I could

---

* I brought some of this substance with me to England, and a mineralogist to whom I shewed it, pronounced it to be Manganese.

infer from them at the same time, that his complaint had taken a still more dangerous turn
than on the preceding day.   Not choosing to
disturb him, I left the place, conjuring them
as well as I could make myself understood,
to follow the directions I had previously given
them, which, however, they still neglected
from one or other of the reasons before mentioned.   As I was coming back to the settlement, one of the native children ran up to
meet me, telling me to follow him, and he
would shew me a large boat which had lately
come on shore; and this was all he could
deliver intelligibly. He accordingly conducted
me to a part of the shore immediately opposite
to the missionary house, and here I found a
whale boat drawn up upon the beach, and
some English sailors standing beside her;
with groups of the natives collected on the
spot to survey their new visitors.   Mr. Kendall, who was here for some time before my
arrival, now introduced me to a Mr. Jones,
the first mate of a vessel fishing in those seas,
the Jefferson, commanded by that Captain
Barnes, on whose conduct towards the natives, I have had before occasion to animad-
vert.   Mr. Jones informed me, that his ship
arrived in the harbour on the Sunday

before, and was now lying off Corroraddickie, thus confirming the statement of the natives who first reported it to us. He said it was four months since they had left Port Jackson, and twenty-six since their departure from England; and that notwithstanding they had been so long at sea, they had not procured more than about nine hundred barrels of sperm oil, which was little better than half the intended cargo.

As this young man had, in a former visit to this part of the island, made himself acquainted with Duaterra, he was now concerned to hear of the severe indisposition of that chief; and as he expressed an earnest desire to pay him a visit, I readily agreed to conduct him to the place. We found him on our arrival wrapped up in European blankets, and in a profuse perspiration; while his disorder was making rapid havoc on his frame, though his mental faculties remained yet unimpaired. He perfectly recollected Mr. Jones, and appearing very glad to see him, observed he should be better in a day or two, and would visit his ship; but, poor fellow! his expectations were too sanguine, and never to be realized; for while he spoke thus confidently, his looks indicated but too plainly, that his hour was fast approaching, and that the only visit he would ever make must be to a premature grave.

As Mr. Jones seemed a young man of an excellent disposition, and gave us a pressing invitation to visit his ship, we did not hesitate to accompany him on board, believing that our compliance would be gratifying to him. We found the Jefferson a very fine vessel of two hundred and fifty tons burden; she belonged, we were told, to a Mr. Roche of Milford Haven, who employed her exclusively in this particular branch of trade.

We spent the night on board this vessel, and next morning, February 17th, Tupee came on board as a visitor. The Captain complained very much, both of this man and his brother Tarra, for having spoiled his trade with the other natives who came alongside with provisions. They incited them, he said, to every species of extortion; and the consequence was, that he was either obliged not to buy from them at all, or to purchase their supplies at more than four times what they were worth. This I had no reason to doubt, having experienced the same myself,

in the case of Themorangha and some others;
but in justice to the brothers above-mentioned, I must say, that for our own part, we
never found them behave towards us in the
manner represented. When we sat down to
breakfast, it was intended that Tupee should
have his after we had done; but whether the
chief considered this arrangement as an affront upon his rank, and was provoked in
consequence, or that the sudden recollection
of some urgent business had prompted his
departure, I know not; but he went off, however, very precipitately, and we rather suspected that he was displeased.

Soon after this, the boat's crew were sent
on shore, to bring off some fire-wood; but
they returned in a very short time, informing
us, that the natives had come down armed to
prevent them from taking any away, and that
they met them with a determined spirit of
hostility. It occurred to us, that this might
have happened through some resentment on
the part of Tupee, who might be glad of such
an opportunity to revenge himself for the
supposed affront; and I therefore went on
shore with Mr. Jones, in order to come to an
understanding with that chief and his brother

the areekee, respecting the unpleasant affair.
—We were met on our landing by both the
brothers, and upon expostulating with them
on the ungenerous selfishness of their withholding the wood when payment was offered
for it, we discovered that they were perfectly
justified in behaving as they had done; the
sailors, as they told us, having taken away
three loads previously, without giving a single
article in return, and would still continue to
do the same, had it not been for the resistance they met with.   This, and not the
resentment of Tupee, as we imagined, was
the cause of the affair in question; but, in
justice to Mr. Jones, it must be observed,
that he conceived the natives were willing to
part with the wood in exchange for some
things he had given them on their coming on
board, which were more than an equivalent
for the required supply.   Had the missionary
establishment not been formed here, which
operated as a check upon the conduct of the
seamen, I doubt not but they would have
resorted to their customary spoliations, in
spite of any prevention on the part of the
natives, who could not have assembled in
such numbers as to repel them in their

desultory incursions. But those Europeans who would act differently, and adopt an equitable line of conduct, either towards these or any other people in the savage state, while at the same time they would secure themselves against imposition, should follow strictly the rule I have laid down in a former part of this work, and which I would here urge a second time; viz. to bargain distinctly for every thing, and to take nothing for granted that is not previously stipulated. By scrupulously observing this rule ourselves, we avoided all disagreeable contentions with the natives; and in our various dealings with them, which were frequent, and in some instances complex, we never had the slightest occasion to complain of their want of punctuality, but found them uniformly strict and regular. The terms being mutually defined, and nothing left to chance, the New Zealanders are as precise as any people in the world; but if the price of any article they have to sell be left to themselves, they will generally make it exorbitant, and oppose any abatement that might be required by the purchaser, insisting upon having their extravagant demand. Yet this is no more

than is done every day by many of their civilized fellow-men, who would pass themselves
on their neighbours as most upright and
conscientious characters, while practising
exactly the same sort of extortion.

The indiscriminate distribution of presents
among savages, I look upon to do more harm
than good ; the articles they receive may
afford them the highest enjoyment for the
moment, as I have frequently witnessed; but
when the first transports are over, they will
prove to them rather a source of anxious disquietude than otherwise, by increasing their
cupidity, which will always be craving after
similar acquisitions.   Besides, it will on most
occasions be utterly impossible to avoid exciting jealousy in some of them, however
impartially the presents may be distributed ;
and those who consider the others more
favoured than themselves, will harbour against
them a poisoned spirit of envious hatred, that
will often break out into open excesses, and
give rise to sanguinary commotions, which
nothing but mutual slaughter can appease.
A third objection to the system of giving
gratuitous favours among such a people is,
I conceive, that it makes them averse to

habits of industry ; for depending on this sort of casual liberality, they neglect those useful employments to which they would otherwise apply themselves, and their exertions being once relaxed, a morbid idleness, with a settled disinclination to labour, are the sure consequences. It is therefore my opinion, that the distribution of presents, while it is obviously injurious to the peace and prosperity of the natives themselves, is likewise extremely unfavourable to the accommodation of the donors, who will not have supplies furnished to them with the same regularity as they would if they withheld their gifts as articles of exchange; whereby the industry of the people, instead of lying dormant, would be set in motion, and the hope of gain would act as an incitement to diligent application. I must, however, observe that, under certain circumstances, exceptions may be made with great propriety: it may be expedient, for instance, to gain the favour of a powerful chief; and, in this case, a present must always be given, being indispensably necessary in point of etiquette, and generally efficacious as to the object. But discretion and judgment will always be the best guides in this respect;

and I would be here understood as objecting
to a promiscuous, not to a particular distribution.

We asked Tupee to return with us to the
vessel, but he declined the invitation; alledging, as an excuse, that he was busy in
building a house; yet it appeared to me, that
he had a decided objection against repeating his visit, though such was his reserve
that he would not disclose it. But his
brother Tarra, whom we invited at the same
time, and who also refused, was more ex-
plicit. He told us that he would never again
go on board Captain Barnes's ship, for that
one of the sailors had presented a pistol to
his breast, and threatened to shoot him; and
we understood from him also, that he had
forbidden his people from taking any supplies to the Jefferson, or having the slightest
communication with that vessel while she
remained in the harbour. That the areekee
was correct in what he said I am perfectly
convinced, for I have myself witnessed several
instances of morose temper on the part of
the crew of this vessel towards some of
the unoffending natives. It is strange how
Europeans should indulge this malevolent
disposition towards savages, when they must

know that it will operate so powerfully against their own interest, setting all ideas of humanity out of the question. Yet this is the case; and, heedless of the consequences to themselves, no less than of the injury they inflict on others, they riot in the unrestrained violence of capricious enormities, consigning their names to infamy by the turpitude of such conduct. It is not without extreme reluctance that I am obliged to advert so often to these inhuman proceedings; but they cannot be too frequently reprobated while a single individual, who claims to be thought civilized, (and particularly if that individual be an Englishman,) continues in the execrable practice of them. Mr. Jones, who had often with pain witnessed the lawless inflictions of his countrymen upon these people, mentioned an instance, which was of itself a sufficient reason why Tarra should never visit any ship commanded by Captain Barnes. The last time his vessel was in this harbour, he said, the King George was in company with her, the Captain of which and Barnes would get drunk together every night, when it was their constant practice to worry and torment such of the natives as happened to be on board, in order to *amuse themselves* during the progress of their sottish inebriation. On one of these occasions, Tarra and his wife, with some of his people, were made the subjects of merriment for the pair of bacchanalians, at the expense of all decency and common feeling. These captains went to the place where the natives had lain down to rest; and after harassing them with all the indelicate and mischievous tricks that a depraved imagination, together with an unfeeling heart, could devise; they compelled them at length to huddle themselves into their canoes at the dead hour of the night, and proceed to the shore; while the poor creatures were glad to run any hazard, provided they could escape from their cruel tormentors. The same pair, after they had thus routed out the harmless natives, now ordered the great guns to be fired off against the rocks, in order to intimidate them from taking that revenge which a consciousness of guilt, even in the midst of their intoxication, made them apprehend. I was assured by Mr. Jones, that for himself he had never in his life spent so disagreeable a time as this; and from

what I could see of him, I am fully persuaded that such barbarous practices were
abhorrent to his disposition.

Returning from the Jefferson, Mr. Kendall
and myself paid a visit to Duaterra, whom
we still found lingering under the increased
violence of his disorder, though perfectly
collected, and fully sensible of every thing
that passed. We made but a short stay, lest
our presence might cause him to talk more
than he could bear from his exhausted state;
but on the following day, February the 18th,
I went again to see him, when he appeared
much in the same state as on the day before,
but somewhat weaker, and I now began to
give up all hopes of his recovery. After
dinner I made another visit to his residence,
feeling a degree of solicitude about him that
urged me upon all occasions to repeat my
inquiries: but the indulgence granted to me
before, was now peremptorily denied; for the
superstition of the taboo had by this time
precluded all access to the presence of the
sick chief; and such was the blind fatuity
of his people, that they gave strict orders
against his receiving those little supplies
which the missionaries were in the habit of
bringing him, and insisted that no human

aid should administer to his wants while he yet survived. The reason of their laying the poor fellow under this horrible interdict, was because they now believed that the Etua had fully determined to destroy him; and for this purpose had made a firm lodgment in his stomach, whence no mortal power durst venture to expel him; nor would he once quit his position, but remain there, increasing the agonies of the sufferer till he thought proper to put an end to his existence. This gross delusion produced the effect that might be supposed; the hapless chief, already too faint and languid, became still more so, by being deprived of that necessary aliment which alone had hitherto served to sustain him under his complaint; and according as the various symptoms assumed a more dangerous aspect, and bespoke a nearer approach to the fatal moment, they blamed their own impiety as having produced them; asserting that the Etua would not yet have fixed himself in the stomach of the chief, had they not in their unhallowed temerity suffered us to see him while he was tabooed against such visitors. I remonstrated with them in urgent terms, and thought to prevail on them to admit me; but it was of no use, they all cried out with one voice, " *nuee nuee taboo taboo*," and forbidding me to approach the shed, they would, as I believe, have killed me on the spot, had I presumed to disobey. Though the immediate family of Duaterra still continued to evince the same deep and bitter affliction as before, still they agreed with his other dependants in excluding him from all further assistance, so awful in their sight was the barbarous superstition by which they were deluded; and leaving him now entirely to the disposal of the Etua, they were studious only about providing for his interment. Expecting his speedy dissolution, they wished to convey him to an adjacent island, where they intended to deposit his remains; but the chief, even weak as he was, opposed this effectually, for anticipating such an event, he kept by him continually the pistols we had lent him when going to the North Cape, and having loaded one of them nearly up to the muzzle, he threatened to shoot the first person who should attempt to take him away. This deterred them all; and none were found who would venture to remove him, though they might easily have done so while he was asleep.

Mr. Marsden, who had heard of the illness of our friend, but was prevented hitherto from visiting him, in consequence of the arrangements he was making for our departure, came on shore on the 19th, for the sole purpose of seeing him; and was not more surprised than concerned at hearing that he was in so hopeless a state, not being previously aware that he was at all dangerously indisposed. Going to his residence, he met at first with the same determined resistance as I did; but as he had considerably more influence with the natives than either myself or any other European that ever visited the island, he found it practicable, after some serious expostulation, to gain admittance, and even prevailed upon them to suffer the missionaries to bring in the usual necessaries as before. These concessions, which were in direct violation of the taboo, would not, I am convinced, have been granted to any other individual but himself; and the authority of my friend with them must have been powerful in the extreme, else they would never have consented to an infringement which they considered so heinous. Mr. Marsden being much attached to Duaterra, could not behold his exhausted state, which left no hope of recovery, without sensations of the deepest regret; and as his feelings were too acute to witness for any considerable time the progressive advances of his fatal malady, he very soon took his departure, repeating his directions to the natives about admitting the necessaries, which, however, the poor chief would not long require.

In the evening, I took a long walk with Mr. Hall, to see some Siberian barley which he had sown in a plantation purchased by him, on his first arrival, from one of the natives. This grain, which he had put in the ground only a month before, appeared in an excellent state of vegetation, and grew now to about five inches above the surface. For the purchase, inclosing, and breaking up of the ground, which consisted of somewhat more than two acres, he had given two axes and a hoe; but this, though to Europeans it may seem a price scarcely worth the name, was here considered a full equivalent.

I went into the town on the morning of the 20th, expecting to see Duaterra, according to the permission that had been granted; but so capricious are savages in most of their proceedings, that they are ever apt to vary, and their promises cannot confidently be depended upon, unless when under the controul of a superstitious awe, or bound by some established usage of the country. I found this to be the case in the present instance; for having now changed their minds, and repented of their admitting Mr. Marsden, as well as of their promised compliance with his request, they returned to their former rigid determination of excluding the profane; and I was therefore obliged to come back without seeing the chief. I made a second attempt on the 21st, but was equally unsuccessful; and upon inquiring what state he was in, the only intelligence I could get was, that the Etua was then preying upon his entrails, and that the chief would be *matou mouee* (killed) as soon as they were all devoured. This notion, much more than the complaint under which they labour, accelerates the death of sick people in New Zealand. So strongly is it impressed upon the minds of their friends, that when the symptoms appear at all dangerous, they think any sort of remedy would be impious; and however afflicted they may be at the loss of them, they never once murmur against the mystical vulture who gnaws them away according to his appetite.

The wife of Mr. King was delivered on

this day of a fine boy; and I was first informed of the circumstance by one of the natives, a man who acted as servant to her mother, Mrs. Hanson. This fellow, who would have made an excellent buffoon, as he possessed all the requisite humour for such a character, met me as I was coming out of the town ; and telling me that Mrs. King had got a *pickeeninnee*, (a child,) he began to describe her groans and expressions while suffering under the pains of labour; and there was such an air of droll mimickry in the indecent representation, that I could not forbear laughing heartily, though I desired him to desist from so unseemly a detail. He descanted in a strain of arch ridicule on the extreme timidity of our countrywomen in this situation, compared with the hardy resolution of the New Zealand ladies. The latter, he said, never experienced any inconvenience from child-birth; but sitting down in the open air, surrounded by a concourse of both sexes, were delivered without uttering a single groan, while the spectators, who stood carefully watching the process, shouted out *tarnee! tarnee!* (an infant, an infant,) as soon as nature had executed her office; when the mother, after cutting the umbilical cord, rose up as if no such occurrence had taken place, and resumed her ordinary occupations. But, said he, " Europee woman be no like New Zealand woman ; she cry out, Measser King ! Measser King ! for *ittee ittee tarnee :*" meaning, that his countrywomen would have more spirit than to use such an exclamation in so trifling an affair as the delivery of a little infant.

Captain Barnes delivered up to Mr. Marsden, on the 22d, two men and a woman, fugitive convicts, who were transmitted from his vessel on board the Active, to be taken back to the colony. The woman was extremely dejected at the idea of being consigned to her former exile, as she entertained hopes of being enabled to contrive her escape from the Jefferson, and secrete herself in this island till the departure of both the ships, where she might enjoy that freedom among the natives, of which she was deprived by the laws of her country, till some fortuitous opportunity might present itself of taking her to England again. She had some short time before solicited the assistance of Mrs. Goshore to effect her purpose ; but this woman, instead of giving her any encouragement, used various arguments to dissuade her from it, yet shewed at the same time, a feeling tenderness in the reasons she advanced. Addressing her in accents of the gentlest sympathy, she would say, while the other pressed her with importunate entreaties, " Me would, Mary, but me got no tea, me got no sugar, no bed, no good things for you; me grieve to see you—you cannot live like New Zealand woman, you cannot sleep on the ground." With these and other arguments, urged in the same pathetic strain, she declined to become the abettor of a project which she knew, when realized, would be attended with so many hardships to the luckless creature who wished to accomplish it.

On going into the town, in the course of the day, I beheld several of the natives sitting round some baskets of dressed potatoes; and being invited to join them in their meal, I mingled with the group, when I observed one man stoop down with his mouth for each morsel, and scrupulously careful in avoiding all contact between his hands and the food he was eating. From this I knew at once that he was tabooed; and upon asking the reason of his being so, as he appeared in good health, and not afflicted with any complaint that could set him without the pale of ordinary intercourse, I found that it was because he was then building a house, and that he could not be released from the taboo till he had it finished. Being only a cookee, he had no person to wait upon him, but was obliged to submit to the distressing operation of feeding himself in the manner prescribed by the superstitious ordinance; and he was told by the *tohunga*, or priest, that if he presumed to put one finger to his mouth before he had completed the work he was about, the Etua would certainly punish his impious contempt, by getting into his stomach before his time, and eating him out of the world. Of this premature destiny he seemed so apprehensive, that he kept his hands as though they were never made for touching any article of diet; nor did he suffer them by even a single motion to shew the least sympathy for his mouth, while that organ was obliged to use double exertions, and act for those members which superstition had paralysed. Sitting down by the side of this deluded being, whom credulity and ignorance had rendered helpless, I undertook to feed him; and his appetite being quite voracious, I could hardly supply it as fast as he devoured. Without ever consulting his digestive powers, of which we cannot suppose he had any idea, he spared himself the trouble of mastication ; and to lose no time, swallowed down every lump as I put it into his mouth; and I speak within compass when I assert, that he consumed more food than would have served any two ploughmen in England. Perfectly tired of ministering to his insatiable gluttony, which was still as ravenous as when he commenced, I now wished for a little intermission ; and taking advantage of his situation, I resolved to give him as much to do as would employ him for at least a few minutes, while, in the mean time, it would afford me some amusement for my trouble. I therefore thrust into his mouth the largest hot potatoe I could find, and this had exactly the intended effect; for the fellow, unwilling to drop it, and not daring to penetrate it before it should get cool, held it slightly compressed between his teeth, to the great enjoyment of his countrymen, who laughed heartily, as well as myself, at the wry faces he made, and the efforts he used with his tongue to moderate the heat of the potatoe, and bring it to the temperature of his gums, which were evidently smarting from the contact. But he bore this trick with the greatest possible good humour; and to make him amends for it, I took care to supply him plentifully, till he cried out *nuee nuee kiki*, and could eat no more; an exclamation, however, which he did not make till there was no more in the baskets. Besides potatoes, they had also at this feast (for such it was considered) muscles and turnips; but the latter had very much degenerated, and become long and fibrous.

Leaving this group after they had finished their banquet, I passed close by the hut where Warree the brother of Gunnah resided, and found him very busy in cutting his wife's hair. This operation he performed with a piece of sharp stone, called by mineralogists Obsidian, or volcanic glass; cutting the fore part quite close, and leaving all the hair on the back of the head untouched. When he had completed his task, which took him some time from the nice precision he observed; he collected together all the hair he had cut off, and laying it up very carefully, went to the outskirts of the town and threw it away. Upon asking him the reason of his doing this, he told me that the hair was tabooed, and could not be left in the town without provoking the anger of the Etua, who would in such case destroy the person from whose head it had been taken. I was going to take up one of the stones he had used, but he charged me not to touch it, telling me that this was also tabooed, and that the enraged deity of New Zealand would wreak his immediate vengeance upon my guilty head, if I presumed to lay one finger on the sacred implement. Laughing at his superstition, I began to exclaim against its absurdity ; but like Tui on a former occasion, he retorted by ridiculing our *crackee crackee* (preaching,) yet at the same time asking me to sermonize over his wife, as if his object was to have her exorcised ; and upon my refusing, he began himself, but could not proceed from involuntary bursts of laughter. I obtained from him without any difficulty one of the stones he had not used, against the transfer of which there was no prohibition.

The ship returned from the Cowa-cowa at a late hour in the evening, and we could hear from the settlement, the natives dancing and singing with great glee upon the deck. The preparations for our departure were now almost completed, and in three or four days more we expected every thing would be in readiness for our sailing.

On the 23rd, Mr. Marsden, whose fears for Duaterra's recovery made him experience a considerable degree of anxiety, came again to Rangehoo to see if there were any hopes of his restoration; but he now found himself debarred from the shed, and the same people who had admitted him before, were on the present occasion deaf to all his arguments, while they opposed his entrance with an inflexible obstinacy. But he was determined not to leave the place without seeing the chief; and finding that remonstrance was of no avail, he resolved to intimidate them with a threat which he never meant to put into execution. He told them accordingly, that if they persisted in denying him access, he would instantly order the guns of the vessel to be made to bear upon the town, and would blow it about their ears, as a punishment for their contumacious prohibition. This threat, which came upon them quite unexpected, produced a sensible change in their behaviour; and though they still refused to admit him, yet they urged their objections in a tone of extreme diffidence, nor could they conceal their panic at the alarming announcement. They now sought to deprecate his anger, and dissuade him from his purpose by many persuasive intreaties; imploring him to consider how much they were in the power of the Etua, whom they durst not have the wickedness to offend, yet whose wrath perhaps they had already provoked, by their irreverent violation of his sacred mandate, in suffering any one not sanctioned by the taboo, to visit a person who was under its immediate influence. Repeatedly urging this argument in suppliant accents, they stood in a state of agitation between contending fears; and though Mr. Marsden heard them with patience, he persevered nevertheless in demanding admittance, and still pretended he would destroy the town if it was not granted. While thus in the minds of these bewildered natives, the terror of the taboo was holding conflict with the alarm of our guns; a young man who had sense enough to despise the absurd prejudices of the others, though nurtured in the midst of them, rose up to support Mr. Marsden, and combat the fanatical delusion of his countrymen. Gunnah, the young man in question, now spoke in a bold strain of sarcastic eloquence, not only against the impropriety of refusing free access to Duaterra, but against the *taboo* itself, which, as he expressed it, was "no good in New Zealand, but only henerecka;" and he told them openly, that it ought not ever again to be feared or regarded. The other natives looked upon Gunnah as a blasphemous sceptic for making this declaration, yet his consequence as a rungateeda had some weight with them; but Mr. Marsden's threat was more efficacious than all, and their fearful scruples being at length obliged to yield to it, they found themselves under the necessity of consenting to his ingress. But I must remark, that it was owing to his discriminating shrewdness in perceiving our enlightened state, and the vast ascendancy it gave us in our different pursuits, that Gunnah inveighed against his native superstition; for I found him when first I arrived at the island, as blind a votary of it as the most deluded of his countrymen.

On getting into the shed, or rather enclosure, which was quite open at the top, Mr. Marsden found the poor chief stretched upon the ground, exposed to the burning rays of the sun, and surrounded as before, by his wives and relations, who watched for his dissolution in silent expectancy. The priest was also in attendance, and made himself very busy in his official capacity, directing the others in all their proceedings, and suffering nothing to be done without his own interference. Duaterra, though so weak that he could hardly articulate a single word, was still in the full possession of his intellectual powers; and upon seeing Mr. Marsden, his languid eyes brightened with an expression of joy, as if the presence of my friend was the last cheering beam of consolation that could light him to the tomb. His frame, which was once so athletic and robust, was now worn away to a skeleton; for the necessary sustenance being withheld from him, there was nothing to support animal life during the intermissions of a severe malady. While thus languishing under the last stage of exhaustion, he begged with indistinct accents that we would send him a little wine; and Mr. Marsden promising that he should have some in the course of the day, withdrew from the place, finding, like myself, the scene too distressing for a longer continuance. Mr. Kendall took him the wine according to promise, and drinking a little of it, he appeared somewhat revived; but it was only a momentary elevation of his spirits, and he soon fell again into the same depressed langour as before. Not having given up all the iron that Mr. Marsden had committed to his trust, he ordered his people to deliver it to us punctually; which, however, they refused, alledging that it was tabooed against the packahâ, who on that account had no right to claim it. But this reason was by no means satisfactory to Mr. Marsden, and insisting upon their surrendering it immediately, they were too much afraid of his resentment, not to comply with the peremptory demand. When Mr. Kendall was going to bring away the decanter that contained the wine, the surrounding group opposed it with indignation; and Duaterra himself intreated that it might be left, declaring it to be tabooed, and that the Etua who was within him, would kill him the sooner if it was removed. To relieve him from this absurd fear, the good-natured missionary consented to leave it; and visiting him again in the course of a couple of hours, he brought him some rice, but which the chief merely tasted, being now too far gone to partake of any kind of food. Mr. Kendall

then offered some of it to his head wife, who
looked extremely ill, as did likewise the
child she was suckling, but he could not
prevail upon her to eat it; she said she was
tabooed, and the priest also refused it for the
same reason.

CHAP. VII.

Duaterra still lingers under his illness—Affecting situation of his head wife and the rest of his family—Escape and recapture of a convict—The Author meets with an accident—Purchase of ground for the missionaries, and curious deed of agreement between the parties—Departure of the vessel from the Bay of Islands on her return to Port Jackson—List of New Zealanders going as passengers—Parting scene between them and their friends —Reflections on taking leave of the missionaries— Further particulars respecting them—Mr. Marsden and the Author go on shore at the North Cape—Interesting view in that part of the island—Jem the Otaheitan, and the son of a New Zealand chief, get on board to proceed to the colony—The vessel sails from the North Cape— Alarm of Themorangha—Incidents on board—Jem's account of the people of the East Cape—The ship arrives at Port Stephen's in New South Wales—Interview there between two of the original natives and the New Zealanders—Return to Port Jackson, and end of the narrative.

THE excellent chief, whose earthly career was so soon to be terminated, still claimed our anxious attention; and I went early on Friday morning, February the 24th, together with Mr. Marsden and Mr. Kendall, to learn if he was yet living, or had been finally released from his sufferings. Arriving at the shed, Mr. Marsden only was allowed to enter, and Mr. Kendall and myself were at first opposed by the natives, though they afterwards consented to admit us. Poor Duaterra, whom we were rather prepared to find rescued by death from the fatal violence of his complaint, than still surviving under the agonies of excruciating pain, was however in the latter situation; and while his bodily strength was completely lost, the paroxysms of his malady returning at short intervals, racked his exhausted frame, and held the last struggles with expiring nature. His head wife was sitting beside him, supporting his head with her arm, and never did my eyes light upon so melancholy a spectacle. She no more appeared the same person I at first beheld her—her eyes, that once kindled with the fire of joyful vivacity, were hollow, dim and suffused with tears; and her countenance, that so lately presented all the marks of serene composure and contented happiness, had now wasted away to the wan emaciation of despair; and a more moving picture of disconsolate affliction never yet drew a tear from the eye of sympathy, than this pitiable creature. How marvellous and inscrutable are the dispensations of Providence! But a few days, and the sun of New Zealand did not rise on a more happy family than that of Duaterra: blessed in the smiles of the affectionate chief, whose health and welfare diffused joy within the circle of his authority, they passed their time in a perpetual round of innocent recreations; and, possessing such necessaries as their habits desired, they were strangers to all discontented cravings, placing the summit of their wishes in the full enjoyment of their simple resources, and having no solicitude about the continuance of their happiness, being as yet unacquainted with the visitations of calamity. Such a few days back was the enviable state of these people, but now how reversed the picture! sorrow, anguish and despair, all legible in every countenance, and the baleful gloom of death hanging over the afflicting scene, and enveloping within its shade the gushing tears of a doleful retinue.

While I was standing beside the chief, with my heart severely distressed at the pangs he appeared to suffer, some of our people were proceeding to take away the empty bottles which had contained the wine and cordials that we had sent him, when he implored me with a look of anxiety which I shall never forget, that I would not suffer them to be conveyed from the place; and we all felt too much for his sufferings to thwart at this moment a superstition which, even while his mind was in the rapid progress of civilization, had pertinaciously adhered to him, and the absurdity of which it was now too late to demonstrate. The bottles were therefore left behind, as were also some other vessels, about which he shewed the same anxious tenacity, because of their having held some nourishment for his use, which laid them under the taboo, and rendered their removal equally impious. I now took my last leave of Duaterra, too well convinced that his life, which was of no less importance to his own people than to the missionaries, must in a very little time* be

* This extraordinary man, whose greatness of mind shone forth with such conspicuous lustre in the midst of that barbarism in which it was enveloped, died shortly after our departure from the island. Selected by Providence to be the instrument of civilization to a race of cannibals, and the harbinger of light to his benighted countrymen, he had scarcely seen the settlement established, and the great work commenced under the auspices of his protection, when he was called off from his labours by the same mysterious power, and saw all the hopes he had cherished, completely destroyed, in the unexpected fate of a premature dissolution. His head wife Dahoo, inconsolable for his death, hung herself almost

at an end; and the sensations I experienced upon this melancholy occasion, I shall not attempt to describe, nor shall I take credit to myself for feeling acutely at a scene which no man, who was not dead to every impulse of sensibility, could witness unmoved.

The presents which this worthy chief had designed for Mr. Marsden and myself were laid up in a store-house, whither we were now conducted by one of his wives, and presented with them in obedience to his particular desire. They consisted of five

immediately after it took place. Mr. Kendall, from whom I received the particulars, assured me in his letter, that she was applauded by all her family and connections, as well as by the whole population of Rangehoo, for this desperate proof of conjugal devotedness. It appears, however, from the subsequent accounts of the missionaries, that it is a common practice in New Zealand, for the wife to destroy herself on the death of her husband; this testimony of her attachment being enjoined here with the same rigour as in many parts of the East, where it has been given from time immemorial. A more detailed account of Duaterra than comes within the plan of this narrative, will be found in No. III. of the Appendix, from the pen of Mr. Marsden, who has drawn it up with all the fervour of friendship, but with all the candour of impartiality. His memoir of the chief will be read with interest by all those who can in the smallest degree participate in the benevolent sentiments of the writer.

elegant mats for Mr. Marsden, and three of
the same texture for myself; while on getting
back to the settlement, I received in addition
a pig, which was brought to me by the
woman whom he had discarded for incon-
tinence. I was not a little surprised to see
her, after her repudiation, have any concern in his affairs; but I should suppose
she had found means to propitiate his resentment, and had been again taken into
favour. One of the convicts, transmitted to
us from the Jefferson, having made his escape
into the woods, we offered a reward to any
of the natives who would bring him in; and
as I was walking on the beach at a late hour
in the evening, a New Zealander, who could
not speak a single word of our language,
came up to me, and from the signs he made,
which were intelligible enough, I could infer
from him that the fugitive was lying in a
bush, at a short distance from the settlement
with Widoua, a native whom I have already
noticed, close beside him. Acquainting
Mr. Kendall with the circumstance, I asked
him to accompany me to the place where
the fellow was lurking; and taking the man
with us who gave the information, we set
out together. On getting to the spot, we

found the runaway concealed in the bush as
was represented, and Widoua beside him,
who remained there only to prevent him from
making his escape, while he sent off the
native to apprise us of his having discovered
him. Bringing off the fugitive, the moment
he was thus delivered into our hands, we
had him put in irons until he could be sent
on board the vessel.

On Saturday, March the 25th, Mr. Marsden repeated his visit to Duaterra, and
found him still breathing, but with all the
symptoms of instantaneous dissolution ; and
being unable to witness the extinction of life
in an individual for whom he had so feeling
a regard, he hurried from the shed, lest he
should expire in his presence. The different
articles belonging to us, which this chief had
in his possession, being now delivered up,
the pistols were returned among them ; and
one of these, which he had still kept loaded
beside him till he was no longer sensible of
his situation, had nearly proved fatal to me
on this day. Wanting to hail the ship, I
took the pistol with me to the beach, in order
to fire it off as a signal for the Captain to
send off the boat ; and, not aware that Duaterra had loaded it till almost the barrel

could contain no more, I resolved to discharge it, without ascertaining its contents, finding it impracticable to pull out the ramrod, which was made firm by the thick coat of rust it had contracted. I found on the beach a great concourse of the natives who had assembled to witness our departure; and Wiveeah being among them, wished me to let him fire off the pistol, which he would take as a particular favour; but not deeming this prudent, I discharged it myself, when it flew out of my hand with a violent explosion, and struck me a blow on the forehead that left me for a few moments in a state of insensibility. Fortunately, however, the part that received the wound was not near either of my temples, else instant death would have been the inevitable consequence; and the public would be spared from awarding either censure or approbation to these pages, whichever may be their fate. I bled profusely, and Mr. Marsden, hastening to my assistance, washed and bound up the wound; but the natives, far from expressing any regret at the accident, only upbraided me with my impiety for meddling with a pistol that was tabooed, and considered me as justly punished by the indignant wrath of the Etua, who could not behold such a flagitious act, without giving some immediate token of his vengeance. Wiveeah, priding himself on his sanctity as a priest, told me with much confidence, that it would not have happened to *him;* and old Tarra, equally presuming in his sacerdotal purity, declared that *he* should most certainly have escaped the accident, but that I who was not a *tohungha*, only met what I deserved.

As this was the last day of our being on shore, we were careful in leaving nothing undone that was connected with our visit to the island, and necessary to be settled before our departure. The land, therefore, on which the missionaries had erected their dwellings, was now regularly purchased; and Mr. Marsden having, in anticipation of the event, brought with him from Port Jackson two parchment deeds, drawn up in proper form, on behalf of the Church Missionary Society, it only remained for him to get them made valid on the part of Gunnah and his brother Warree, to whom the ground belonged. For this purpose, the ingenuity of Shunghi furnished a ready contrivance; and that chief drawing upon the deeds a complete representation of the *amoco*, or tattooing of

Gunnah's countenance, to which the latter set his mark, it served as the ratifying symbol of the agreement. These deeds Mr. Kendall and myself witnessed on the part of the settlers; and a native, whom they called a carpenter, drew the *amoco* of one of his cheeks, as a corresponding testimony for the New Zealanders. The ground, which consisted of about two hundred acres, Gunnah and Warree now declared to be tabooed to all but the white people; and henceforth the natives were not allowed to enter it without the concurrence of the missionaries. The following is an exact copy of the agreement, which is, perhaps, one of the most curious documents * ever yet presented to the public.

* It is rendered particularly singular by the tattooed symbol, which is not here given, because of its similarity to one of which a fac-simile will be found in another part of this work. Mr. Marsden has, I should think, made a mistake with respect to Gunnah's name, in calling him Ahoodee O Gunna, which appears to me to be a misnomer, the word *Turee*, and not *Ahoodee*, being the preceding part, which was usually omitted for the sake of brevity. That young man, who was only a rungateeda, is styled king in this deed, in anticipation of his succeeding Duaterra, as sovereign of the district, during the minority of Tippahee's daughter, to whom it belonged. But the land sold by him and his brother to the missionaries, was their own independent property, and subject in no particular to the existing chief of Rangehoo, though within his territory.

" Know all men to whom these pre-
" sents shall come, That I, Ahoodee O
" Gunna, King of Rangee Hoo, in the Island
" of New Zealand, have, in consideration of
" Twelve Axes to me in hand now paid and
" delivered by the Rev. Samuel Marsden, of
" Parramatta, in the territory of New South
" Wales, given, granted, bargained, and
" sold; and by this present instrument do
" give, grant, bargain, and sell unto the
" Committee of the Church Missionary
" Society for Africa and the East, insti-
" tuted in London, in the kingdom of
" Great Britain, and to their heirs and suc-
" cessors, all that piece and parcel of land
" situate in the district of Hoshee, in the
" Island of New Zealand, bounded on the
" south side by the bay of Tippoona and
" the town of Ranghee Hoo, on the north
" side by a creek of fresh water, and on the
" west by a public road into the interior;
" together with all the rights, members, privi-
" leges, and appurtenances thereunto belong-
" ing; To have and to hold, to the aforesaid
" Committee of the Church Missionary So-
" ciety for Africa and the East, instituted in
" London, in the kingdom of Great Britain,
" their heirs, successors, and assigns, for ever,

" clear and freed from all taxes, charges,
" impositions, and contributions whatsoever,
" as and for their own absolute and proper
" estate for ever :

> " In testimony whereof, I have, to these
> " presents thus done and given, set
> " my hand, at Hoshee, in the Island
> " of New Zealand, this twenty-fourth
> " day of February, in the year of
> " Christ one thousand eight hundred
> " and fifteen.

Signatures to the grant. { THOS. KENDALL.
{ J. L. NICHOLAS."

Before we repaired on board, Mr. Marsden baptized, in the presence of the natives, the child of which Mrs. King had been lately delivered ; and they evinced during the ceremony, a kind of fearful apprehension for the safety of the infant, mingled with astonishment at the rites they beheld, but behaved at the same time with the greatest propriety, and did not in the smallest degree interrupt the clergyman. The crowds that flocked from all parts of the surrounding country to witness our departure, nearly comprised the whole population within several miles of the bay; and there were many present, who had previously come from remote districts. The missionaries intending to accompany us to the mouth of the harbour, we now took leave of their families, who wishing us a safe return, were evidently touched with regret at the separation; and getting on board the vessel with several of the chiefs, in the midst of a fleet of canoes, we stood out for the opening of the bay.—From the chiefs who were on board we received the warmest assurances of friendship; and as Duaterra was probably now no more, they pledged themselves to do all that he would have done for the mission, had he survived, and to defend it in every instance against any hostile assailants. These promises were extremely gratifying to us, and we had no apprehensions of their fulfilment, which we knew the missionaries by their prudent conduct would be enabled to secure.

Those chiefs and common men who had previously obtained leave to return with us to Port Jackson, from the desire they expressed of visiting the packahâ's country, were now mustered upon the deck, when they appeared in the order here subjoined.

Tupee, brother to Tarra, the areekee of the
Bay of Islands.

Themorangha, the chief of Heckrengha.

Thewranghee, brother to Korra-korra, the
chief of Parro.

Tenana, a warrior and relation of Shunghi.

Totoree, servant to Tupee.

Shara, servant to Themorangha.

Mokiki, a subject of Korra-korra.

Tonghomuroo, a subject of Duaterra.

Atoo, a lad of fourteen years of age, and
son to Tekoki, the chief of the Cowa-
cowa.

Kyterra, a lad of twelve years of age, and son
to Pomaree.

These passengers being now to take leave
of the different friends who had accompanied
them to the vessel, a scene more affecting
than that which ensued between them was
probably never beheld. Regarding each
other with looks of despair, as if their separation was to be eternal, and the present their
last interview on this side of the grave, they
burst into tears; and then rushing into the
arms of one another, mutually indulged the
affliction of their hearts; while each manly
countenance, hung with agonized sympathy

on the neck of some distracted friend. Thus would they remain for some moments, when tearing themselves away from each other, as if in obedience to some fatal impulse, they would stand apart, and utter such doleful lamentations, as would force the most callous heart to participate in their anguish. The demand upon my feelings was but too severe, yet could I not help paying it to the full; and indeed there was no European present, not excepting the most obdurate sailor on board, who was not more or less affected. No length of time can ever efface from my memory the look of unutterable woe that was pictured in the countenance of Tekoki, when he came to take leave of me; with feelings so overpowered, that he was unable to utter a word, and the big drops rolling down his cheeks, he shook me by the hand, and turning towards his son who was standing by, directed my attention to him with an imploring anxiety of feature, that seemed to say, "Will you not be a friend to my little boy? will you not protect him from danger?" I felt the silent request with a poignancy not to be described; and the afflicted parent got into his canoe in an absolute state of convulsive agony. Poor Shara, the servant of Themorangha, sat upon the deck, watching the canoe that carried back his friends to the shore, until it got quite out of sight; and he continued sobbing the whole time, as if his heart would burst at the separation. I was heartily glad when all the canoes had taken their departure; and such a parting as this was, I shall never again, I hope, have occasion to witness. From the excessive anguish displayed in this scene, I expected every moment that the passengers would change their minds, and return back with those friends for whom they shewed so moving an affection, and by whom they were in turn so tenderly beloved; but not one of them swerved in the least from his original determination; and however severely afflicted they appeared, their desire to see Port Jackson was too powerful for their regret. But I cannot help noticing, that in the general expression of inconsolable distress, Pomaree was the only person who shewed no concern; he took leave of his son with all the indifference imaginable, and hurrying into his canoe, paddled back to the shore, a solitary exception to the affecting sensibility of his countrymen. Bustling and avaricious, he was a total stranger to all the softer feelings of the heart; and this savage, like too many hardened beings in civilized life that I have myself met with, was formed of stuff that no trial could move to tenderness, no affliction to sympathy.

At one **P. M.** we anchored in ten fathoms water, close to the innermost of the little islands on the south-east of the entrance of the bay; and being now to bid our last fare-well to the Missionaries, who had accompa-nied us thus far, we could not see them return without sensations of regret, however pleasing to us was the prospect of the good they were likely to effect. This feeling was reciprocal, and they parted with us as with the friends of their heart, whom they never again expected to see; yet were they recon-ciled to the event by the important object that demanded it. But in thus adverting to those estimable men from whom we were now finally separated, it may be permitted me to make a few remarks, which, though unconnected with the direct tenor of this work, are called for at the same time as a tribute of justice, due not only to the indi-viduals in question, but to their zealous brethren in the various other parts of the world, who have cheerfully undertaken the same noble task, that of bringing deluded man to the knowledge of himself as well as of his Maker.

Of the few characters who devote themselves exclusively to the service of their fellow-beings, there is none perhaps who acts from motives more purely disinterested than the Missionary, yet none is more liable to misrepresentation. Looked upon by the generality of mankind, who are incapable of appreciating his views, or being even charitable to his principles, as either a visionary enthusiast or an imposing hypocrite, he proceeds on his laborious vocation, cheered only by the conscious sincerity of his own heart, and the pleasing approbation of that small number of worthy men, whose sentiments are warmed with a congenial fervour. Yet would those people who are so ready to attribute undue motives to the Missionary, and to decry that zeal for his fellow-creatures by which he is actuated, but take the trouble to reflect for a little time on the appalling difficulties and severe privations he has so often to encounter, they would perhaps be more sparing of their censures, and not speak contumeliously of a character who is generally found without reproach. Would they but suffer their thoughts to accompany him through all the dangers of an inhospitable or destructive climate, through all the dreary haunts of uncivilized man, or through regions pregnant with disease and death; then would they render justice to his intentions, and regard him, not as a fanatic or hypocrite, but as the mild instructor of the ignorant, and the faithful servant of a beneficent deity. His exertions too, it must be observed, are bounded by no smaller sphere than the globe itself: wherever man has dared to penetrate, there has the Missionary made his way; and whether we look upon him seated on the frozen coast of Greenland, or under the burning heat of an African sun, or whether we view him in climes still farther remote, amidst the most repelling loathsomeness of savage life, every where will he be found cheerful, happy and indefatigable in the prosecution of his labours. It can never affect the unsullied character of the general body of Missionaries, that some worthless individuals may have usurped the name, and imposed upon religious societies to serve their own private purposes; the turpitude of such impostors should no more be adduced as a proof of aggregate culpability, than the nefarious wickedness of one servant in a family should be charged equally upon all the others, though they look upon it with abhorrence.

Deeming it necessary to say thus much of Missionaries in general, whose character I have too often heard aspersed without the slightest foundation for the slander, I shall now proceed to notice some few particulars respecting our friends who are settled in New Zealand; and if any men have ever given unequivocal proofs of disinterested philanthropy, these certainly have evinced them. With all the means necessary to secure a competent independence in their own country, where they enjoyed from their earliest childhood those comforts which England above any other nation affords,—with the progressive improvements of the arts, and the grand inventions of original genius, presenting each day before them something useful, elegant or noble,—with the fond endearments of social ties, and the cheering converse of private friends who felt interested in their welfare;—with these motives to detain them, and others too multifarious for me to enumerate, they departed at the call of Religion and Humanity, to dwell in an island of cannibals, remote from their native shore as the very extremity of the globe. Here sequestered amidst savage wilds are these worthy men contented to fix themselves for life; here are they willing to endure all the revolting habits of barbarism; and here do they cheerfully forego every thing that can render existence desirable, provided they can realize the grand object for which they have thus gone into voluntary exile. In the commencement of this work, I stated the pursuits in life of these Missionaries; and I have been credibly informed, that the profits they derived from them were such as to make them independent of their present emoluments. Mr. Kendall, before he engaged in the service of the Church Missionary Society, was the master of a respectable school in the vicinity of London, which not only afforded him the means of supporting his family in comfort, but left a handsome sum annually, which he was enabled to lay by for future exigencies; so that had he chosen to remain in his own country, he could always have lived above want, and ultimately perhaps in comparative affluence. His attendance on the ministry of the Reverend Basil Wood, whose celebrity as a divine, and excellence as a man, are so generally acknowledged, was the first incentive that kindled in his mind a zeal for missionary labours, and induced him to devote the remainder of his life to the service of his dark fellow-creatures. He did not, however, adopt this resolution in the precipitate ardour of an inflamed imagination; but weighing coolly and deliberately the circumstances on both sides, he found a sense of duty to the many prevail over the selfishness of individual interest. As little were Mr. King and Mr. Hall influenced by pecuniary motives in becoming Missionaries; the former, as I have understood, was in easy circumstances, and the latter, I know from unquestionable authority, was in the receipt of four hundred a year at New South Wales, where he resided for four years, and was acquiring that sum by his business as a builder and carpenter. It is evident, therefore, that even in money matters, without taking the various other considerations into account, this man must be a considerable loser by attaching himself ·to the mission; but to give one instance of disinterestedness more forcible than another may appear invidious, and I think I may confidently repeat it, that not one of these excellent individuals ever engaged himself for the arduous task he has undertaken, with the least view to his personal advantage. Thus exiled by their own free will in the service of humanity, they repine not at the loss of friends, connections and civilized intercourse; but calmly submitting to these privations, than which none can be more severe, they urge in a barbarous land the work of enlightenment with unremitting perseverance, and look for their reward in the conscious rectitude of an approving heart, and in the grateful respect of every good man. That their zealous efforts will eventually be crowned with success, I fondly anticipate; and in bearing this imperfect testimony to their merit, I have only done that which any person having a similar opportunity of appreciating it, could not possibly omit, particularly in the affecting moment of a final separation.

The convict who had secreted himself on board our vessel when we left Port Jackson, and whom we intended to take back with us to the Colony, made his escape two days before; dreading nothing more than the idea of returning to the place of his banishment.

Mr. Marsden and myself went on board the
Jefferson, where we had a search made for
him, but without success, as he had not, so
far as we could ascertain, concealed himself
in any part of that ship, and we conjectured
that some of the natives might have afforded
him a retreat. We had now on board the
two men, together with the woman, who
were transferred to us by Captain Barnes,
besides the two wretched fugitives who had
surrendered themselves to us soon after our
arrival at the island. Our friend Gunnah,
who had remained with us hitherto, now
took his leave of us, and much to our surprise, without the least symptoms of regret.
This we could not attribute to any want of
sensibility on his part, having seen how much
he was affected at parting with us but for a
short time at the Cowa-cowa, when he cried
like a child, and sobbed as if he was bereft
of all earthly consolation; but the reason, I
believe, why he shewed no such proofs of
tender feeling on the present occasion, while
he was never more to behold us, was that he
had learned, from a longer intercourse with
us, to assume our fortitude, which he thought
more becoming than the lachrymose wailings
of his countrymen, and in consequence either

repressed his emotions, or stifled them altogether. He was a great admirer of " *Europee
fashion,*" and I am persuaded that this par-
tiality had occasioned the seeming unconcern
with which he parted from his *Europee*
friends. At six P. M. it being high water,*
we again got under sail, with a light breeze,
and the weather cloudy, and at eleven
P. M. Point Pocock bore south-west, distant
three miles.

We found ourselves on Sunday, February
the 26th, at two A. M. close by the Cavalles,
and at noon the south point of Doubtless
Bay bore south, distant three leagues. Our
Indian passengers had not yet recovered
their spirits after the parting scene with their

* It is high water in this bay at the full and change of the
moon about eight o'clock, and the tide then rises to eight feet
perpendicularly. It appears, from such observations as I was
able to make of the tides upon the sea coast, that the flood
comes from the southward, and I have reason to think that
there is a current which comes from the westward, and sets
along the shore to the S. E. S. S. E. as the land happens to
lie.—*Hawksworth's edition of Cook's Voyages,* vol. ii. p. 370.

For the information of future navigators along this coast,
it may be worth remarking, that the soundings are deep, close
to the shore, both on the eastern and western sides of this
island, contrary to what is generally met with in the other
islands of the Pacific Ocean, which are either surrounded by
reefs of coral, or have flats near the sea shore, and which
consequently render the approach to them very dangerous.

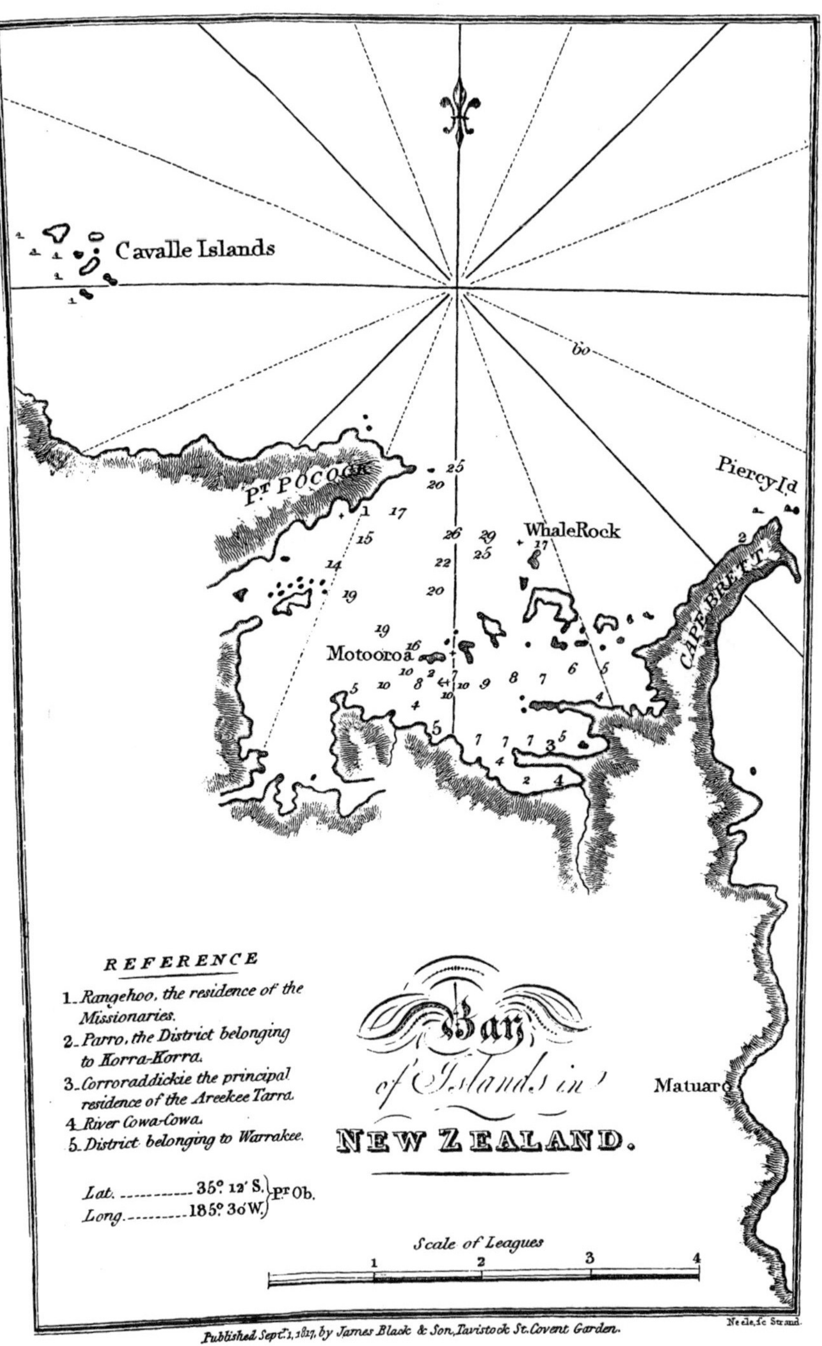

Cavalle Islands
Piercy Id
Pt POCOCK
WhaleRock
CAPE BRETT
Motooroa
Matuaro
60

REFERENCE
1. Rangehoo, the residence of the
Missionaries.
2. Parro, the District belonging
to Korra-Korra.
3. Corroraddickie the principal
residence of the Areekee Tarra.
4. River Cowa-Cowa.
5. District belonging to Warrakee.

Lat. _________ 35° 12' S.
Long. _________ 185° 30'W.
Pr Ob.

Bay
of Islands in
NEW ZEALAND.

Scale of Leagues
1   2   3   4

Published Sept. 1, 1817, by James Black & Son, Tavistock St. Covent Garden.
Neele, sc Strand.

friends, and they remained the whole day in a state of gloomy pensiveness.

Wishing to procure a quantity of flax, which Jem the Otaheitan had promised to have in readiness for us on our return, we lay to under the west side of the North Cape, on Monday the 27th, at seven A. M. expecting every moment that his canoe would put off from the shore. He was, however, in the interior, though at no great distance, as we were informed by some of the natives, who visited us in two canoes; and we also learned from them that he had several baskets packed up with flax for us, and that he looked out continually in expectation of the vessel. Mr. Marsden having a wish to go on shore, I accompanied him in one of the canoes, together with three of our passengers; and the natives conducting us with considerable skill and dexterity, through a very heavy surf, in which I thought there was imminent danger of our being upset, landed us at the foot of some lofty hills. Ascending the highest of these, we came to one of the sweetest views I had seen in New Zealand. Below us was a beautiful valley, formed like the arena of an amphitheatre, and open to the northward, and commanding a bold prospect of the expansive main. This valley was laid out in neat enclosures, and planted with the coomera and potatoe; and at the foot of the hill was built a small village, close to which ran a meandering stream that emptied itself into the ocean. Besides the village, there were also houses scattered in different directions, that added considerable interest to the scene. The sides of the hills were cultivated in some places to their very summits, and in others covered with beautiful trees and shrubs, harmonizing in attractive unison with improved lands. The majestic appearance of the ocean, with the bold promontory that forms the North Cape, running out to some distance from the coast; the uncommon neatness and regularity of the cultivated lands; the picturesque form of the valley, with its clear and beautiful stream winding its way till it lost itself in the sea; the varied and pleasing foliage of the different coppices scattered on the sides of the hills,—these gave altogether such an interesting singularity to this view, as must strike the most tasteless observer with admiration.

As I had outstripped my friend Mr. Marsden, I waited here until he came up;

when a party of the natives advanced towards
me, and among them an old woman who
began dancing before me, and made remarks which called forth the laughter of her
companions. It is probable she was exercising her wit upon the packahà, and as I
gratified her turn for raillery by laughing
in concert with the merry group, we all
very soon got into good humour with
each other. Mr. Marsden joining us, we
descended the hill, and proceeded to the
valley, where one of the young men who
had come on board the vessel when we were
here before, shewed us the governor's pro-
clamation which Mr. Marsden had given to
him. We walked along the beach for about
two miles, in expectation of meeting Jem;
the cliffs that bound the coast on this part of
the island are formed of hard nodules of a
dark stone in a clayey cement, and rise to
the elevation of about one hundred feet, and
are nearly perpendicular. The wind coming
on to blow fresh, we returned to the canoes,
anxious to get on board, when we were overtaken by Jem, who on coming up to us,
immediately discharged his musket in the
air, and expressed himself much pleased that
he was so fortunate as to meet with us before

our departure. He told us, that if we would consent to detain the vessel till the ensuing day, he would bring us the flax, which was ready to be sent on board, and Mr. Marsden agreed to the proposed delay. Getting into the canoe, we reached the ship about four o'clock, and just in time, for it now blew so very hard, that we should not have considered it safe to have ventured from the shore in the frail little bark that conveyed us to the vessel. The three passengers who had attended us in our excursion having imprudently separated from us, without mentioning the place they intended going to, we were obliged to leave them behind. I should have observed, that in the valley I had lately visited, I saw the flax-plant in greater perfection than I had hitherto met with it any where else. It grew by the side of the stream, and was not less than eight feet in height, and the leaves from four to five inches broad.

After plying continually to windward during the night, we got quite close in under the land on the morning of the 28th; and at eleven A. M. Jem came on board, bringing with him thirteen baskets of flax, and accompanied by our three passengers, who were delighted with the opportunity of regaining the ship, which they supposed they had entirely lost by their heedlessness. With these came also another passenger, a young lad named Toopannee, brother to the principal chief of the district, who wished us to take him with us to Port Jackson. The flax which Jem had collected amounted in weight to three hundred pounds, and was well prepared. By a calculation* which we now made of the value of the entire cargo, it appeared that it would produce at the Colony, the sum of four hundred and fifty-one pounds four shillings; after deducting the enormous duty of one shilling per foot, to which the timber was subject. But as the future cargoes of timber will come for the greater part in plank, they will be much more valuable, and I have little doubt but the vessel will in time amply repay the Missionary Society, for the expenses they have incurred. They must, however, get this

---

* The following is the estimate we made:

	£.	s.	d.
4848 feet of timber at 2s. 6d. per foot - - 606	606	0	0
Duty, 1s. per foot (deduct) - - - - - 242	242	0	0
	364	0	0
1344 lbs. of flax, at 1s. per lb. - - - - 67	67	4	0
Fish and pork - - - - - - - - - - 20	20	0	0
Total value of the cargo - - 451	451	4	0

exorbitant duty upon the timber taken off, which I should suppose might be easily effected by a proper representation to the Secretary for the Colonial Department. We now made sail, steering west by north, and at noon the North Cape bore east by south, distant five leagues. As the frequent repetition of dates with the ship's bearings, must be uninteresting to the reader, I shall omit, during the remainder of the voyage, that detail of incidents which I have hitherto given in a daily form; noticing such circumstances as come within my purpose, without any further regard to the period of their occurring, than is absolutely necessary to preserve regularity.

Our passengers, as we proceeded, resumed their wonted good humour, and two of them, Atoo and Kyterra, were remarkably lively; but Toopannee, the lad who had lately come on board, remained quite sullen and gloomy, nor did he appear either grateful for our endeavours to cheer his spirits, or sensible of our friendly attentions towards him. He seemed of a dull, morbid disposition, and had none of those amusing peculiarities with which in the other savages of his age we were so frequently entertained.

We experienced on the 4th of March, a smart gale of wind, and our New Zealanders, who had never before ventured to any distance from the shore, were much alarmed at the tossing of the vessel. Themorangha in particular expressed his fear in the greatest agitation, and as if he had not another moment to live. Coming upon deck with the tears streaming from his eyes, and trembling from head to foot, he told the captain that the ship was *nuee nuee pagata*, (too heavily clad, meaning that she carried too many sails,) and that the *racaw* (mast) would certainly break. The captain, however, told him there was no danger, but this did not remove his alarm, which still continued till the weather got settled, and he became more familiarized to the boisterous element. The female convict, whom we had taken out of the Jefferson, being employed as servant in the cabin, had learned to keep our savage guests in excellent order; and she maintained over them a sort of absolute authority, to which they were all very willing to submit, except when any thing was said or done, which the chiefs, or those among them who were allied to chiefs, imagined had a tendency to lessen their consequence. A slight of this kind,

whether involuntary or designed, would instantly set all wrong; and their pride was so
sensitive, that a look or a word was enough
to excite them to indignation The boys,
though busily assisting in the several menial
offices of the cabin, yet could not bear to
think that they were derogating in the
smallest degree from their patrician dignity;
and to call one of them a *cookee*, while he
was either scrubbing the floor with a mop,
or washing the plates, would make him at
once give up the degrading task, and cry out
that he was *nuee nuee rungateeda;* nor would
he resume his employment till some person,
wishing to compose his agitated pride, would
assure him that it was not unsuitable to a
gentleman. Though the New Zealanders, as
a people, are remarkable for their equanimity,
yet I have often observed in some of them
a contrary disposition; and Tupee, while he
was one of the most shrewd and intelligent of
his countrymen, was at the same time extremely irritable and capricious. Being refused on one occasion some sugar for his
tea, he poured out all the maledictions he
could utter upon the servant who had the
charge of it, and retired to his sleeping place
to indulge his sulky humour. Here he re-

A fac-simile of the Amoco or tattooing on the face of a New Zealand chief, as drawn by himself on board the ship Active, March 9th, 1815.

mained growling by himself till Mr. Marsden took him the sugar, which instantly had the effect of making him get into better temper. In speaking to this man respecting the illness of Duaterra, we could learn that both he and Themorangha ascribed the origin of it entirely to the resentment of Warree, the seducer of his wife; who they said never ceased invoking his Etua, to take vengeance on the chief for the flogging he had given him, till his prayer was granted On the opposite side will be found a fac-simile of the tattooing on Themorangha's countenance, which is a perfect representation of the lines, as drawn by himself with a pen, which I directed him to use for the purpose, and which he now handled for the first time in his life.

On the 13th of March, being in Lat. 32° 48″ S. Long. 157° 4″ E. the weather became tempestuous, attended with thunder and lightning; and as Mr. Marsden performed divine service before the ship's company, Themorangha supposed that he was praying for the squalls to cease, but that his Etua was angry with him, and would not listen to his entreaties. Not so, he said, with the priests of his country; for when any of them happened to be overtaken by a storm at sea, he had only to call upon the Etua of New Zealand, and the elements were immediately hushed in peace; but they had more power, he asserted, than our *tohungha*, whose supplications were obviously of no avail, as the bad weather still continued. Of Jem, who on our first interview with him, had excited our prepossessions in his favour, we were now led to entertain still higher opinions, having an opportunity of forming a closer estimate of his character. We found him a young man of much good sense, as well as politeness, and more intelligent than we could have expected, even allowing for his previous intercourse with the Europeans. He told us he had been on Shoupah's expedition to the East Cape, and that the whole force which that chief had mustered together amounted to a thousand men, who, setting out in their canoes from the river Thames, which was the general rendezvous, proceeded against an unoffending people, a great part of whom they murdered and devoured, after they had first ravaged their country and burned their habitations. I asked Jem if he had partaken of the horrid banquet; but he appeared shocked at the idea, and assured me that nothing in life could prevail upon him to taste human flesh. He added, moreover, that he was by no means a willing agent in this scene of slaughter, but that he was obliged to declare himself for Shoupah, who, if he did otherwise, would most certainly make him a victim to his resentment. He described the people of the East Cape as much more ingenious and active than any of the other tribes in New Zealand. Their houses, he said, were larger and better built, and their plantations more extensive, than were any where else to be met with in the island; besides, the best mats were made there, as were also the most finished and complete war instruments. Of these latter, the pattoo pattoo, made of jade,* is the most remarkable; but I found that Jem, though very shrewd in other particulars, had fallen into an absurd notion which prevails among the natives respecting it. They assert it to be made of the internal substance of a fish, which, being boiled over the fire, dissolves into a glutinous liquid, and is thus

---

* This stone is the same which is called by Captain Cook, in his account of New Zealand, the green talc. There is a fine specimen of it in the British Museum in its rough state, as taken from the rock; and I have now by me chisels, earrings, and some other articles made from it.

moulded into the shape of the pattoo pattoo, while it assumes a hard consistence by being left exposed to the air. It is surprising how this notion is so generally assented to in this part of New Zealand, when its absurdity might be so easily detected by the admission of the people who make the instrument in question; but it would appear to me that these countenance the error from some motive of private interest. Jem observed likewise, that the people of the East Cape, though very numerous, were yet of an unwarlike turn of mind, and preferred peaceful and regular habits to the predatory mode of living that was followed by the rest of their countrymen. But this disposition, with the resources produced by their superior skill and industry, served only to expose them the more readily to the devastating incursions of their rapacious neighbours, who conspired to despoil them of that property which they wanted courage to defend.

Nothing particular having occurred during the preceding days, we found ourselves on Tuesday, March 21st, full in view of the coast of New South Wales, when, taking advantage of the wind and the favourable state of the weather, we were enabled at noon to approach within seven leagues of Port Stephen's. At three P. M. we got under the lee of one of the three islands which lie off the entrance of that port, and anchored in five fathoms water. Mr. Marsden and myself, taking all our New Zealand friends along with us, landed on the narrow neck of land that forms one side of the harbour of Port Stephen's; and walking across this spot, we got a fine view of the haven, which is very extensive, running a considerable way up the country. The land on each side is low for many miles, till it swells gradually into high grounds, known by the name of the Blue Mountains. Here we saw that elegant plant the gigantic lily, but not in flower; and we found also immense quantities of a creeping plant,* that bears a large bean, and the same which Captain Cook mentions as being so serviceable in curing his people of the scurvy,† while he was lying in Endeavour River.— Leaving the New Zealanders by themselves, we walked along the shore, where we discerned, at some distance, two of the original natives approaching towards us: we made signs to them to come up, which they did

* The Glycene Rosea.
† See Hawksworth, vol. iii. p. 187.

with apparent diffidence, when we immediately conducted them to our rude passengers. The poor creatures, when they beheld the New Zealanders, who were arrayed in their war-mats, with their spears and other instruments of destruction about them, were dreadfully alarmed, and stood trembling in every joint. Their fellow-savages, however, did every thing that they thought could re-assure them, and dispel their apprehensions; they were going to nose them, but the latter not understanding this mode of salutation, our friends desisted from the attempt, and shook hands with them, as a more intelligible demonstration of friendship. They then danced and sung to them, and tried every means to remove their fears, while the natives acknowledged their kindness, by continually calling out *bougerree you, bougerree you!* (very good you,) yet shaking all the time with unabated alarm. Seeing, however, that no injury was intended, they began by degrees to recover their confidence; and Mr. Marsden, telling them that they must conduct us on the ensuing day to Newcastle, which was about fifteen miles distant from this place, one of them started up, and reeling about like a drunken man, attempted to sing, but his voice failing him almost at the moment he began, he became for a short interval as completely mute as if nature had never furnished him with the organs of sound. The New Zealanders stared at him with astonishment, and I thought he was mad; when at last the poor fellow, regaining the use of his tongue, pointed to his cheek, and clapping his belly with his hand, cried out *bougerree, bougerree!* (very good,) to the mirthful surprise of every body present, except one New Zealander, who regarded him with cool indifference.— This man having given him some tobacco, believing it to be the most acceptable present he could offer, perceived that its narcotic effects had caused a temporary suspension of his faculties, and that he was now beginning to recover, which our passenger explained to us in a manner that was highly diverting.— These men, like the rest of the original natives of this country, were perfectly naked; and according to the general practice, had the front tooth knocked out. The miserable appearance they presented, furnished matter of conversation to our New Zealand friends: as we proceeded to the ship, they eagerly inquired whether they cultivated the coomera or potatoe, and if they had plenty of pigs; and being told that they were too idle to work, and had not a single pig in the world, they expressed both pity and contempt at their wretched mode of living.

The wind shifting to the northward, we got under sail, at ten A. M. on Wednesday, March 22d, and stood along the coast. The weather on this day was finer than we had experienced it for some time, and continued throughout uncommonly serene; and we admired the view of the coast from the Coal River to Port Jackson, which was bold and striking. From the former place to Bird's Island, which lies close to the main land, and is about midway between it and Broken Bay, the coast presents a low ridge of land running parallel with the sea, and backed by lofty hills covered with timber. Opposite to Bird's Island is a considerable tract of flat country, but said to be very barren; the heads of Broken Bay rise with an abrupt and rugged ascent, but the coast becomes more level to the westward. The last day of a voyage which to me never once appeared tedious for a moment, being now arrived, the morning of Tuesday, March 23d, brought us within three leagues of the harbour of Port Jackson, when Mr. Marsden being anxious to get on shore, I accompanied him in the boat, and landing at the South Head, we walked into Sydney. Here we proceeded, in the first instance, to pay our respects to the Governor, after being absent four months—the time allowed to Mr. Marsden for his leave of absence.

Having thus closed the narrative part of this work, I shall subjoin, as a conclusion to it, such further observations on New Zealand as appear to me necessary to complete the object I have proposed to myself; which is, to draw the attention of the British Public to a nearer and more perfect view of that interesting island.

SUPPLEMENTARY

OBSERVATIONS.

———

CHAP. VIII.

Of the first discovery of New Zealand—Its situation, extent
and soil—General face of the country—Hills and mountains—Climate contrasted with that of New South Wales
—Particulars of each—Vegetable productions—Fossils
and minerals—Quadrupeds, birds and insects—Fish, abundant and of various species.

THE island of which I have hitherto treated
was first visited in 1642, by Abel Jansen
Tasman, a Dutch navigator who sailed from
Batavia for the purpose of making discoveries in the Pacific Ocean. Arriving on the
eastern side of it, on the 24th November, he
explored the north-eastern coast, and entered
a strait, or passage, of about five leagues
broad, and separating two islands from each
other, to which he gave the general name of
New Zealand. Being attacked by the bar-

barous natives almost immediately after he had anchored; and having three of his men killed on the spot, and a fourth mortally wounded, (as has been stated in the commencement of this work,) he did not attempt to land upon the island; but sailed away, after he had given it the above-mentioned name, and imposed the appalling designation of *Murderers' Bay* on the inhospitable harbour. It was supposed, from the period of its first discovery, to the time of the enterprising Captain Cook, that the strait entered by Tasman separated an island from some vast southern continent; but the British navigator, who sailed round both islands in the years 1769 and 1770, has completely removed this geographical error. He made three more voyages hither in 1773 and 1774; and in these, while adding to his own celebrity as an indefatigable navigator and excellent commander, he has enabled some philosophical minds to extend the limits of science, and advance the progress of human research. The two islands that go by the name of New Zealand are situated between the latitudes of 34 deg. 22 min. and 47 deg. 25 min. south, and between the longitude of 166 deg. and 180 deg. east.

Upon referring to the map of this country, it will be seen that Eaheinomauwe, or the northern island running from the North Cape, which is in latitude 34 deg. 20 min. south, to Cape Palliser, in 41 deg. 36 min. south, contains 436 miles in length; and taking the medium breadth, which varies from five miles at Sandy Bay to 180 at the East Cape, at about 60 miles, this extent will include 26,160 square miles, or 16,742,400 square acres; while T'Avai Poenammoo, the southern island, extending from 41 deg. 30 min. to 47 deg. 25 min. south, stretches 360 miles in length, and estimating its medium breadth at 100 miles, contains not less than 36,000. square miles, or 23,040,000 square acres.— These islands, therefore, taken together, will give an area of 62,160 square miles, or 39,782,400 square acres. Such, as nearly as I can make the calculation, is the extent of both islands; and the reader will see what an ample scope there is here for the industry of civilized man to exert itself, particularly when it is considered that nature has been as liberal to New Zealand in every other respect as in the dimensions she has assigned to it. The general face of the country, so far as we had an opportunity of exploring it, is undulating; and the hills rise with a varied ascent, from inconsiderable eminences to lofty mountains. A continued chain of hills runs from the North Cape to the River Thames, and extends, as would appear from Captain Cook's survey, through the whole country, from north to south; while, in taking the latter direction, these hills gradually swell into mountains, the highest of which, according to Doctor Forster, is Mount Egmont,* lying

* "The highest of all the mountains which we saw in the course of this voyage is, in my opinion, Mount Egmont, on the northern isle of New Zealand, whose summit was covered with snow a great way down, and almost constantly capt with clouds, though, at intervals, we saw its top very distinctly. In France, in about 46 deg. of north latitude, the line of eternal snow is found at the height of about 3,280 or 3,400 yards above the level of the sea. On the Pico de Teyde, on the Isle of Teneriffe, in about 28 deg. of north latitude, the snow is to be met with at the height of 4,472 yards. Mount Egmont is very nearly in 39 deg. of south latitude; but as we constantly found that in southern latitudes the cold is much more intense than in the corresponding degrees of the northern hemisphere, I will suppose the climate of Mount Egmont equal to that of France, and, therefore, the line of snow to be at the height of 3,280 yards; and as the snow seemed to occupy one third of its height, the mountain will be 4,920 yards high, or 14,760 feet, which is somewhat less than Dr. Heberden found the Pico of the Isle of Teneriffe to be. The summits of the mountains in the interior parts of New Zealand, both in Queen Charlotte's Sound and in Dusky Bay, we found constantly covered a good way down with eternal snow. We

in latitude 39 deg. 16 min. south, longitude 179 deg. 45 min. east, and said to resemble in its appearance the Peak of Teneriffe, being also of the same elevation. The whole of the northern island, if we except a few spots on the western side, appears admirably well adapted for the purposes of cultivation ; but the southern island, into which we had not an opportunity of penetrating, is described by Captain Cook as mountainous, and apparently barren. Yet though this part of the country might have presented to his eye a less vivid surface than the northern quarter, still this should not be taken as a certain indication of its barrenness; and from the astonishing height of the trees found growing upon it, as well as from their great abundance, it would seem that the soil must be rather fertile than otherwise; and were it

observed these snow-capt heads all the way along, when we sailed from Dusky Bay to Queen Charlotte's Sound, in May, in the year 1773 ; and we took notice of the same circumstance in the same year, in October, on the other side of the southern isle, when contrary storms brought us a good way along its south-east shore, almost as far as Banks' Island. This I believe sufficiently proves that these mountains form as it were one continued chain, running throughout the whole southern isle, and that they are little inferior in height to 12 or 14,000 feet."—*Forster's Observations*, p. 32.

properly cleared and tilled with the necessary care, the husbandman, in my opinion, would have no reason to complain of its sterility. In our excursions into the interior of the northern island, we found that the soil varied in its quality, but generally appeared extremely fertile ; the hills were composed, for the greater part, of a stiff clay ; and the valleys consisted of a black vegetable mould, producing fern of the most luxuriant growth, while the swamps which we occasionally met with, were of trifling extent, and might be drained with little trouble or expense.—There was one feature in the country which every where struck us with admiration, and that was the fine rich verdure of the landscape wherever we turned our eyes, and which gave us at the same time a high opinion of the genial influence of the climate. This opinion was the more strongly impressed upon our minds, by contrasting the bright mantle of green that extended over the country now lying before us, with the parched and arid lands of New South Wales, where at the same season of the year, I have seen vegetation completely destroyed for want of moisture, and the labours of the agriculturist appearing only a dreary expanse of unprofitable tillage.

As the Bay of Islands lies within a few miles of the same parallel of latitude with Port Jackson, we were at a loss to account for so remarkable a difference in the climate between both places; and I could attribute it only to their topographical situations being dissimilar. The country of New South Wales, though undulating like that of New Zealand, yet has no hills of equal elevation with it; nor any of sufficient height to attract the dense clouds from the incumbent atmosphere, with the exception of the Blue Mountains, which extending from sea to sea, in the shape of a semi-circle, have, until a very late period, formed the boundaries of the colony. Yet even these are of no considerable height, nor does it appear that rain falls more frequently in their neighbourhood than in any other part of the adjacent country. The immense extent of land beyond these mountains, which stretches to the northward for nearly two thousand miles, must have a material influence on the climate in this quarter, and its powerful effects are but too often experienced. The situation of New Zealand is altogether different from that of the small part of New Holland at present colonized. Both the northern and southern islands are for the greater part extremely narrow in proportion to their length. At the Bay of Islands, it is scarcely thirty miles across from the eastern to the western side, and in many parts not quite so much; while in one place, as has been shewn, the breadth declines even to five miles. The winds, therefore, from the eastward and the westward bring with them the exhalations drawn up from the boundless extent of ocean on both sides; and these being attracted by the high lands that run through the whole extent of the country, fall down in refreshing showers, and afford an abundant supply of moisture. Having thus accounted for what appears to me to be the cause of that genial humidity which produces such invigorating effects on the vegetable kingdom in New Zealand, I shall now proceed to describe more particularly the nature and temperature of the climate, as likewise of that of New South Wales; as it may be worth the reader's attention to see how widely different the seasons may be found in two countries lying within nearly the same parallels of latitude. I have besides a stronger motive for this contrast, which is to shew that the former country is in this respect far better adapted for an European colony than the latter.

From the accounts of the missionaries, who visited the Bay of Islands in the midst of winter, and from our own observations during our residence there in the summer season, I do not hesitate to assert, that there is perhaps no country in the world that can boast of a finer and more regular climate than this part of New Zealand. Though not removed further than eleven degrees from the verge of the tropics, and where, in the midst of summer, the rays of the sun fall almost vertically, yet we did not find even in the hottest months of the year, the heats to be at any time excessive, or unfavourable to vegetation; and the air was so delightfully bland and healthful as to act powerfully upon the animal spirits. Mr. Kendall, who happened to have a thermometer in his possession, observed to me, that he had not seen the mercury, during his residence on shore, rise higher at any time than 74°, or fall below 63°; and he informed me, that in his first visit to this part of the country, which, as has been stated, was in winter, the cold was by no means severe; and the plantations looked as green and flourishing as they would in the latter end of spring, or beginning of summer, in our own country. This verdant and fertile appearance was not in the least diminished by the heats of summer; for there were occasionally soft and mellow showers that descended to refresh the lands, and we experienced also three or four days of continual rain. The herbage therefore never for a moment lost that rich freshness so pleasing to the eye of the beholder, and the prospect in every direction was cheering and attractive. The mildness of the climate in this part of the country appears equally to extend to that bordering on Queen Charlotte's Sound, where the vegetables which Captain Cook had sown in a previous visit, were found by him on his return remarkably vigorous; having stood the winter without being otherwise affected by it than as it added to their strength; though if left exposed during the same season in England, they must certainly have perished. In this part, notwithstanding that it lies as far south as 41°, and in the vicinity of the snow mountains, yet no frost could be seen during the time the Resolution and Adventure remained here, which was till the 6th of June, almost the very depth of winter. The climate, at the further end of the southern island, must, from its situation, partake of a much greater degree of cold than the other parts, and is subject, it appears, to heavy and continued rains; for Captain Cook observes, that " during the stay the Resolution " made in Dusky Bay, which was for six " weeks and four days, only one week of " continued fair weather was experienced, " and all the rest of the time the rain pre- " dominated, insomuch that they never expe- " rienced above two fair days in immediate " succession; but notwithstanding which (he " adds) the crew recovered their health very " fast; and perhaps the climate was less " noxious to Englishmen, than it would have " been to any other nation, from being so " analogous to their own."* From the re- marks here offered, it will be seen that the climate of New Zealand, taking the country through its whole extent, is mild and tem- perate, and consequently particularly favour- able to the growth of whatever productions the soil may be adapted to yield.

* Hawksworth, vol. i. p. 99.

The climate of New South Wales, of which I am now to speak more in detail, has, as would appear from the united testimony of some of the earliest settlers, been subject of late years to considerable periodical changes. That it was formerly much more kindly and genial than it is at present, I have some reason to believe; but to what causes the phenomenon of its deterioration may be ascribed, I shall not take upon myself to investigate. I should think, however, from the general face of the country, that the climate at best must have been dry and unfavourable to agriculture. The land springs are extremely scarce, and there are few or none of those small running streams which are always to be met with in countries plentifully supplied with moisture, and which serve both to embellish and fertilize the landscape. Upon my landing in the colony, at the latter end of the year 1813, I found the settlers plunged in the deepest distress from the continued and excessive droughts that had prevailed. For the ten preceding months it was almost one uninterrupted season of parching weather, the consequence of which was, that the crops were nearly destroyed, the water pools in many places dried up, and the grass had become so sapless and withered as to afford little or no nourishment. The cattle were dying in great numbers all over the country, and the meat that was brought into the market was of such an indifferent quality as to be both disgusting to the eye, and insipid to the palate. Fortunately, however, this state of things was at length to experience some change for the better, and about a month after my arrival, the earth was revived by heavy showers, which were productive of considerable service; but these were not of long continuance, and the atmosphere, resuming its usual severity, denied almost entirely any further supply of moisture during the two ensuing years that I remained in the country. The heavy dews, however, which fell in the night time, tended to keep the herbage in a sort of sickly vegetation, in defiance of the burning heat of the sun during the day; and were it not for these the markets could not have been supplied even with the provisions, bad as they were, which the farmers brought in. A gentleman of my acquaintance at Sydney, kept a journal of the state of the weather for twelve months, and from the copy of it, which I subjoin, the reader will be enabled to form a tolerably accurate opinion of the temperature in this part of the world.

ABSTRACT of a METEOROLOGICAL JOURNAL, kept at Sydney in New South Wales, from October 3d, 1813, to October 3d, 1814.

	Thermometer.			Baromr.	Days of Rain.	Days of fine Weather.	Wind.							
	High	Low	Mean	In. D.			W.	S.W.	S.	S. E.	E.	N.W.	N.	N.E.
1813.														
Oct.	78	60	69	30.07	7	22	6	3	5	3	3	4	1	4
Nov.	84	66	75	29.91	4	26	1	2	10	4	2	3	5	4
Dec.	86	70	78	29.91	3	28	1	8	12	4	0	2	2	9
1814.														
Jan.	88	73	80	29.74	4	27	5	0	6	15	7	0	2	20
Feb.	87	73	80	29.91	5	23	2	2	10	4	0	2	4	17
March	82	68	75	30.07	13	18	0	2	18	17	1	0	1	3
April	73	62	67	30.04	9	21	3	9	16	7	1	4	5	5
May	69	51	60	30.09	4	27	11	17	8	5	0	4	0	5
June	66	52	59	30.00	3	27	10	19	8	2	2	5	0	6
July	61	43	52	29.57	2	29	19	15	6	0	1	6	1	0
Aug.	68	47	62	29.93	3	28	17	10	1	1	0	4	5	7
Sept.	70	52	61	30.01	4	26	9	12	16	5	3	5	4	6
Oct.	73	55	64	29.90	0	2	0	1	2	0	0	0	0	0
Ann. Mean			68	29.93 Ann. Mean	61	304	84	100	118	67	20	39	30	86

Brilliant Days . . . 278
Cloudy 26
Rainy 61
____
365

Thus it will be seen what a very small quantity of rain fell during the period of which this journal kept an account, and in a country where the heat of the sun is so intense as to require frequent and plenteous showers to counteract its parching influence. But even this small quantity was only partially diffused, and of the sixty-one days of rain, which the above journal notices, there were not, I believe, more than a dozen of continued rain that extended generally over the whole face of the country. Before this period, however, such heavy rains used to fall in the month of March, as to cause the two principal rivers in the colony, the Nepean and the Hawkesbury, to overflow their banks; laying the country round for many miles completely under water, and sweeping away in one common destruction the varied produce of the farmer's industry. These floods have occurred at irregular intervals, varying from three to seven years and upwards; and at the time I am now treating of, (1813,) there had elapsed an intermediate space of four years. But since my return to England, I have learned that in the beginning of the year 1816, a flood, the most destructive of any that has ever yet been experienced at the colony, took place there, and carried off in its irresistible torrent not only the labours of the husbandman, but also houses, mills, bridges, and every building that stood to intercept its desolating progress. The loss occasioned by these floods must be very considerable; in March, 1806, there was one that destroyed property to the amount of at least thirty-five thousand pounds, but what the injury done by this recent inundation might have been, I am not aware.

The prevailing winds in the summer season are from the south and south-west; those in the winter from the north-east and south-east. A destructive and suffocating wind is sometimes experienced from the north-west; and during its continuance, which is seldom long, the atmosphere is so dreadfully oppressive as to be almost insupportable. This pernicious wind equally extends its baleful effects to the animal and vegetable kingdoms; and on the 1st of January, 1814, such a specimen of it was experienced here as produced the most distressing sensations, during its continuance, on the animal system. The sky, suddenly changing its appearance, became lurid and gloomy; the thermometer rising to 114 deg. occasioned a heat which it was impossible to endure, without feeling the blood in a raging ferment, and the whole frame was agitated with a burning restlessness which sought in vain for some mitigation. The vegetables in the gardens of Sydney were nearly all destroyed; and a gentleman, a friend of mine, had two birds suffocated in their cages by the pestilential heat with which the atmosphere was impregnated. It appears to me that this wind, which is similar to the sirocco experienced on the shores of Italy and Sicily, originates probably in the same cause; and as the latter, in passing over the sandy desarts of Africa, brings with it the intolerable heat of these regions, so the former perhaps, being wafted over tracts of equal sterility, though yet unexplored, comes charged with a suffocating vapour, attracted from them at that season of the year when the sun is most intense. In the winter months, which are exactly the reverse of ours, the greatest cold being felt in May, June and July; the frosts are rather constant, and water is frequently found congealed into ice half an inch in thickness: the morning and evening at this time of the year are sharp and piercing, the thermometer falling to 44° and 42°, and rising at noon to 62° and 66°; yet this disproportion in the temperature is a singularity perhaps peculiar to this climate: but the change, which is felt very sensibly, is neither conducive to health nor comfort. From the foregoing statement, the reader will perceive that the flattering accounts given by Europeans of the climate of New South Wales, have been in a great degree exaggerated; while the temperature of New Zealand, to which that country in a geographical situation is analogous, may be justly commended for its mildness and salubrity. But to conclude this contrast, on which enough has been said for my purpose, I shall now proceed with my remarks on the latter country alone.

New Zealand, thus favoured with a fertile soil and fine climate, is rich in various natural productions, some of which are extremely valuable. Having, in the course of the preceding narrative, noticed these only in a desultory manner, according as they presented themselves in the occasional excursions I made through the country, I shall here consider them in a more regular form, offering my remarks on the vegetable and mineral kingdoms under one general head. In the vegetable kingdom, there is no production that is so much calculated to strike the traveller with admiration as the trees of

amazing growth, which rise in wild luxuriance all over this country. Pines of different
descriptions, and which are utterly unknown
to Europeans, are here to be met with, soaring
to a height which leaves no similarity between
them and the tallest that ever grew on the
mountains of Norway; and those species,
which bear the uncouth names of the cowrie,
the totarra, the towha, and the zarida,
afford such a supply of valuable timber as the
profusion of some ages to come will not be
able to exhaust. Here are also several kinds
of trees of inferior growth, though not less
excellent in their quality; and many of them
are admirably well adapted for ornamental
works requiring a fine grain, the wood being
of this nature, and susceptible of a high
polish. According to the different situations
in the country, the timber appears to vary;
" thus, (says Dr. Forster,) a fine shrubby
" tree at Dusky Bay, or the Southern ex-
" tremity, (T'Avai Poenammoo,) which there
" grows in the lowest part of the country,
" dwindles to a small inconsiderable shrub
" at Queen Charlotte's Sound, or the Northern
" End, where it is only seen on the highest
" mountains." But this difference is not to be
ascribed to the soil, else the reverse would

be the case, and the timber would grow to a larger size in the northern quarter, as being the most fertile, and would be stunted in the opposite direction; it is caused only by the variations of the climate happening to be more favourable to those particular species of trees in different degrees of temperature. The trees which the natives chiefly make subservient to their purposes, are, besides the different species of pine above mentioned, the henow, from which they extract a black dye, the towha, a tree resembling the sycamore, the *river river*, the grain of whose wood is similar to that of the beech, a species of the cork-tree, called by these people vow, a large tree named eckoha, and another termed kycata, a tall and beautiful tree, together with many others which are both curious and serviceable. The trees here specified, according to the names assigned to them by the natives, have not, I believe, been classified as yet by any botanist; and the scientific gentlemen who may hereafter visit this country, will find the same difficulty in methodizing their labours as those did who accompanied Captain Cook; no distinguishing order being made out since that period of several productions, with which the latter were totally unac-

quainted. The supple-jack is to be met
with in all parts of the woods; and there is
here also a species of the myrtle similar to
that found in various parts of New South
Wales. Another species of it grows in the
country about Dusky Bay, an infusion of
which was drank by the crew of the Endeavour, as a substitute. for tea. The leaves of
this shrub have a pleasant aromatic flavour
at the first infusion, but yield a strong bitter
when the water is poured on them a second
time. Besides being aromatic, they have
the same astringent properties as tea, and
they were generally used instead of that
plant by all the ship's company of the Resolution, who are supposed to have derived the
most salutary effects from it towards the
restoration of their health, which was very
much impaired on their arrival in these
regions. This shrub is a remarkable instance
of that influence of climate which I have
already noticed: in the midst of a thick
forest, where it is properly sheltered from the
weather, it becomes a considerable tree,
growing very frequently to the height of
thirty or forty feet; while in exposed and
elevated situations, it never rises above six
feet; though as it grows generally in more

favourable spots, its usual size is from eight to ten feet, and something more than nine inches in circumference. The branches produce no leaves, and only the stem bears them; the flowers, which are white, expand themselves at the top, when the shrub is in full bloom, and have to the eye a very pleasing effect.

Of the other trees noticed by Capt. Cook and the gentlemen who accompanied him in this part of New Zealand, is one resembling the American spruce fir, and from the leaves of which a very wholesome liquor was brewed. This was called the New Zealand spruce fir, from its similarity to the former tree, and is represented as growing to a great height, with long pendant branches, covered with articulated leaves in a flourishing state of verdure. They found here also several small shrubs, which are not to be met with in the other parts of the country; and among them was a new species of the dragon-tree, the central shoot of which partook at once both of the flavour of cabbage and of an almond kernel.* The supplejacks, it appears, from the accounts of these

* Forster, vol. i. p. 176.

gentlemen, are, in this place, no less than from fifty to sixty feet long, every where obstructing the passenger; and I have before stated how great an annoyance we found them in making our progress through the forests. In New Zealand there are no trees that yield a fruit fit to be eaten by Europeans; though there are some few which the natives themselves prize very highly for the sort they produce. But fructiferous trees of any description are here very scarce, and perhaps not more than three or four species could be found in the country.

Besides the common fern which supplies the natives with their ordinary food, there is here likewise the fern-tree, so called from having its leaves similar to those of that weed; and which also affords them an edible substance. The part of it eaten by these people is the root, which they bake between hot stones, in the same manner as they dress their potatoes; and when thus prepared, its flavour is considered better than that of a turnip. In the centre of this tree is found a tender pulp, which is extremely succulent, yielding, when cut, a juice of a reddish colour. The trees of this country being thus particularized, with as much accuracy as it was in my power to describe them, from so limited a knowledge of their numerous varieties; I have only to add, that it is impossible to imagine, in the wildest and most picturesque walks of nature, a sight more sublime and majestic, or which can more forcibly challenge the admiration of the traveller, than a New Zealand forest.

The native herbage of this country, as far as we could perceive, is confined to a few species, and there are two principal obstacles here to the growth of any kind of grass in the forest lands: the first is, the rank exuberance of the trees which infects the soil; and the next, the exclusion of the rays of the sun by the impenetrable thickness of the foliage; so that the woods afford nothing that can serve as pasturage for cattle. The herbaceous productions indigenous to the country are, wild celery, canary grass, wild parsley, plaintain grass, a species of ray-grass, the *ensata* or flag, the phormium tenax or flax-plant, and a species of the fern. On the banks of the rivers we observed various plants, which we are entirely unacquainted with, having never seen them either in Europe or New South Wales. The esculent roots, cultivated by the natives, and which have been given to them by Europeans, are the potatoe, the cabbage, the turnip, and the *tacca*, a species of the yam. The only grain they have in the country is a little Indian corn, which they have likewise received from European navigators, as well as the pumpkin or gourd, and this they cultivate for the purpose of converting it into drinking vessels.

With respect to the fossils of New Zealand, I observed the sides of the numerous coves about the Bay of Islands, were for the greater part composed of a soft argillaceous kind of stone that scraped easily with a knife. This was intersected with veins of a greenish hue, and was of a lamellated conformation, and appeared related to that class of stones called steatites, as described by Kirwan in the first volume of his work on Mineralogy, p. 138; resembling very much the soap-stone which I afterwards had an opportunity of seeing in China, and which in that country is worked up into a variety of ornaments. The only perceptible difference was in the coloured veins, and in the degree of hardness. Some of the rocks adjoining Rangehoo had veins of a dark-brown colour which would not yield to the knife, and in which the pre-

sence of iron might easily be perceived:
when detached from the rock, they had very
much the appearance of that metal, strongly
oxided, or in a state of rust. The softness
of these rocks is the cause of the frequent
perforations we observed as we coasted
along the shores, and which produced an
uncommonly picturesque effect. In one of
our excursions into the interior, we fell in
with some huge masses of quartzose rock;
and in the bed of the Wyetanghee, and on the
shores of the fresh-water lake Morberrie, I
observed that the stones were of a greyish
hue, and exceedingly porous, containing in
their different cavities small crystals adhering
to the sides, when broken. At the North
Cape, the cliffs which bounded that promontory were composed of hard nodules of a
black and hard stone, imbedded in a clayey
cement. The jade we had no opportunity of
seeing in its natural state. I procured one
or two pieces of pumice-stone, which the
natives make use of in polishing their spears,
halberts, and other war instruments, as
likewise obsidian or volcanic glass. But it
does not appear that these substances are
produced in New Zealand; for though I
made repeated inquiries among the natives as

to the existence of volcanoes in this country, I could not ascertain that any had ever been known here. Yet in a rude sketch of Eaheinomauwe or the Northern Island, which Korra-korra drew for me upon paper, he described between the East Cape and Queen Charlotte's Sound, a high island on the eastern side, which at intervals vomited forth fire and smoke, and from which place I should suppose the above volcanic substances were procured. Among the curiosities which we purchased of the natives, were some axes made of porphyry, and others of a dark-coloured stone; but the most valuable ones were cut out from the jade, as were also a variety of small ornaments, which in particular attracted our attention for the ingenuity they displayed.

From the opinion of geologists, that mountains running for any considerable distance in one uninterrupted direction, are more likely than those that are broken and segregated, to contain metallic veins, I should think it very probable that the continued chain of lofty hills, which extends from one end of New Zealand to the other, comprising a space of more than seven hundred miles, will, when explored, be found pregnant with some valuable ores. It is the opinion of Dr. Forster, than whom few writers were more prepared to consider the subject philosophically, that the species of fossils found in the mountains of these islands,* being of the primogenial kind, and not decomposed by the action of subterraneous fire, indicate the presence of the richest metallic veins. Iron, that most useful of all metals, and without which the labours of man must be tedious and inefficient, is found in considerable quantities in the neighbourhood of Mercury Bay ;† and manganese,

* " The mountains of New Caledonia are the most likely to contain the richest metallic veins; and the same opinion, I suspect, may be formed of the mountains in New Zealand. For the metallic substances, in all the other volcanic isles, are probably destroyed and scorified by the violence of the subterraneous fire: those in New Caledonia and New Zealand seem to be as yet undisturbed, as the species of fossils, prevailing in these two isles, are substances, which mineralogists have hitherto looked upon as primogenial, in which all the metallic veins on our globe are constantly found. I speak of veins only, and not of flat-work or floors, which contain likewise sometimes metallic ores, but have an origin different from that of the primogenial mountains."—*Dr. Forster,* p. 28.

† " We found thrown upon the shore, in several parts of this Bay, great quantities of iron-sand, which is brought down by every little rivulet of fresh water that finds its way from the country, which is a demonstration that there is ore of that metal not far inland."—*Hawksworth,* vol. ii. p. 348.

as we have already seen, is met with near the banks of the Cowa-cowa. We could not perceive any stratum in the country that had the appearance of coal; but I think it not unlikely, that when the country is better known, some mines of it may be discovered. But should this not be the case, there can be no want of fuel, as the extensive forests will afford a supply for ages to come.

The animal kingdom in New Zealand includes but few species; and the quadrupeds, in particular, are very scarce, as has been shewn in page 125 of this volume, where their number is given on the authority of Doctor Forster, with the addition of one animal, the guana, of which he does not take notice, but which I have reason to suppose exists in the country. The birds, though not so numerous in the part of the country that we visited as in the southern quarter, still deserve the consideration of the zoologist, some of them being as enchanting in their song as they are beautiful in their appearance. The poe, with its pendent tufts of white feathers, of which an accurate drawing is given in Cook's Voyages, charms with its delightful notes the romantic wilds of New Zealand; and it is not too much to say of this native

warbler, that no successful rival can be found
for it among the woodland songsters of Europe. This bird was brought to us for sale
by the natives, in small cages made of wicker-
work. We saw two or three beautiful species
of the parrot and the paroquet, a small bird
resembling the sparrow; and we occasionally
met with that singular species of the duck
which I have described in the narrative, as
remarkable for having the beak, legs and
feet of a bright red, and the eyes encircled
with a rim of the same colour, while the body
was of a fine glossy black. In the marshy
grounds, and on the banks of the rivers, we
observed the wild-duck in considerable numbers, and some small birds of the most beautiful plumage. From the feathers which line
the garments of some of the chiefs, it would
appear, that there is here a species of the
cassowary, but we did not see any in our
excursions. The feathers are precisely the
same as those of the emu in New Holland,
except being somewhat smaller. Among the
sea-fowl which are generally to be met with
upon the coast, we noticed the shag, the gannet, the albatross, and three or four species
of the petrel. In Dusky Bay, the small birds
are represented as being exceedingly nume-

rous; and they were found by Captain Cook's party, so very tame and unacquainted with the presence of mankind, that they betrayed no distrust whatsoever, and even hopped on the ends of the fowling-pieces. There was shot in this bay a white heron, that answered exactly to the description given by Pennant, in his British Zoology, of a bird formerly found in England. Towards the southward there are also water hens of a large species, rails in vast numbers, cormorants, oyster-catchers, or sea-pies, penguins, and some other sorts of aquatic birds. From this part of New Zealand thirty-seven new species of birds were brought away on the return of Captain Cook. The country will now have to boast of every species of domestic fowl known in Europe; for the missionaries took with them great numbers of turkeys, geese, ducks, and common fowl, so that in the course of a few years these will be numerously pro-pagated, and supply the natives with a new article of diet.

The few insects found in the Bay of Islands do not warrant the supposition that any great variety of them can be met with in the other parts; and those which I observed were, the butterfly, the beetle, the flesh-fly, the common fly, and a small sand-fly that infested the numerous coves of the bay.— This latter insect was excessively troublesome to us, by its settling on the instep and about the ancles, and biting those parts in such a manner as to prove very painful when we were warm in bed. We sometimes met with mosquitos, but these were rarely to be seen, and the inconvenience we experienced from them was but trifling. So far as I could ascertain, there are no noxious reptiles in any part of New Zealand.

During the short stay which I made in this interesting island, I had repeated occasions to observe the great abundance of fish that every where visited the coast; and, indeed, so immense a supply is here provided for the use of man, as must inspire him with admiration and gratitude for the liberality of nature. Nor is the profusion more remarkable than the variety; and there is no part of the world where the epicure who understands the qualities of this species of food, could more readily select a treat for his discriminating palate, than on the shores of New Zealand. Captain Cook justly remarks, that ample amends are made to the natives of this country, by being thus furnished with the inexhaustible resources of the deep, though denied a supply of land animals.*   Sailing

* " For this scarcity of animals upon the land, the sea, however, makes an abundant recompence; every creek swarming with fish which are not only wholesome, but equally delicious with those of Europe. The ship seldom anchored in any station, or, with a light gale, passed any place that did not afford us enough with hook and line to serve the whole ship's company, especially to the southward: when we lay at anchor, the boats with hook and line, near the rocks could take fish in any quantity; and the seine seldom failed of producing a still more ample supply: so that both times when we anchored in Cook's Strait, every mess in the ship, that was not careless and improvident, salted as much as lasted many weeks after they went to sea. Of this article the variety was equal to the plenty; we had mackerel of many kinds, among which, one was exactly the same as we have in England.— These came in immense shoals, and were taken by the natives in their seines, who sold them to us at a very easy rate. Besides these, there were fish of many species which we had never seen before; but to all which the seamen very readily gave names: so that we talked here as familiarly of hakes, bream, cole fish, and many others, as we do in England; and though they are by no means of the same family, it must be confessed that they do honour to the name. But the highest luxury which the sea afforded us, even in this place, was the lobster, or sea cray-fish, which are probably the same that in the account of Lord Anson's voyage are said to have been found at the Island of Juan Fernandez, except that, although large, they are not quite equal in size. They differ from our's in England in several particulars; they have a greater number of prickles on their backs, and they are red when first taken out of the water. These we also bought every where to the northward, in great quantities, of the natives, who catch them by diving near the shore, and finding out where

round the whole extent of coast, he found as he proceeded, shoals of the most excellent fish; and I must observe, that while we remained here, our table was not only plentifully but luxuriously supplied. The fish, however, which are in common use among the natives, are snappers, bream, the beneecootoo, the parrot-fish, cray-fish, the herring, the flounder, and a fish resembling the salmon, but much inferior to it in flavour. In some of the coves were large flats, which, at low water, had beds of cockles, muscles and other shell fish. The muscles were of immense size, and the natives relished them exceedingly.

The foregoing is a summary account of

they lie with their feet. We had also a fish that Fregier, in his voyage to the Spanish Main in South America, has described by the names of elefant, pejegallo, or poison coq, which, though coarse, we ate very heartily. Several species of the skate, or sting-ray, are also found here, which are still coarser than the elefant; but as an atonement, we had among many kinds of dog-fish, one spotted with white, which was in flavour exactly similar to our best skate, but much more delicious. We had also flat-fish, resembling both soles and flounders, besides eels and congers of various kinds, with many others, of which those who shall hereafter visit this coast will not fail to find the advantage; and shell-fish in great variety, particularly clams, cockles, and oysters."—*Hawksworth*, vol. iii. p. 35.

the natural productions of New Zealand, classed with some regard to perspicuity of arrangement; and the next subject to which I shall briefly advert, is the origin of the natives—one, which though no writer can develope with precision, yet nevertheless deserves inquiry.

CHAP. IX.

THE page of history sufficiently informs us, that to trace with accuracy the rise and early progress of certain nations, is not only a difficult but a hopeless task; and this happens even with respect to countries who have preserved records of their origin; for in these documents the historian will often find much to reject, and still more which he cannot reconcile. Rome, which was afterwards the mistress of the world, could refer only to mythological fiction for the first dawnings of her power, yet was Livy obliged to content himself with this ideal authority. If such, then, has been the case with the historian of an empire which carried the arts of civilization to the highest pitch, the writer who would follow up a people sunk in the deepest gloom of barbarous ignorance, to the source whence they first emanated, while he has no written language to direct him, nor any fixed data for his arguments, may justly expect indulgence, even though erroneous in his research. It should be considered that correlative analogy is his only guide; and on the merits of this alone must depend all the strength and applicability of his reasoning.

Having therefore premised thus much, I shall now proceed to consider which of the various nations on the globe appears with most probability to have furnished the population of New Zealand, as well as of the other islands in the same ocean, which I shall afterwards prove to be of the same stock. In surveying the several nations of the world as delineated on the map, the first country that presents itself, which from its relative situation would seem likely to have supplied a race of inhabitants to this island, is New Holland; to which it is more immediately connected by proximity of distance than to any other extensive land, the space between them being little more than three hundred leagues. But there is such a total dissimilarity in every particular between the natives of both these countries, as to leave no doubt upon my mind that they are two distinct races, entirely unconnected with each other.

During my residence in the colony of New South Wales, I had frequent opportunities of conversing with the original inhabitants, and observing their habits and mode of living. Of these people, therefore, I can speak from my own experience, which is further corroborated by the accounts of Captain Cook, and more particularly by those of Collins and of Flinders. The wretched and improvident habits of these people, and their total ignorance of the art of cultivation, and of any of the means which contribute to raise the existence of human beings superior to that of brutes, must leave them considerably behind the natives of New Zealand, sunk even as the latter have always been in utter barbarism. The people too of this continent appear totally incapable of exercising their reasoning faculties, while the New Zealanders, considering their abject state, are uncommonly shrewd and argumentative. The difference likewise of the form of their bodies, of the lineaments of their countenance, together with the dissimilarity of their language, must afford testimony that the natives of New Holland are not one common race with these islanders. Besides, it is evident that these people could never have ventured to any distance from the shores of their native country without the certainty of inevitably perishing; their embarkations being so wretchedly constructed, consisting merely of the bark of a tree twisted together at each end, and kept apart in the centre by sticks placed across. To this I may add the total inaptitude they evince for imitation, as well as their disinclination to manual labour, which leads them rather to subsist on the most loathsome fare, than procure the necessaries of life by the exertion of a little activity. Wandering about in a state of nudity and starvation, they have seen, without profiting in the smallest degree by it, the example of European industry before their eyes for the last thirty years; and it appears from the accounts of the late Captain Flinders, who circumnavigated the whole of this coast, that the character of the natives is equally abject in every part as in that which is colonized. It is clear, therefore, that this is not the country to which New Zealand is indebted for its population ; and in pursuing our inquiry, we are led to a more distant land, the vast continent of America.

But as little shall we find that these islanders owe their origin to any part of the western hemisphere. When the Spaniards, in the beginning of the sixteenth century, possessed themselves of those fertile regions which lie contiguous to the southern ocean, it appears that they found but two states or kingdoms* who had acquired any degree of national importance from the extent of their population, and the progress they had made in civilized pursuits; and from the traditions preserved among these singular people, it would seem they had not originated more than three or four centuries before the arrival of their ruthless invaders. The rest of this immense continent was thinly occupied by a few scattered tribes dispersed at considerable distances from each other; yet all of them differing so much in physical and moral appearances from the inhabitants of the South Sea Islands, as not to afford the slightest grounds for supposing an identity of extraction between them. In the dic-

* See Dr. Robertson's History of America, vol. ii,

tionaries of the Peruvian and Mexican languages, there is not a single word which seems
at all analogous to any of the oral expressions
of the people in the Pacific Ocean; and it is
worthy of remark, that when the Spaniards
touched at some of the islands in this ocean,
shortly after the discovery of America, they
found these as populous as they are at this
day.   Reasoning then from analogy, it does
not appear that either New Holland or the
continent of America, has furnished the population of these islands; and still discussing
the subject upon the same principle, we
must proceed to another region, and getting
into the islands of the Indian and Chinese
seas, look with a greater probability of
success for such a similarity between many
of the nations there, and the islanders in the
south seas, as would reasonably induce the
belief of their being of one common origin.
This similarity I shall explain in the proper
place, observing here, that the inhabitants of
these islands, though dwelling in situations
so remote from each other, appear to me to
be descended from a once powerful people,
who, formerly speaking the same general language, migrated from the continent of Asia,
and settled in the Indian Archipelago. Here

gradually degenerating into barbarism, from a high state of civilization, the consequence most probably of their seclusion from the continent, they spread themselves, I should suppose, in distinct tribes over the adjacent islands, while the spirit of enterprise led them in successive migrations to those of the southern ocean, where they ultimately passed to the last stage of moral degradation. That the New Zealanders are of the same race with the people of the tropical isles, I think, is unquestionable; and so striking a resemblance do they bear in their manners and customs, as well as in the conformation of their bodies, to the natives of Otaheite, of the Society Isles, of the Marquesas, the Figis, the Tonga, or Friendly Isles, and of Easter Island, that it is impossible not to consider them the offspring of the same primitive stock. They are likewise identified with them in their superstitions and their systems of theogony, which are only modifications of a common belief originally assented to by the whole of them, and altered in the lapse of time according to caprice or circumstance. But what appears conclusive on the subject is, that all these islanders speak one general language, the variation in the words being only dialectical, while in many of them no difference is perceptible.* Climate and situation must be supposed to influence their habits, but the difference is never so great as to preclude an obvious similarity in most particulars. The natives of New Zealand must, therefore, be necessarily classed with the other islanders in the same ocean; and while we consider the whole as one race disparted into several small nations, and respectively adopting institutions with different degrees of barbarism, though similar in the aggregate; it will be proper at the same time to take a survey of the people, from whom, according to the opinion I have advanced, they have deduced their origin. This appears necessary before I advert to those analogous particulars in the moral and political economy of both, which I shall have occasion to notice in support of my argument.

Among the various nations which we find dispersed in the Indian and Chinese seas, that of the Malays is decidedly the most considerable; possessing the greater part of

---

* The reader will find some examples of this in the vocabulary which I have added, where the New Zealand and Tonga words are compared.

the shores of Sumatra, Java, and Borneo, besides the numerous smaller islands lying in the same regions. These people have been generally considered as the aborigines of the peninsula of Malacca, whence they were supposed to have migrated at certain periods, and gradually extended themselves over the different islands they now occupy; but this opinion is disproved by the written traditions of the people themselves, by which it would appear that they derive their origin from the south-eastern part of the island of Sumatra.* These traditions are corroborated by the testimony of Europeans who have resided on the peninsula of Malacca, and who de-

---

* " The original country inhabited by the Malayan race, (according to the authorities of the Malayan books,) was the kingdom of *Palembang*, in the island of *Indalus*, now Sumatra, on the river *Malayo*, which flows by the mountain named *Maha-meru*, and discharges itself into the river *Tatang*, (on which Palembang stands,) before it joins the sea. Having chosen for their king or leader a prince named *Sri Turi Buwana*, who boasted his descent from *Iskander* the Great, and to whom, on that account, their natural chief Demang Lebar Daun submitted his authority, they emigrated under his command (about the year 1160) to the south-eastern extremity of the opposite peninsula, named *Ujong Tanah*, where they were at first distinguished by the appellation of orang de-bawah angin, or the Leeward people, but in time the coast became more generally known by that of *Tanah Malayo*, or the Malayan land."—*Marsden's Sumatra*, p. 327.

scribe the people inhabiting the interior parts as a perfectly distinct race from the Malays, and to be similar in every respect, except in stature, to the Caffres of Africa. The Malays, therefore, appear to be only a tribe of the people I have mentioned, as having formerly emigrated from the continent of Asia, and given inhabitants to these islands as well as to those of the Pacific Ocean. Though the population both of Sumatra and Java is divided into various small nations, differing from each other in language, manners and customs, yet sufficient evidence is afforded by them severally to shew that they may be all traced to the same source. The difference of language* among the whole of them consists

* " Besides the Malayan, there are a variety of languages spoken in Sumatra, which, however, have not only a manifest affinity among themselves, but also to that general language which is found to prevail in, and to be indigenous to all the islands of the eastern sea, from Madagascar to the remotest of Capt. Cook's discoveries, comprehending a wider extent than the Roman or any other tongue has yet boasted. Indisputable examples of this connexion and similarity I have exhibited in a paper, which the Society of Antiquaries have done me the honour to publish in their Archæologia, vol. vi. In different places it has been more or less mixed and corrupted, but between the most dissimilar branches, an evident sameness of many radical words is apparent; and in some very distant from each other in point of situation, as for instance, the Philip-

merely in the change and omission of certain vowels, in the facility or difficulty they find in pronouncing the consonants, and in the adoption of new words to express new ideas, which distinct habits and varied circumstances must naturally suggest. From what part of the Asiatic continent the islands were originally peopled, cannot be ascertained by any positive authority; some have asserted, but without much probability of truth, that Africa is the quarter whence the migration took place to them; and that some tribes, who were banished from Egypt,* came down the Red Sea, and after coasting along the peninsula of India, settled themselves in the Archipelago. But there are no corroborating circumstances to support this opinion; and Mr. Raffles, in his history of Java lately published, supposes, apparently on better grounds, " the tide of population to have " flowed towards these islands from that " quarter of the continent lying between

pines and Madagascar, the deviation of the words is scarcely more than is observed in the neighbouring provinces of the same kingdom."—*Marsden's Sumatra*, p. 200.

* Middlekoop's Collection, vol. ii. p. 65.

" Siam and China ;"* while he adds, at the same time, that all the islanders in the Indian

* " The inhabitants of Java seem to owe their origin to the same stock, from which most of the islands, lying to the south of the eastern peninsula of Asia, appear to have been first peopled. This stock is evidently Tartar, and has by its numerous and wide spreading branches, not only extended itself over the Indian Archipelago, but over the neighbouring continent. ' To judge from external appearance, ' that is to say, from shape, size and feature,' observes Dr. Francis Buchanan, in his notices on the Birman Empire,* ' there is one very extensive nation that inhabits the coast of ' Asia. It includes the eastern and western Tartars of the ' Chinese authors, the Calmucs, the Chinese, the Japanese, ' and other tribes inhabiting what is called the Peninsula of ' India beyond the Ganges, and the islands to the south and ' east of this, as far at least as New Guinea.'—' This nation,' adds the same author, ' may be distinguished by a short, ' squat, robust, fleshy stature, and by features highly different ' from those of an European. The face is somewhat in shape of ' a lozenge, the forehead and chin being sharpened, whilst at ' the cheek-bones it is very broad. The eyebrows, or super- ' ciliary ridges in this nation, project very little, and the eyes ' are very narrow, and placed very obliquely in the head, the ' external angles being the highest. The nose is very small, ' but has not, like that of the negro, the appearance of being ' flattened; and the apertures of the nostrils, which in the ' European are linear and parallel, in them are nearly cir- ' cular and divergent; for the septum narium being much ' thickest towards the face, places them entirely out of the ' parallel line. The mouths of this nation are in general

* Asiatic Researches, vol. vi. p. 219. Octavo edition.

Archipelago appear to him to have had the
the same native origin; thus affording his

‘ well shaped; their hair is harsh, lank and black. Those of
‘ them that live even in the highest climates do not obtain
‘ the deep hue of the Negro or Hindoo; nor do such of them
‘ as live in the coldest climates, acquire the clear bloom of
‘ the European.’

“ The Javans are to be included under this general description, but possessing many peculiarities which mark them
as a race distinct, though still retaining general traces of
a common origin. The less civilized of the tribes inhabiting
the islands, approach so nearly in physical appearance to that
portion of the inhabitants of the peninsula, which has felt least
of the Chinese influence on the one side, and of the Birman
and Siamese on the other, and exhibit so striking an affinity
in their usages and customs, as to warrant the hypothesis, that
the tide of population originally flowed towards the islands
from that quarter of the continent lying between Siam and
China. But at what æra this migration commenced, whether
in the first instance it was purely accidental, and subse-
quently gradual; or whether originally it was undertaken
from design, and accelerated at any particular periods by
political convulsions on the continent, we cannot at present
determine with any certainty, as we have no data on which
to rely with confidence. It is probable, however, that the
islands were peopled at a very remote period, and long before
the Birman and Siamese nations rose into notice.

“ Whatever opinion may be formed of the identity of the
tribes inhabiting these islands and the neighbouring peninsula, the striking resemblance in person, feature, language
and customs, which prevails throughout the whole Archipelago, justifies the conclusion, that its original population
issued from the same source; and that the peculiarities which
distinguish the different nations and communities into which
it is at present distributed, are the result of a long separation,

respectable testimony to what I have said upon the subject. Yet from whatever part of the continent these islands first received inhabitants, it is certain that the original colonists were not only superior in every respect to the present race, but as I have observed before, had arrived at a high state of civilized improvement. This fact is sufficiently demonstrated by the traces of architectural structures which they have left behind them; and there are found in Java and Sumatra ruins of this description,* which do

local circumstances, and the intercourse of foreign traders, emigrants, or settlers."—*Raffles' History of Java*, vol. i. p. 57.

* " High up on the river Batu-Bara, which empties itself into the straits of Malacca, is found a large brick building, concerning the erection of which no tradition is preserved amongst the people. It is described as a square or several squares, and at the corner is an extremely high pillar, supposed by them to have been designed for carrying a flag. Images, or relics of human images, are carved in the walls, which they conceive to be Chinese (perhaps Hindoo) idols." —*Marsden's Sumatra.*

The following extract is taken by Mr. Raffles from the Report of Captain George Baker, of the Bengal Establishment, who was ordered by the government at Java to visit the ruins in the neighbourhood of Brambanan:—" The " sepoy who attended me, and who had resided two years " among the Bramins and Benares, and of a corps of up- " wards of eight hundred sepoys, was acknowledged to be " the best acquainted with such subjects, informed me that " similar figures were common guardians of the entrance to as much credit to their genius as to their amazing powers of execution. These people appear likewise to have brought with them the Hindoo form of worship; and in the island of Java it is still followed by a small tribe,* who have preserved it to this day, through the various revolutions of succeeding ages. That insular situations, by precluding an enlarged and general intercourse with mankind, tend to impede the progress of the

" the temples of India, and seemed perfectly well acquainted " with their history, purpose, and distinctive accompaniments ; " but he was lost in surprise at the number, magnitude and " superior execution of those at Brambanan, to which he " said, that India could in no respect furnish a parallel. " Every thing here, he said, was manifestly the work of the " gods, as no human power could have effected such things. " The temples at Brambanan are entirely composed of plain " hewn stone, without the least mixture of brick, mortar, " or rubbish of any-kind, even in the most extensive solid " masses, or to fill up the floors and basements of the largest " structures."—Vol. ii. p. 8, 9.

* " To the eastward of *Surabaya*, and on the range of hills connected with *Gunung Dasar*, and lying partly in the district of *Pasuruan*, and partly in that of *Probolingo*, known by the name of the Teng'ger Mountains, we find the remnant of a people still following the Hindoo worship, who merit attention, not only on account of their being (if we except the *Bedui* of Bantam, who will be hereafter noticed) the sole depositaries of the rites and doctrines of that religion existing at this day on Java, but as exhibiting an interesting singularity and simplicity of character."—*Raffles' History of Java*, vol. i. p. 329.

human mind, is a fact that needs no elucidation; and as the improvement of man in
his aggregate as well as in his individual
capacity, depends entirely upon the scale of
his social communication, it cannot be considered an anomaly in the history of his
species, if we find him retrogressive with
respect to intellectual attainments, in proportion as this is curtailed. The original
inhabitants of these islands came from the
continent well versed in all the arts of civilization existing there at the time of their
migration; but their successors, neglecting
to cultivate these arts after they had been
introduced, and having no connection with
the country whence they first came, gradually
lapsed into utter ignorance, till branching
off into savage tribes, they sought out territories in more distant regions, and proceeded to the Southern Ocean, with no other
guide to direct them than the fearless spirit
of adventure.

Having offered these remarks on the
people of the Indian Archipelago, I shall
now endeavour to trace the connection between them and the natives of the South
Sea Islands; and the reader, I am disposed
to believe, will perceive with me such a close

affinity between them, as will lead him to conclude that both are but one and the same race, existing from adventitious circumstances, under different shades of character. But my object being to trace the origin of the New Zealanders, I shall particularly advert to them in the assimilation which I am to submit; yet availing myself at the same time of any illustrative features in the character of the other islanders in the same ocean, with whom I have shewn them to be identified.

In taking a view of society, as it is constituted in New Zealand, we find three orders who rise in graduated distinction above the common people. These orders are, beginning with the lowest, rungateedas, chiefs, and areekees. The rungateedas claim an ascendancy over the multitude, together with many political privileges, in consequence of their being allied by birth to the chiefs; and the latter, though inheriting independent sovereignties, are nevertheless obliged by the recognized usage of the country, to lend their services to the areekee or principal chief, whenever he thinks proper to make war, no matter whether the motives be just or otherwise. The cookees, or inferior class, though by far the most numerous, as is the case in every country, are held by each of these orders in a state of complete vassàlage, though in some few instances they have an independent interest in the ground they occupy. Here is a mode of government entirely analogous to that which prevails in the islands of the Indian seas, and very much so among the Malays,* where the chief authority is vested in the rajah, whose rank resembles that of the areekee of New Zealand, and who commands the services of the pangeran, or heads of the dusums or villages. These latter correspond exactly with the subordinate chiefs above-mentioned; and like them, they acknowledge a superior, though with respect to their possessions they are independent of his controul. In both regions the system of government (if government it may be called) is evidently feudal; and the power exercised by the privileged classes in each, is nearly similar in every respect. The peculiar homage also which is paid to superiors in the islands of the Archipelago, is offered with equal veneration by the natives of some of the South Sea Islands,

* See Marsden's Sumatra, p. 350.

those of Tonga* in particular. Mr. Raffles thus describes the deference which the Javans pay to rank. " The respect shewn to su-
" perior rank in Java is such, that no indi-
" vidual, whatever be his condition, can stand
" in the presence of a superior, neither can
" he address him in the same language in
" which he is spoken to; and the same re-

* " The respect which is shewn to Tooitonga, and the high rank which he holds in society, is wholly of a religious nature, and is far superior when occasion demands it to that which is shewn even to the king himself; for this latter, as will by and by be seen, is by no means of the most noble descent, but yields in this respect to Tooitonga, Veachi, and several families related to them; and if the king was accidentally to meet any chief of nobler descent than himself, he would have to sit down on the ground till the other had passed him, which is a mark of respect that a common peasant would be obliged to shew to any chief or egi whatsoever; and for this reason the king never associates with any chief superior to himself, and always endeavours to avoid meeting them; and they, in like manner, endeavour to avoid him, that he might not be put to the trouble of sitting down while they passed: for if any one were to forego this ceremony in presence of a superior egi, some calamity from the gods would be expected as a punishment for the omission. Sitting down is with them a mark of respect, as standing up is with us, before a superior; upon the principle perhaps, that in this posture a man cannot so readily attack or assassinate the person in whose presence he is; or it may be, that in this posture lowering his height, is significant of his rank or merit being humbled in the pre-sence of the other."—*Account of the Tonga Islands,* vol. ii. p. 82, 83.

" striction applies to the family of each
" subordinate chief. Were this mark of
" respect confined to the royal family alone,
" it might perhaps find a parallel in other
" eastern countries, where it is usual for the
" subject to prostrate himself before the sove-
" reign; but in Java the nature of the govern-
" ment is such, that each delegated authority
" exacts the same marks of obeisance, so
" that from the common labourer upwards,
" no one dares to stand in the presence of a
" superior. Thus when a native chief moves
" abroad, it is usual for all the people of
" inferior rank, among whom he passes, to
" lower their bodies to the ground till they
" actually sit on their heels, and to remain
" in this posture until he is gone by. The
" same rule is observed within doors; and
" instead of an assembly rising on the en-
" trance of a great man, as in Europe, it
" sinks to the ground, and remains so during
" his presence."*

The reader cannot fail to observe, from the
note which I have subjoined respecting the
Tonga people, and the statement here quoted
in reference to the Javans, how very great is the

---

* Raffles' History of Java, vol. ii. p. 308.

similarity between them in one particular; and I shall now mention another which will appear still more remarkable. The practice of shampooing is well known to prevail not only in the Indian islands, but all over the continent of Asia; and it is a singular coincidence that the same identically exists at Otaheite and the Tonga Isles, though under a different name. This practice, which is supposed by the Asiatics to contribute very much to the healthful vigour of the individual who submits to it, simply consists in pressing the hands and fingers upon the body and limbs, so as to compress but not to pinch them. The Chinese and Malay barbers are thought to excel all the other practitioners of the East in this art, which is considered a necessary substitute for exercise during the hot weather: but at the baths, the persons who are in attendance perform it so roughly, as frequently to make the joints and even the vertebræ of the back crack with a sudden jerk, which, to people not accustomed to it from their childhood, is a sensation by no means agreeable. In the account given by Captain Cook, who submitted to this operation at Otaheite, for a rheumatic pain, which it effectually removed; we shall find it performed exactly in the same manner as in the East. Being visited by several women, who came for the purpose of offering him their friendly services in this respect, he observes, " At first I thought this numerous train of " females came into my boat with no other " view than to get a passage to Matavai; " but when they arrived at the ship, they " told me they intended to pass the night on " board, for the express purpose of under- " taking the cure of the disorder I complained " of; which was a pain of the rheumatic " kind, extending from the hip to the foot. " I accepted the friendly offer, had a bed " spread for them upon the cabin floor, and " submitted myself to their directions. I " was desired to lay ·myself down among " these. Then as many as could get round me " began to squeeze me with both hands from " head to foot, but more particularly on the " parts where the pain was lodged, till they " made my bones crack, and my flesh be- " came, a perfect mummy. In short, after " undergoing this discipline about a quarter " of an hour, I was glad to get away from " them. However, the operation gave me " immediate relief, which encouraged me to " submit to another rubbing down before

" I went to bed ; and it was so effectual that I
" found myself pretty easy all the night after.
" My female physicians repeated their pre-
" scriptions the next morning before they went
" ashore, and again in the evening when they
" returned on board, after which I found the
" pain entirely removed ; and the cure being
" perfected, they took their leave of me the
" following morning. This they call *romee*,
" an operation which, in my opinion, far
" exceeds any thing of the kind that we may
" use externally ; it is universally practised
" among the islanders. being sometimes per-
" formed by the men, but more generally by
" the women. If at any time one appears
" languid and tired, and sits down by any of
" them, they immediately begin to practise
" the *romee* upon one's legs, and I have
" always found it to have an exceeding good
" effect." * This operation, according to Mr.
Anderson, the surgeon who accompanied
Captain Cook, is resorted to at the Tonga
Islands as a soporific, and is known by the
name of *tooge tooge*. The manner of per-
forming it is somewhat different from that
which is practised at Otaheite, but the general
principle is strictly the same. " When sup-

* Hawksworth, vol. ii. p. 63.

" per was over," (observes that gentleman,
speaking of a night he had spent among the
natives,) " abundance of cloth was brought
" to us to sleep on, but we were a good deal
" disturbed by a singular instance of luxury,
" in which their principal men indulge them-
" selves, that of being beaten while they were
" asleep. Two women sat by Tuttafaihie,
" and performed this operation, which is
" called *tooge tooge*, by beating briskly on
" his body and legs with both fists, as on a
" drum, till he fell asleep; when once the
" person is asleep they abate a little in the
" strength and quickness of the beating, but
" resume it if they observe any appearance
" of his awaking. In the morning we found
" that Tuttafaihie's women relieved each
" other, and went to sleep by turns. In any
" other country it would be supposed that
" such a practice would put an end to all
" rest, but here it certainly acts as an opiate,
" and is a strong proof of what habit may
" effect."* Thus do we find a practice mutually prevailing in the remote nations I have
assimilated, which it is impossible not to
recognize as identical, and as strongly cor-

* Hawksworth, vol. i. p. 323.

roborative of their being of the same original descent.

In proceeding to examine the other instances in which a similarity exists between these nations, we shall perceive them to be equally striking. The eastern practice of women destroying themselves upon the death of their husbands, I have already noticed as prevailing in New Zealand ; and it seems also to have extended to some -of the tropical isles, being found in the Figis, and having formerly been observed in the Tonga Islands by prescriptive * usage. The remorseless tyranny exercised over the lower orders in many of these islands, partakes of the cruel character of Asiatic despotism; and here, as in the East, do we find the lives † of the

---

* " It used to be the custom at Tonga, when the divine chief, Tooitonga, died, to strangle his chief wife ; but this absurd practice was left off during Mr. Mariner's time."— *Account of the Tonga Islands*, vol. i. p. 342.

† Finow, observing one of the natives busily employed in cutting out the iron fid from the main top-gallant mast, and as he was a low fellow, whom he did not choose should take such a liberty, he was resolved to put a stop to his work ; so speaking to a Sandwich islander, who was amusing himself on deck by firing off his musket, he bade him try to bring that man down from aloft. Without the least hesitation, he levelled his piece, and instantly brought him down dead: the shot entered his body, and the fall broke both thighs and fractured

multitude solely at the disposal of the supreme head of the government—there being the same arbitrary power, the same abject slavery. Many of the traditions, too, of the New Zealanders, which have come down to the present day through ages of obscurity, and interwoven with the vagaries of their deluded imaginations, are yet sufficiently plain to afford probable evidence of their being derived from a people who had been familiar with the Mosaic account of the creation. It is not too much to suppose that this account might have been transmitted from Egypt to the interior of Asia; and that the original emigrants might have brought it with them thence to the islands where they settled. This much I can vouch for, from my own knowledge, that the people of New Zealand are generally impressed with the belief, that the first woman was formed of one of the ribs of a man; and as I have

his skull; upon which Finow laughed heartily, and seemed mightily pleased at the facility with which it was done. When Mr. Mariner understood the language, he asked the king how he could be so seemingly cruel, as to kill the poor man for so trifling a fault: his majesty replied, that he was only a low vulgar fellow (a cook;) and that his life or death was of no consequence at all to society.—*Account of the Tonga Islands,* vol. i. p. 59.

observed before, when adverting to these traditions, it is an extraordinary coincidence, that *heevee*, a word so similar in sound to the name of our common parent, should be their term for bone. Their tradition likewise respecting the creation of the first man* is particularly remarkable; and the custom of sprinkling their children with water at the time they name them, is certainly referable to some other cause than a barbarous institution. The oldest men throughout the country have been acquainted from their youth with these traditions; and I could not learn that they ever at any period received the least information from Europeans, which could have given rise to them. The scrupulous regard which the natives of New Zealand pay to the graves of their dead, is equally observed among the Sumatrans; and the native clothing of the latter people is precisely the same, both in texture and material, as that worn by the Otaheitans,† and which is made of the papyrus tree. As

---

* See vol. i. p. 59.

† " The original clothing of the Sumatrans is the same with that found by navigators among the inhabitants of the South Sea Islands, and now generally called by the name of Otaheitan cloth."—*Marsden's Sumatra*, p. 49.

many of the words connected with the theogony of the Sumatrans have been ascertained to come from the Sanscrit,* it is not improbable that, following up the analogy between the two countries, we might be justified in ascribing similar terms among the New Zealanders to the same origin; and perhaps the word *dewa*, which signifies *deity* in the great original language of the East, might have given rise to the *etua* of the latter people.

But it is among a people who inhabit that part of Sumatra bordering on the straits of Malacca, and who have preserved their genuineness of character from the first period of their origin to the present time, that customs and institutions obtain, which, in the aggregate, resemble those in New Zealand almost to identity. The people I allude to are the Batta nation; and I shall conclude this inquiry with stating some instances of coincident similitude between them and the New Zealanders. Looking, in the first place, at their respective forms of government,† we

---

* See Asiatic Researches, vol. iv. p. 223.

† " The government of the Batta country, although nominally in the hands of three or more sovereign *rajahs*, is effectively (as far as our intercourse with the people enabled us to ascertain) divided into numberless petty chiefships, the heads

shall find that they are, with very little deviation, completely similar; the superior autho-

of which, also styled *rajahs*, have no appearance of being de-
pendant upon any superior power; but enter into associations
with each other, particularly with those belonging to the same
tribe, for mutual defence and security against any distant
enemy. They are at the same time extremely jealous of any
increase of their relative power; and on the slightest pretext,
a war breaks out between them. The force of different kampongs is notwithstanding this very unequal, and some rajahs
possess a much more extensive sway than others; and it must
needs be so, when every man who can get a dozen followers,
and two or three muskets, sets up for independence. Inland
of a place called *Sokum*, great respect was paid to a female
chief, or *uti*, (which word I conceive to be a liquid pronunciation of *putri*, a princess,) whose jurisdiction comprehended
many tribes. Her grandson, who was the reigning prince,
had lately been murdered by an invader; and she had assembled an army of two or three thousand men to take revenge.
An agent of the Company went up the river about fifteen miles,
in hopes of being able to accommodate a matter that threatened materially the peace of the country; but he was told by
the uti, that unless he would land his men, and take a decided
part in her favour, he had no business there; and he was
obliged to reimbark, without effecting any thing. The aggres-
sor followed him the same night, and made his escape. It does
not appear likely, from the manners and dispositions of the
people, that the whole of the country was ever united under
one supreme head. The more powerful rajahs assume authority over the lives of their subjects. The dependants are
bound to attend their chief in his journies, and in his wars;
and when an individual refuses, he is expelled from the society, without permission to take his property along with him."
—*Marsden's Sumatra*, p. 374.

rities claiming a certain allegiance from the numerous petty rulers, while the latter are in every respect independent of each other, and possess an absolute controul over the lives and properties of their subjects. In the Batta country, as in New Zealand, female succession is recognized; and here is also a class similar to the rungateedas, diverging from the rajahs, or chiefs, in the junior branches of their families. The government, therefore, of the Batta people, considered in all its parts, approaches nearer than even that of the Malays to the system of polity existing in New Zealand. In the *kampongs*, or fortified villages of these people, we see almost an exact description of the New Zealand hippahs. Constructed like the latter upon elevated ground, they are fortified with large ramparts of earth planted with brush-wood; and outside these ramparts, or mounds, is a ditch, on each side of which rises a high palisade of camphor timber. The whole is encompassed with a hedge of prickly bam-boo, which, when it arrives at a certain growth, is so very thick as entirely to con-ceal the town from the view of the spectator. The natives of Batta, influenced by a similar propensity for war and rapine, live as the New

Zealanders do, in a state of perpetual hostility among each other. There appears also a correlative affinity between these two nations, with respect to their systems of mythology; the Battas acknowledge three deities as rulers of the world, whose names are Batara-Guru, Sora-Pada, and Mangalla-Bulang. The first of these may be classed with the chief deity of the New Zealanders, Mowhœeranga-ranga; and of the other two they entertain precisely the same ideas as these latter people do of their gods Towackhee and Mow-heemooha—the one having rule over the air between land and sky, and the other over the earth. The Batta people have likewise, in common with the New Zealanders, a great many inferior deities, whom they have invested with local authority; and they entertain some vague notions of the immortality of the soul.

But, in addition to these characteristic assimilations, I have to observe, that the Battas, as well as the people of New Zealand, devour the dead bodies * of their ene-

* Mr. Marsden, in adverting to this horrible practice as it prevails in Sumatra, observes exactly as I have done with respect to the New Zealanders: "They do not eat human flesh as the means of satisfying the cravings of nature; for

mies—a practice which, though it renders them abhorrent from civilized man, yet connects the two nations in a unity of revolting

there can be no want of sustenance to the inhabitants of such a country and climate, who reject no animal food of any kind, nor is it sought after as a gluttonous delicacy. The Battas eat it as a species of ceremony, as a mode of shewing their detestation of certain crimes, and as a savage display of revenge and insult to their unfortunate enemies." He quotes the following instance of cannibalism in that country, from the information obtained by Mr. Holloway from Mr. W. H. Hayes, an officer in the East India Company's service.

"In the month of July, 1805, an expedition, consisting of Sepoys, Malays, and Battas, was sent from Tanapuli against a chief named Punei Manungum, residing at Negatimbul. about thirty miles inland from old Tanapuli, in consequence of his having attacked a kampong under the protection of the Company, murdered several of the inhabitants, and carried others into captivity. After a siege of three days, terms of accommodation being proposed, a cessation of hostilities took place, when the people of each party, having laid aside their arms, intermixed with the utmost confidence, and conversed together as if in a state of perfect amity. The terms, however, not proving satisfactory, each again retired to his arms, and renewed the contest with their former inveteracy. On the second day the place was evacuated; and upon our people entering it, Mr. Hayes found the bodies of one man and two women, whom the enemy had put to death before their departure, (being the last remaining of sixteen prisoners, whom they had originally carried off,) and from whose legs large pieces had been cut out, evidently for the purpose of being eaten. During the progress of this expedition, a small party had been sent to hold in check the chiefs of *Labusukum* and *Singapollum*, (inland of *Sibogah*,) who were confederates of

barbarism.   The same principle, too, of inhuman revenge is the actuating cause in both ;
but the cannibals of the Batta country offer,

Punei Manungum.   These, however, proved stronger than
was expected ; and making a sally from their kampongs,
attacked the sergeant's party, and killed a sepoy, whom he
was obliged to abandon.   Mr. Hayes, on his way from Negatimbul, was ordered to march to the support of the retreating
party ; but these having taken a different route, he remained
ignorant of the particulars of their loss.   The village of *Singa-*
pollum being immediately carried by storm, and the enemy
retreating by one gate, as our people entered at the opposite,
the accoutrements of the sepoy who had been killed the day
before, were seen hanging as trophies in the front of the
houses ; and in the town-hall, Mr. Hayes saw the head entirely scalped, and one of the fingers fixed upon a fork or
skewer, still warm from the fire.   On proceeding to the village
of *Labusukum,* situated little more than two hundred yards
from the former, he found a large plantain-leaf, full of human
flesh, mixed with lime-juice and Chili pepper ; from which he
inferred that they had been surprised in the very act of feast-
ing on the sepoy, whose body had been divided between the
two *kampongs.*   Upon differences being settled with the
chiefs, they acknowledged, with perfect *sang-froid,* that such
had been the case, saying, at the same time, ' You know it is
our custom ; why should we conceal it?' "—*Marsden's History*
of Sumatra, p. 463.

" In the *sapiyau,* or building in which the *rajah* receives
strangers, we saw a man's skull hanging up, which he told us
was hung there as a trophy, it being the skull of an enemy
they had taken prisoner, whose body (according to the custom
of the *Battas*) they had eaten about two months before."—
Extract from Mr. Charles Millar's Journal of a Journey into
the Batta Country. Marsden, p. 370.

by a more horrible enormity, still greater violence to our feelings than those of New
Zealand; for they not only gorge themselves
with the flesh of the enemies they have slain
in battle, but also tear asunder the dead
bodies of their criminals, with which, in separate parties, they glut their appetites. In
their domestic institutions, these people
equally approximate to the New Zealanders;
the men, who are allowed as many wives as
they can support, lead comparatively an idle
life, while the women are obliged to do all the
drudgery, and are treated as complete bond-
slaves. The females are held exactly in the
same degraded state in New Zealand, where,
though a man takes a number of wives, none
of them but the head wife is allowed the
least privilege, as I have already shewn.—
Adultery is punished among the Batta people with exile; and in aggravated cases, with
death. The mode of wearing the dress in
this country is the same as prevails in New
Zealand; it is made of cotton cloth, manufactured by themselves, and tied round the
waist, while another garment of the same
material hangs down the body suspended
from the shoulder. These garments are dyed
with mixed colours. The New Zealanders

generally dye their inferior mats with red ochre; and work borders round the better kinds, in which they contrive to blend three or four colours with much taste and ingenuity. The Battas are certainly more advanced in knowledge than the New Zealanders; they have a written language, and many of them are found who can both read and write; they have likewise subjected to their use the services of the horse and the buffalo; and they have some defined ideas of trade and commerce: but with these advantages, which they owe entirely to place and circumstance, they are still hardly raised above the condition of wild savages. In drawing this scale of comparison between two nations so little known, I do not mean to assert that the New Zealanders are descended from the Batta people, but that they are coeval with them, and have sprung from the same continental origin to which, according to the preceding inquiry, the population of their respective countries must be referred. How far this inquiry is conducted upon just grounds, I shall leave it to the public to determine, while I cheerfully submit to the candour of their decision.

CHAP. X.

Reflections on the population of New Zealand—Causes that
tend to diminish it or prevent its increase—General remarks on the character of the natives—Further particulars as to the expediency of colonizing the island—Conclusion.

In taking a first view of civilized society, as
its various artificial wants are contrasted
with the simple requisites of savage life, we
should be led to suppose that the human
species is much more likely to be multiplied
in the latter than in the former state, where
obstacles, proceeding from so many accidental causes, act as a check to the extension of
mankind.   Among cultivated nations, the
numbers who neither enter into the marriage
state, nor give themselves up to illegitimate
connections, are very considerable; pruden-
tial motives, untoward circumstances, ascetic
devotion, together with numerous other reasons, conspire to make a vast body in every
civilized country resolve upon a life of perpetual celibacy; while dissolute habits, with
their attendant distempers, render too many
others, of both sexes, incapable of adding to

the population. It should therefore be thought, that in uncivilized countries, where nature never meets with any of these obstructions, and where a sufficiency of food (the only requisite) might be raised for the inhabitants, with comparatively little labour, the advance of propagation must be very great; yet this is by no means the case, and New Zealand affords a striking instance of it. From the many natural advantages which this country possesses, it might be supposed that it would contain a crowded population; but it happens quite otherwise; and so far as we could judge from observation and inquiry, we found the scanty number of natives entirely disproportioned to the vast extent of territory they inhabited. In the Bay of Islands, to which our means for information on this subject were chiefly confined, we beheld the population composed of small communities, living apart from each other, and when taken collectively, their aggregate number was but trifling. The people of Kangehoo did not amount to more than three hundred souls, and this was the largest community of the entire; while in the principal town belonging to the areekee Kangeroa, which stood about twenty miles in the interior, we could find, when we visited it, only fifty or sixty inhabitants; and four hundred was the greatest number the place could possibly contain, though it was the grand capital and seat of the supreme chief of this quarter. With the exception of two or three places, the villages in the neighbourhood of this bay that were best peopled, contained but from fifty to one hundred inhabitants, and the greater part of them had only from twenty to thirty. The rival forces which were mustered together under the chiefs Henou and Wiveeah, and which formed the largest assemblage of warriors I had seen in the country, did not amount collectively to more than four hundred, though comprising all the male population of the surrounding districts. Our final departure from Range-hoo, which attracted the natives from the banks of the Cowa-cowa, the Wycaddie, and other remote parts of the interior, collected at most (exclusively of the subjects of Duaterra) only five hundred people, who came to take their leave of us; so that the country in general appeared to us to be very imperfectly supplied with inhabitants.

But though we may form an accurate opinion as to the amount of population, whether great or small, which New Zealand contains, still as our knowledge of the country is confined almost exclusively to the sea-coast, any numerical statement of this amount cannot be given with precision. Doctor Forster, who has computed the population of the different islands in the South Sea, has fixed that of New Zealand through the whole extent at one hundred thousand souls; but though I conceive this estimate to be fully equal to the number of the inhabitants, yet I will suppose them at present one hundred and fifty thousand. Taking, therefore, the latter amount as the ratio of calculation, we shall find that Eaheinomauwe, or the Northern Island, which contains 16,742,400 square acres, will have remaining, for the support of each individual, a space of between seventy and eighty acres, after one-third is deducted for rivers, marshes, and those high lands which cannot be brought into cultivation; and if, in the time of the Romans, one acre was found sufficient for the maintenance of one person, Eahēinomauwe will be found capable, when acted upon by the industry of man, of furnishing food for upwards of seventy times its present population. The Southern Island is of still larger extent; and consequently, upon the same principle, must afford a greater number of acres for each inhabitant. Thus it will be seen how immense is the disproportion between the population of this country and the space it includes; and the causes of it are to be traced to the barbarous and unorganized state of society among the natives. Nature has been liberal to them in every respect, but they have not learned to avail themselves of her bounty; and their institutions, like those of every savage people, are all of them hostile to her purposes. The principal causes which retard the increase of population in New Zealand are the following:—the degraded state in which the women are held; the universal practice of polygamy among the higher classes; preposterous superstitions; the frequency of suicides; and the people not being united under one head, but divided into small independent tribes under their respective chiefs, whose jealousy of each other involves them in perpetual hostility. The limits of this work will allow me only to advert cursorily to each of these causes; yet even were I not thus circumscribed, I might, perhaps, be readily excused for not entering into an elaborate disquisition on the subject.

In proportion as nations advance or retrograde in civilization, so we find the female sex treated with a greater or less degree of gentleness and attention. Countries distinguished for their refinement* are also conspicuous for admitting women to their proper rank in society; and it is only in states where rudeness and barbarism are found to exist, that those beings, who were designed by nature to be the solace of man in his progress through life, are made wretched slaves to his presumptuous tyranny. Thus it happens in New Zealand, where woman is born only to labour incessantly for her task-master; and though, while health remains, she exerts the whole of it in his service, yet the period soon arrives, when hardships and privations exhaust her frame, and she becomes incapable of further drudgery. The term of procreation is also short from the same cause; and most of the women of this country cease at

* "That women are indebted to the refinements of polished manners for a happy change in their state, is a point which can admit of no doubt. To despise and to degrade the female sex, is the characteristic of the savage state in every part of the globe. Man, proud of excelling in strength and in courage, the chief marks of pre-eminence among rude people, treats woman, as an inferior, with disdain."—*Robertson's History of America*, vol. ii. p. 103.

an early age to bring forth children. But let it not be supposed from these remarks, that the New Zealanders treat their women with wanton cruelty, while they oblige them to perpetual toil; it is far otherwise, and they conceive they are only claiming the right they are entitled to as superior beings, in making them, as an inferior species, work instead of themselves. In fact, considering the respective attributes of each people, they do not at all differ in this particular from the Swedish peasantry, who oblige their women to do all the agricultural labours, as well as various others of a masculine description. Most savage tribes, I rather think, are unconscious of any severity towards their women in thus consigning them to toilsome servitude; and it is fortunate for the latter, that they never consider it an injustice or degradation.

With respect to polygamy in New Zealand, as it operates against the progress of population, it must be observed, that the higher orders form an interested conjunction with several women, none of whom, except her who is emphatically termed the head wife, can be said to experience any of the enjoyments of matrimony; living with their nominal husbands in the degraded state I have described, and as handmaids to the favoured spouse. Though obliged, when once married, to submit for life to conjugal restraints, (death, under certain circumstances, being the sure consequence of any dereliction,) still, as they are generally neglected for the head wife, the intercourse between them and the men who claim their fidelity is unfrequent, which of course must be unfavourable to the propagation of the human species. The gross superstitions of these people have a powerful tendency to abridge the natural period of their existence. No sooner does a person arrive at a certain stage of illness among them, than they place the unhappy creature under the wrath of the Etua; and, incapable of accounting for the disease with which he is afflicted, as of applying a remedy to it, they can only consider it as a preternatural visitation of retributive justice, which it would be impious to resist by any human expedient. Many a poor sufferer who, with a little ordinary attention, might be soon restored to health and vigour, is devoted by this horrid superstition to perish in the very midst of his kindred, without a single effort being made for his recovery. But his death is not the only loss which the community sustains at the time it happens; his wife, though she durst not administer that simple aid which might have rescued him from a premature grave, is obliged to immolate herself at his dissolution, as an indispensable test of her faithful attachment. With the above causes, on which 1 have severally commented, I must now notice the feudal chieftainships, as tending to keep this country always low in point of numbers. Were the inhabitants of New Zealand all subject to one ruler, or did they form one undivided republic, they would not be liable to those jealousies and barbarous dissensions to which their present incongruous system of polity gives rise; and those lives which are now so often lost to avenge the quarrels of the petty chiefs, would then be preserved, and rendered valuable to society. In all barbarous nations the impulse to hostility is easily provoked; and in one where the whole population is divided into independent tribes, occasions of disagreement will too frequently occur. Hence in New Zealand there are always furious struggles for separate interests, which have a considerable effect in diminishing the number of its inhabitants, though certainly not in the degree that might be supposed, from the character and temper of the hostile parties. Violent and ungovernable as they generally are, when recourse is had to arms, yet, as has been shewn in the Narrative, they are sometimes willing to come to a peaceable accommodation; and it may be ascribed to these occasional adjustments, that much greater havoc is not made upon the population. The preceding appear to me to be the chief causes why a country of such extent and such advantages as New Zealand is so thinly peopled; and having thus briefly examined each of them, I shall now offer a few general remarks on the character of the natives, while I afterwards recur, as I promised, to the subject of establishing an European colony among them, which must conclude these additional observations.

The motives by which man in the savage state is liable to be actuated, are so very undefined that it is impossible to give an exact account of his character, wanting, as it does, that consistent stability and regular tenor, which are necessary for a minute delineation. It will be proper, therefore, without making any categorical statements as to particulars, which in most cases are variable, to consider his general conduct as it is influenced by those decided principles of action which he inherits from nature, in common with the civilized part of his species. Estimating the people of New Zealand by this rule, we find them superior to most savage tribes in some of the qualities they possess, yet are they rendered abhorrent, at the same time, by atrocious enormities, which, however, it would be unjust to attribute to innate cruelty. Divided as a nation by the form of their government, they are split into rival associations, who are taught from their infancy to cherish a spirit of ferocious hostility against each other; and implacable vengeance becomes a necessary duty, to which they are reconciled by habit, while they indulge it without remorse. But in his social and domestic relations, where the full force of the human heart is allowed to prevail, no man can be more amiable than the New Zealander. Seated in the midst of his family or friends, he appears gentle, conciliating and affectionate; and, far from exercising a severe controul over his dependants, he behaves towards them upon all occasions with affability and mildness, abject and insignificant as they are held in his estimation. In this respect the New Zealand chiefs are particularly distinguished from the higher classes in the Tonga Islands, who treat the multitude, in many instances, with wanton cruelty, as we have seen in the case of Finow, the king of those islands, who ordered the cookee or plebeian to be shot, without the least provocation that could justify such an act. Neither the areekees, nor the subordinate chiefs of New Zealand, are ever known to imbrue their hands in this unwarrantable manner in the blood of their followers; and whenever the latter transgress, they usually punish them with a spirit of lenity and moderation, consigning them to death only for crimes which they consider heinous. The tenderest parental affection (an impulse wisely ordained by nature) is remarkable among all classes, high and low, in this country. The chiefs carry their children upon their backs, taking them from their mothers at an early age, that they may not be an incumbrance to them in their laborious employments. It must be allowed, however, that the men make excellent nurses, and have a peculiar art in the management of their infant offspring. I have never seen any father fonder of his child than the chief Wiveeah appeared to be of a fine boy, whom he brought with him on his back, in one of his visits to us; he evinced the gentlest attention to the little creature, while it clung with its arms round his neck, and seemed to rest perfectly happy in his indulgent care. In their respective tribes, these people are not provoked to anger without some very serious cause, their natural disposition being tranquil and equable; but when they form separate coalitions, the most trivial circumstance will act as an incitement to ungovernable violence. Native courage, that peculiar characteristic of all savage nations, they possess in an eminent degree; but it is never tempered with mercy, nor softened down by compassion. In battle they rarely give or expect quarter, and when the conflict is over, their revenge is not sated till they shew themselves more than ordinary barbarians, by devouring their victims—the last outrage they can offer to humanity.

Superstition is natural to man, and it exists under distinct forms in different countries. Civilized nations are not exempt from its influence, nor is it to be expected that they will be, as long as some men are born with weaker minds than others. Its growth, however, has been considerably checked, if not destroyed, in all countries where science has made progress; and I am persuaded, there cannot now be found in Scotland half the number of seers, that might be met with in that superstitious quarter of Great Britain a century ago. In New Zealand, as in other countries where the people are utter strangers to the first principles of knowledge, the grossest delusions prevail, and the word *taboo* very frequently decides the actions of a whole race. To follow this word through its several diversified meanings, would be to detail minutely every circumstance that regards the political and moral economy of these people; a task I am by no means prepared for: it not only regulates their institutions, but likewise their daily labours, and there is scarcely a single act they perform, with which this momentous dissyllable does not interfere. Yet though it subjects them, as the reader must have seen, to many absurd and painful restrictions, it is nevertheless found particularly useful in a nation so irregularly constituted. It serves them in the absence of laws, as the only security for the protection of persons and property, giving them an awful sacredness which no one dares to violate; and by its powerful influence, restraining even the most cruel

and rapacious plunderers.   It were fortunate
for the natives, if they were all under the
sanction of this mystical guarantee; but
this is not the case, the protection it affords
being confined only to certain orders, with
whom it is revocable at pleasure, though in
their various concerns, the taboo, as I have
stated, affects the general body of the population.   This superstition serves in a great
measure to consolidate the limited power of
the areekees over the inferior chiefs; for instance, if one of the former class thinks
proper to taboo any ship coming into the
harbour, none of the latter must dare
think of holding the least communication
with her, or of supplying her with provisions, while the interdict continues.   The
same holds good with respect to whatever
else the areekee chooses to exclude from
common intercourse, and the prohibition
being generally understood, is never upon
any account contravened.   When they go to
war, I rather think that the taboo is either
suspended for a time, or that it permits their
hostilities; but as the tohungha or priest is
the arbiter of all their delusions, he takes
care, I have no doubt, to suit them to the
genius of his votaries, if not to their con-

venience. The New Zealanders make no idols, nor have they any external form of worship; their conceptions of a supreme power being shewn only in the veneration they have for the above-mentioned superstition, and in the single word *taboo* all their religion and morality may be said to consist.

In his daily occupations, the New Zealander seldom applies himself to his work for any length of time together; for not setting any adequate value on time, it is quite a matter of indifference to him at what period his task is finished, provided it be ultimately completed. Desultory in his general mode of living, he has no fixed hours by which to regulate his proceedings; and following nature in every thing but the moderation she enjoins, he eats to excess when he is hungry, goes to sleep when he finds drowsiness and lassitude steal upon him, and joins in the dance or song when prompted by the effervescent flow of the animal spirits. Those chieftains who are more advanced in years, usually spend the day in conversation, being seated on the ground under the open air, while they have collected round them a social circle, who are admitted to the freedom of converse, and avail themselves of the indulgence with incessant loquacity, the cookees bringing refreshments at stated intervals, of fern-root and potatoes. The women, though doomed to a state of degraded and toilsome servitude, are under no restraint in the presence of the chiefs; and mingling in their festivities during the hours of relaxation, they seem for the time to forget their inferiority, nor upon these occasions does any thing happen to remind them of it. With the manners, habits and customs of these people, the reader has been occasionally made acquainted in the detached accounts given in the preceding Narrative; and confining the present remarks to their general character, I shall conclude them by observing summarily, that in his peaceful pursuits, the New Zealander appears social, cheerful, friendly and hospitable, disposed to kind offices, and faithful to his engagements; but war effects a total transformation in the man, and it is then only that he becomes a cruel, furious and untameable savage.

CONCLUSION.

REVERTING now to the subject of forming an European Colony in the fine and fertile country of New Zealand, I shall proceed to submit those additional remarks with respect to it, which the restricted order of the Narrative precluded me from offering in the first instance. The motives which can induce a civilized community to emigrate to a remote and barbarous land, I am well aware, must be particularly forcible; they must originate either in immediate necessity at home, or in the peculiar facilities which the foreign region offers, of procuring an easy independence in a shorter time and with less trouble than it could be realized in the mother country. Man is not yet so complete a cosmopolite as to forego his connections, and the land of his nativity, without sensations of regret; and however indigent may be his circumstances, and however cheerless the country that gave him birth, he rarely departs as an emigrant but with a sort of melancholy dejection, nor can he always abstract his heart even from the associations of his poverty. It cannot therefore be supposed, that a colony of Englishmen (for such I would wish them to be) would proceed to New Zealand without the strongest inducements; yet from what has been already made known of that country through the medium of the Church Missionary Society, a considerable number of persons * in England are become desirous of going out there as settlers. Without hazarding any opinions inconsiderately, I have no doubt but an English Colony in New Zealand might soon become flourishing and happy: the space being so ample for their industry, the soil so fertile, the climate so salubrious, they would have every natural advantage in their favour; and I shall now state some particulars in detail, which certainly hold out a rational encouragement.

The whole of the northern part of New Zealand, and much of the southern likewise, are admirably adapted for the growth of every kind of grain, as also of various other

---

* I am authorized by the Reverend Mr. Pratt, Secretary to the Church Missionary Society, to state, that there are at this moment a vast body of persons in one town in England, who are anxious to proceed with their families to New Zealand.

productions; and the vine, the olive, the orange, the citron, with all the choicest fruits of the countries in the South of Europe, might be produced here in the greatest abundance by proper cultivation. In fact, there is scarcely any production that can stimulate man to exertion by rewarding his industry, which this country, with moderate labour, could not furnish, if we except those plants which require the heat of a tropical sun to bring them to perfection. The immense surplus of the native productions of the country, above what would be required for the use of the colonists, would be extremely valuable in a commercial point of view. The timber of its extensive forests finds at this time a quick sale in the market of Port Jackson, where it is cut up into scantling, and preferred to the timber of that place, which from its hardness is difficult to be worked, and from the quantity of its gum-veins occasions a considerable waste. When a free communication is opened with the Spanish Colonies on the south-west coast of America, which from the present posture of affairs in that part of the world, may be reasonably anticipated as an event very likely soon to take place, a fine field for speculation would present itself to the colonists of New Zealand, from which country timber has been already carried thither; and I believe with considerable advantage to those commanders of vessels who have taken it. Wood being scarce in these colonies, is always sure to bear a high price; and the settler at New Zealand receiving his payment in specie, would be enabled to purchàse those European commodities which are necessary for the comforts of life, as well as for its more refined enjoyments. For the smaller timber which abounds here, a ready market is open at Calcutta, where the heavy native wood is not adapted for the yards and topmasts of vessels; and when I left Port Jackson, Mr. Marsden had it in contemplation to have always a supply of spars for the ships that came from India. Though the timber in the part of the country that we visited is not fit for the purposes of ship-building, which requires wood of considerable firmness and solidity to resist the destructive action of the worm and the violence of the elements, yet on the Southern Island the timber is much stronger and of a closer grain. A vessel of 150 tons burthen is said to have been constructed some years back in Dusky Bay, but 1 have not been able to learn how far it answered the expectation of the builder. However, from what Captain Cook states respecting the timber in this quarter, I am disposed to believe that ships both durable and substantial might be built from it.

The fisheries of this country would be an invaluable source of wealth in themselves; and the vast quantities of fish which they would supply for exportation might be sure, I should think, of finding a market in the Spanish and Portuguese colonies. The two species of the whale so very valuable, the one for its sperm or head-matter, the other for its oil, are frequently met with in these seas, so much so, that New Zealand has been for many years accounted one of the best stations for procuring those prodigious animals. Should the Government at home not deem it expedient to allow the colonists to avail themselves of this lucrative traffic, but confine it exclusively to the vessels fitted out from England; still it would be of advantage to the settlement, as these vessels would put in upon their coast for provisions, in preference to Port Jackson, where, from the heavy charges of the port duties, and the almost general want of principle among the trading part of the inhabitants, the expenses to which commanders of ships are necessarily liable, become a serious drawback upon the profits of the voyage. The ursine-seal or sea-bear, and the sea-lion, are found in congregated herds to the southward; and on *Campbell* and *Macquarie Islands*,* which are situated at no great distance from the southern part of New Zealand, the valuable furs of these animals are found in great plenty, and are now made by the colonists of New South Wales a most profitable article of commerce either in England or in China, to which latter country they are frequently exported. The settlers at New Zealand, from the contiguity of their situation, could possess themselves of a great share of this trade, and con-

---

* *Macquarie Island* was discovered in 1811. It lies nearly in a straight direction from north to south, being eighteen miles in length and six in breadth. Lat. 54° 45′ S. Long. 159° 42′ E. At the distance of eight leagues from the north point of this island, in a north-east direction, are some smaller islands called the *Judge and his Clerk;* and from the south of *Macquarie Island*, and at the distance of nine leagues, are some others denominated the *Bishop and his Clerk*. Campbell Island lies in Lat. 52° 41′ S. Long. 169° E. When Macquarie Island was first discovered, the persons left on it to shoot seals, killed not less than eighty thousand of them.

sequently participate in the profits which are already derived from it.

That singular species of the flax-plant, which I have already described as peculiar to this country, is, from the strength and firmness of its fibre, the great abundance that each plant produces, the little trouble required in preparing it, and the facility with which it may be cultivated, another very considerable resource of which the colonist might avail himself. From this plant, which I do not hesitate to pronounce the most valuable of its kind of any ever yet known, he would not only be enabled to supply himself with an excellent material for the fabrication of linen, canvas and cordage for every purpose, but would, when a regular intercourse was established with the mother country, find it a most advantageous article of export, as the sale of it in England would be always certain and profitable. When in the course of time the settlers would be enabled from the augmented strength of their numbers, to search for new sources of wealth in the bowels of the earth; it is very probable that the long chain of hills which I have before adverted to as likely to contain metallic ores, may yield treasures far beyond what the

most sanguine hopes of the miner could
venture to anticipate. But without at all
considering these treasures, which are only
contingent, New Zealand possesses so many
obvious resources which are defined and
certain, as would render it one of the fittest
places in the world for an industrious and
enterprising colony.

It may be urged perhaps as an objection
against forming any considerable settlement
in this country, that the natives being a brave
and warlike race, would look with jealousy
on the colonists, as threatening at some
future period to destroy their liberty and
independence, and would therefore take
every opportunity to harass them in the progress of their acquisitions, by continued acts
of hostility and depredation. But from
what I have seen of the disposition of the
New Zealanders, I do not believe that there
would be any cause for apprehension in this
respect. The security of the colony would
entirely depend upon the settlers themselves :
for by conducting themselves towards these
people in a kind and conciliatory manner,
they might easily secure their attachment
and prevent their suspicions: but if by
adopting a contrary demeanour, they should

have the imprudence to provoke their resentment, the very worst consequences might be
expected to ensue. As landed property is
accurately defined in New Zealand, there
being among the chiefs a mutual recognition
of their respective territories, and an understanding that no encroachment is to be
made on any without the general consent,
it would be necessary to enter into a regular
agreement with one of the areekees for a
certain portion of land ; which in the absence
of a legal obligation, should be secured to
the colonists by the superstition of the *taboo*,
and the limits properly ascertained. In this
purchase there would be no difficulty, as
they might get a very extensive tract of
ground ceded to them for a small number of
axes and implements of agriculture, their
natural wants rendering these articles much
more precious in the estimation of the New
Zealanders, than specie is with us as a cir-
culating medium. Their next measure should
be to gain the confidence and friendship of
the areekee from whom the purchase was
made, and also to enter into alliances with
the chiefs in the vicinity of the settlement,
who would feel a degree of pride in being
admitted to a close intercourse with Euro-

peans, and would readily co-operate with them in repelling any remote tribes, who might come for the purpose of rapacious aggression.   These chieftains might readily be prevailed upon to assist them with their people in the cultivation of their lands; and for this purpose, houses should be built for them, rations regularly served out to them, and they should be treated in every respect upon an equality with the white inhabitants; care being taken at the same time that the labour required from them should not be exacted with severity, as their present desultory mode of living could not be expected to be changed at once into a constant and regular habit of application.

The limits of this work will not permit me to go into a more enlarged detail, on a subject which I would again hope may attract the attention of the Government, at a time when so many valuable members of society are pining all over the nation in extreme indigence.   By the colonizing of New Zealand, the cause of humanity would be served in a two-fold manner; provision would be made for a distressed class of enlightened mortals, and the civilization of a fine race, who are now sunk in utter ignorance, would by such an event be rapidly accelerated.

----◆----

ON THE LANGUAGE OF NEW ZEALAND.

THE reader will perceive from what I have said when discussing the origin of the New Zealanders, that the several nations in the Pacific Ocean, which I have classed with them as belonging to the same source, speak only different dialects of the same language. That of New Zealand is soft and harmonious to the ear, from the alternation which it employs of the vowels and consonants, and there are rarely perceptible in it any harsh or discordant sounds. The subjoined Vocabulary was compiled by Mr. Kendall, previously to my departure from New South Wales, at which place it has been printed by order of Mr. Marsden, who sent several books of it to New Zealand for the instruction of the children there. The compiler derived considerable assistance from a copious collection of words in the Otaheitan language, with which he was furnished by one of the Missionaries, who had resided for some years at Eimeo. This collection formed a vocabulary consisting of nearly two thousand words, the greater number of which had so close an affinity to those of New Zealand, that Mr. Kendall found it necessary to make but little alteration in the most of them, and in some none at all. The genius and construction of the two dialects appear to be perfectly the same, and the like identity is observable in the extensive vocabulary of Tonga words collected by Mr. Mariner, and compiled under the judicious care of the gentleman who edited his work. But the similarity of sound between the words of these dialects would be still more apparent, had the several vocabularies been collected by one individual; the perceptions of different persons are not alike, and hence variations may arise where none originally were found to exist. I observed when at New Zealand, that the Missionaries would not only differ from each other in the spelling of the same words, but likewise in the pronunciation of them; a circumstance which must always happen when a new language is to be learned with no other standard of instruction than the ear. In the words which I have inserted from the Tonga dialect, there are some which, corresponding in import with those of New Zealand, have exactly the same spelling, and others which vary in the spelling, but shew a radical analogy in the sound. From the dialect spoken in New Zealand, I should not think the language of the South Sea Islands a copious one, nor does it seem either forcible or energetic.

As Mr. Kendall is at present applying himself strictly to the study of the New Zealand language, it is probable he will furnish us in some time with a copious and enlarged account of it, and add considerably to the following collection of words, for which we are indebted to his industry.

A VOCABULARY

OF

ENGLISH AND NEW ZEALAND WORDS,

THE LATTER BEING COMPARED WITH SOME OF THOSE IN THE TONGA LANGUAGE.

English.	New Zealand.	Tonga.
The conjunction *and*	A	
An interjection of surprise	Aa!	
You	Acquoi	Aco'y
A leaf	Arou racou	Lo acow
A needle	Ahou	Hooi
A line	Ahho	
Fire	Ahe	A'fi
When	Ahaa	Afé
What	Aaha	Coihá
Where	Ahéa	
Liver	Atta	A'te
Gall	Apóua	
The Supreme Being	Attúa nue, or Etua	Hotoóa
A bolt	A-deuo	
Health	A-oura	
Night	Apo	Bo-oo'li; Abó (to-night)

English.	New Zealand.	Tonga.
Small	A-itte	
Great	A-nue	
Ill	A-mattee	Mahagi
Short	A-poto	
Long	Aroa	Lolo'a
Large	Aráhe	Láhi
Paddle	Ahoy	Fo'he
Walk	A-ire	E'va
To run	A-horo	
To dig	A-tea	
To flow	A-párre	
To ebb	A-teeneo	
To draw the fishing-line	A-he	
To fling a stone	A-hapa	
To-morrow	Appopo	
The day after to-morrow	Attootida	
The fourth day	Awhákkee	
The fifth day	Awhákkee nuee	
To make	Ahángha	
Right	Amátto	Toto'noo
Winking with one eye	Akamo	
A working tool	Akoko	
The act of carrying a person on the shoulder	Amo	
To carry on the shoulder	Amoéa	
Left	Amóue	
The rainbow	Anúanúa	
Close, narrow	Ape, ape	
A sail	Arara	La
Blunt	Aquorree quoe	
An orphan	Apánne	

English.	New Zealand.	Tonga.
Affection, love	Aróha	O'fa
Fern-root	Aróhhe	
Fever	Attooto	
I (personal pronoun)	Aou	Au
A current	Aou	
To roll as a ship	Ahoodoo	
To tattoo the skin	Amoko	
The tongue	Araro	Ele'lo
To kick	Awánno	
A superior chief	Areekee	Egi
Morning	Attanta	
Evening	Attaiä	
Sweet potatoe	Coomera	Gooma'la
Phoca, or seal	Cakenno	
A worm	Cootoo-cootoo	Géle-moo'too
A rush	Coopoo bung- hahoü	
The nose	Eshoa	I'hoo
At, for, in	Epeep	
Yesterday	Enanáhee	Aniáfi
To sit down	Enho	
East wind	Etoughi	
Oil	Enu	Lolo
A bone	Evee	
Within	E-roto	Gi-lóto
Without	E-wáhho	
Fine day	E-rapi	
Hand	Díngha díngha	Low-ni'ma
A handful	Díngha ta hi	
To pour out	Díngha héa	
A boil	Fafa	Váca-fáwha

English.	New Zealand.	Tonga.
Handkerchief	Hey	
A spirit	Hie	
The paps	Hoo	Hoo'hoo
A cave	Hana	A'na
A road	Hara	Ha'lla
The first woman	Heena	
To nurse	Heeke téa	
Fish	Heeka	I'ca
To row or paddle	Hóyea	Towa'lo
To give	Homi	My
Shore	Hoota	Oo'ta
The stomach	Hooma	
Rain	Hooa	Oo'ha
Concealment	Hoona	
An old woman	Hadoodoohee	
Crooked	Haháppa	
To gape	Hamama	
To run	Hahouma	
A skull	Hánghángha	
To thunder	Haroorooke	
To sigh	Hatarane	
A comb	Headoo	He'loo
Strong	Hékkaha	
Skin	Hehékko	
To banter	Hengorékka	
Diving	Herookoo	Hoo'goo
To jump	Herérre	
Come hither	Haromai	
Hot	Hiráttoo	
To sail	Hoyáttoo	
Deep	Hohonoo	Lo'lo'to

English.	New Zealand.	Tonga.
To skin	Heoheoro	
Head	Hoopoka	
Pillow	Hoolúngha	Aloo'nga
Helm	Hoolúnghee	
Sand	Hunuippoo	
To turn over	Hurehéa	
To pull off	Hunnowhéa	
Hair, feathers	Hooroohooroo	Low-oo'lo
Thigh	Hoowha	
Spittle	Howheinee	A'noo
To stand up	Hetoo	
A battle-axe	Hohiecker	
Halbert	Hennee	
To-day	Iheenee	Hea'ho'ni
To walk	Ire	
Go away	Ire attoo ra	
A human body	Ko-evee	
Language, or to speak	Ko-raro	
Rain over	Ka-mou	
Rainy	Ka-hooa	Oo'hai'a
Within	Ka-roto	Gilo'to
Without	Ka-wáhho	
The belly	Kopoo	
The neck	Kákkee	
Laughter	Kátha	Cáta
A rat	Keóuree	
A louse	Kootoo	Goo'too
The chin	Kówhi	
A file	Kánnee	
A hole	Kowôu	
The arms	Koomoo	

English.	New Zealand.	Tonga.
Flesh	Keko	Cano
Bad	Keno	
Belch	Koopa	
To swim	Kóukou, or cow-cow	Caccow
A basket	Kétta	Cato
Sharp	Kaquoe	
Breakfast time	Ki-átta	
Dinner time	Ki-awátta	
Arm-pits	Kaka	
Supper time	Ki-aíei	
Fire	Kapoola	
Victuals	Kiki	Meá-ky : *mea,* things, *ky,* to eat
Good	Ka-pi	
High	Ka-teheikaka	
Anger	Kadíddee	
Strong	Kaha	
Beneath	Kedárro	Gi la'lo
Rough	Koekoekee	
To snore	Knunghoro	
Suicide	Kohoodoo	
To smell	Kakkakárra	Na'moocaca'la
Wet	Kamakoo	Vicoo
Raiment	Kákkahow	
Seed	Kakánna	Too'nga
Enough	Ka-tedúra	
Forward	Kamooa	
Behind	Ka-moode	Gi-moo'i
Swift	Ka-térre	

English.	New Zealand.	Tonga.
A girl	Ko-teedo	
The eye	Kónnohe	
The little finger	Koloíite	
The thumb	Kolomadua	
Tired	Kanénghe	
No	Kioure	
To stink	Kapedo	Eho; elo
Broken	Ko-aquárre	
To gape	Kouhada	
To nip	Keneteá	
By and by	Keamow	
To stoop	Korropeko	
Finished	Kamootoo	
Plenty	Keamaha	
To fall	Katakka	
To squint	Kakawah	
To cry	Katanghe	Tángi
To fly	Koarérre	
Red	Kaphwéddoo	
A working tool	Kahadoo	
A pigeon	Kookoopa	
Straight	Katikka	
Through	Kapoota	
To put in the fist	Kamotéa	
Throat	Kurrokurro	
Spear	Kokíddee	
A four-legged animal	Koráddee	
To make	Kamáhe	Gna'hi
A rock	Kamakka	Foo-ma'cca
A cloud	Kappooha	
A stone	Kowáttoo	

English.	New Zealand.	Tonga.
Broken	Kowátte	Fétchi, (to break)
A penguin	Korolah	
A fishing-net	Koopéngha	Cobénga
A table	Kyhingha	
A residence	Kahingha	Nofoa'nga
Flax-plant	Koráddee	
Above	Kedúngha	Gi-aloónga
Cray-fish	Kahouda	
A pot	Koeshooa	
A foot-path	Kapékka	
Sweat	Kokówa	Caca'va
Sweet	Karékka	
All gone	Koapów	
Gone	Kadedo	
Rotten	Karakka	
To run away	Kahóuma	
To see	Kakítta, tickee tickee	
To make sharp	Keaquoe	
A bird like a woodcock	Koohákka	
Make haste	Kahahoro	
Old man	Kurroheika	
To shout	Karánghateá	
To sprinkle	Kowewea	
Potatoes	Korrapuna	
A ship	Kipookee	
The fundament	Koomoo	Hílo
Skin	Kudee	Gíli
The back of the neck	Kakee	
Barbed spear	Kecker	

English.	New Zealand.	Tonga.
A rib	Larra	
An owl	Looloo	Loo'loo
Clean	Ma	Ma
A sweet thing	Maarékka	
A round thing	Maaporotákka	
Spots or eruption of the skin	Maddehow	
Finger nails	Mattekóokoo	
Warm	Mahánna	Mafa'nna
Idle	Mángherre	
To jump ashore	Mahoota	
Grained	Mángha	
Calm	Marreeno	
Disturbance	Maneanea	
Breath	Mannówha	Mana'va
Moon-light, &c.	Marámma	Mahi'na
Cold	Makkadéde	
Blind	Máttapo	
North wind	Matanghi	
A knife	Maurippe	
Death	Mattéréoa	
A bait	Mahoonoo	
A sail	Mamáddoo	
To look earnestly	Mattatowha	
Afraid	Mattakkoo	
A dream	Moenárkoo	
A grandson	Mokopoona	
Fat	Momona	
White	Ma (or ka-ma)	
Sleep	Moe	Mo'he
Light, not heavy	Mama	Mámá

English.	New Zealand.	Tonga.
A bird	Manoo	Ma'noo
The mouth	Mánghi	Ma'änga, mouthful
A shark	Mángho	A'nga
Black	Mangho	
A cough	Marree	
Dry	Marokee	
Face	Matta	Mátta
A fish-hook	Mattow	Matou
To understand	Matou	
Illness	Mattee	Mahagi
A parent	Madua	
Thread	Míllo	Fi'lo
Salt water	Moana	
A bed	Moongha	
Flax	Moka	
An ulcer	Momói	Mama'hi
Blaze (of flame)	Moora	
The lips	Mootoo	Lo gnoo'too
Fighting with fists	Moto	
A low island	Motoo	
The first man	Mouee	
Father	Madua-tanee	Tammy
Mother	Madua-why-enee	
Urine	Mimme	Mími
A man of colour	Mangho tan-gata	
A gun-lock	Mootoo-pararo	
A bait for fish	Maoonoo	
Common	Noa	

English.	New Zealand.	Tonga.
Small	Noe noe	
Great	Nue nue	
A wave	Naddoo	Gna'loo
A sand-fly	Nammoo	
A button	Narkee	
Last night	Napo	
Fat	Narko	Gnáco
A fly	Nárro	La'ngo
Of	No	
Whose	Nawké	
A scratch	Nattoo	
A tooth	Nehoo	Ni'fo
To bite	Nau (or gnaw)	Oo'-oo
A sharp point	Oka	
Life, health, &c.	Ora	Möoo'i
Who	Owhi	Coha'i; ah'ae
The ground	Oronownee	
A valley	Oworoha	
A river	Owah	
A rope	Orahikee	
Father	Pa	
Night	Po	
Dirt	Paddoo	
A bell, drum, &c.	Páhoo	
A war club	Pattie	
The ball of the hand	Parlo	
The breech	Papa	
To kill	Patua	
To get upon the back	Pekou	
A cockle	Pippee	

English.	New Zealand.	Tonga.
The navel	Peto	Bi'to
A knot	Pona	
To tie a knot	Ponaæa	
A cabbage	Poka	
The wrist	Punapuna	
A ship's block	Pookoo	
An anchor	Poongha	
A hat	Poti	
Short	Poto	Nono
Smoke	Powha	
A sow thistle	Poowha	
A mountain	Pooka	Möoo'nga
A musket	Poo	
To fire a musket	Poohéa	
The shoulder	Pooka-hieve	
A box	Pophaw	
The beard	Pihow	
The outside mat that they wear over the shoulder.	Pagata	
A pipe for smoking	Pohee-pohee	
A white man, (the flea is also called by this name, as they assert it to have been first introduced into their country by Europeans —the turnip is likewise called packahâ from its whiteness)	Packahâ	

English.	*New Zealand.*	*Tonga.*
A muscle	Pooréffas	Chicoo'coo
The green-stone (jade) of which they make their axes, pattoo-pattoos, and ear ornaments	Pooheenau	
A parrot	Powhytarnee	
A duck	Panada	
A great gun	Poodee whennah	
The sun	Ra	La'ä
The forehead	Rie	Láë
Long	Roa	Lo'a ; lolo'a
Timber	Racóu	Aco'w
The sky, or heaven	Ránghee	L'angi
Great	Ráhe ráhe	La'hi
They three, or more	Ratoo	
They two	Rahooa	
To itch	Rákkoo rákkoo	
Sweet	Rékka-rékka	
Brains	Roro	Oo'to
Flaggy grass	Roupo	
A scratch	Rakkoo rakkoo	Maco'hi
A gentleman	Rungateeda	
Rest	Ra-tabboo	
A female deity in the moon	Rona	
Wind	Shou	
A good wind	Shoupi	
A bad wind	Shoukeno	
Excrements of the nose	Shoopa	

English.	New Zealand.	Tonga.
To wash	Shoroea	
To dance	Shákka	
South wind	Shou-houdoo	
West wind	Shou-dāno	
A tree	Tee	
Lewd	Tei	
An oyster	Teo	
To write	Tue tue	
Sacred	Tábboo tabboo	
To weep	Tánge tánge	Tan'gi
Biscuit	Tarro	
Grass	Táddoo tád-doo	Mahoo'goo
To forsake	Tiwa	
A little boy	Tamittee	
An infant	Tarnee	
A brother and sister	Tana	Tehina (brother)
A door	Tattou	
To hang by the neck	Tárrona	
A lie	Tékka tékka	
To row	Tohéa	Towa'lo
A whale	Tohora	Tofou'
An albatross	Toroá	
A bird	Toohee	
A stone	Toka	Ma'ca
An axe, &c.	Tokee	To'gi
A root	Toomoo	Too'boo (to take root)
Blood	Totto	Ta'wto
To bake	Touna	
A large spear	Tow	

English.	New Zealand.	Tonga.
To nod	Túngho	
The elbow	Tuka tuka	
The knee	Turee	To'oi
Dung	Tuti	Ta'e
Deafness	Tooree	Too'lli
A stick	Tókko tokko	Va aców
To strike	Tókko tokke-héa	
To fetch	Tara	
A man	Tungata	Tangata
Sea biscuit	Tarro	
Iron	Tokee	
The back	Tuararo	Too'a
Water	Whi	Vy
Nail	Wou	Fao
A woman	Whyeenee	Fafi'ne
A star	Whittoo	Fetoo'
A spirit	Whidooa	Hotoo'a
Land	Whénua	Fonnoo'a
A leg	Whitohi	
A mosquito	Whiro	
Milk	Whihoo	Hoo'hoo
A cause	Wauga	
Lightning	Weeda	
Veins	Wóuwa	
Hail	Wháttoo	
A house	Warree	Fa'lle
The bowels	Wakou	Gua'ców
The tail	Whiro	I'goo
Thunder	Watteeteeda	
The mouth	Wahha	

English.	*New Zealand.*	*Tonga.*
Sweet water	Whydecka	
The heart	Watteemau-nowha	
A friend	Wanhoungha	

SENTENCES.

English.	*New Zealand.*
What do you want?	Aána ra?
Run to me	Kahoro mi
Run to me	Kahoro mi ra
Run away	Kahoro attoo ra
I am bad	Kakeno aou
I am good	Kapi aou
Art thou well?	Koea ta oura?
Art thou ill?	Koea ta mátte?
I am well	Koou ta oura
I am ill	Koou ta mátte
The sun is set	Kapo tu ra
I love thee	Karoha aou ke eakoe
I hate thee	Kakeno aou ke eakoe
I love the man	Karoha aou ke ta tungata
I love the woman	Karoha aou ke ta whyeenee
I am very hungry	Kamátte aou e te eaki
I am very thirsty	Kamáttee aou e ta whi
Wilt thou drink water?	Kaenu a koea ta whi?

English.	*New Zealand.*
Yes! I will drink	Ai! kaenu aoa
Fetch some good water	Tara ta whi maoude
Fetch some sea water	Tara ta whi moana
Get thou up and go away	Wakkateeka a koe ire
Go thou	Ire attoo ra
Sit thou	Ekona ra
What dost thou want here?	Aána a koe ekona?
Go away	Ire attoo ra
To-morrow return	Appopo ka yooke mi
Where art thou going?	Kohaa a koea ka ire?
I am going to Tippoonah	Aire éna ou ke Tippoonah
Where dost thou eat?	Kohaa a koe a kiei?
Above at Ranghee Hoo	Kedunga e Ranghee Hoo
How many?	Toko hea?
Good is the word of the great Atua to me	Kapi ta koraro no ta Atua Nue ke ou
God is the name of the great Atua	God ta ingoa no ta Atua Nue
Jesus Christ is the son of the great Atua	Iesus Christ ta tamo neke no ta Atua Nue
Great is the love of Jesus Christ	Kanue ta Aroha no Iesus Christ
Great is the love of Jesus Christ to me	Kanue ta Aroha ke a ou no Iesus Christ
The way of God is good. The way of man is bad	Kapi ta Hara no God. Kakeno ta Hara no Tungata
Thou art a good friend to me	Wanhoungha pi eakoe ke a ou
Thou art a bad friend to me	Wanhoungha keno eakoe ke a ou

English.	*New Zealand.*
Thou and I are good friends	Wanhoungha pi taooa
A friend to me	Wanhoungha ke ou
Thou art my elder brother or sister	Tuakunna koe ke aou
I am thy younger brother or sister	Tana aou ke a koe
I am thy elder brother or sister	Tuakunna ou ke a koe
Thou art my younger brother or sister	Tana koe ke aou
Behold! Jesus Christ is the great and good Atua, the great and good friend to white and black men; to all men	Na! Iesu Christ ta Atua Nue, ta Atua Pi, ta wanhoungha Nue, ta wanhoungha Pi ke ta no-tungata na, Pakkahah, ke ta na tungata maoude, ke ta tungata katoa katoa
The little boy does not wash his hands and face	Tamitee aquorre shoroe na díngha díngha a matta
Wash thou thy hands and face	Shoroe akoe na díngha dingha a mátta
It is very cold. I go to warm myself at the fire	Kamátte ta makkadede. Ka-ire aou kahenina e ta áhe
In the morning, breakfast ended, sail	Attaata keaki, kamootoo, kahoy
When does the canoe come? to-morrow?	Ahaa hoowhi ta wauga? Appopo?
Yes! to-morrow it comes	Ai! appopo hoowhi
When does the man come? the day after to-morrow?	Ahaa iremi attao tungata? Attoo tida?

English.	*New Zealand.*
When do the people come to fight?	Ahaa hoymi ta na poohee e ta towha
The men are afraid they will not come	Aquorre ahoymi na tungata komattákkoo éna
Give me one fish-hook and two nails	Homi ati mattou, kadooa wou
I will give none	Aquorre ra hoáttoo
Give me some pork, bread and potatoes	Makoo ta ti wáhhe pork, tarro a na korropuma
Take some	Taneida
What are you talking about?	Aaha ta kohootoo a koraro?
What do you two want here?	Aáua kodooa ekoua?
We are looking about us	A titteedo no a nano
Where art thou going?	Kohaa a koe a ka ire?
I am walking about	A yooke yooke éna aou
Make a fire	Touna ta áhe
Make a fire	Touna wakkoúdea ta áhe
Go tell the man to come to eat	Tara ta tungata ka iremi keaki
I do not know the English language	Aquorre aou a matou ta kóraro no England
I do not see the English language	Aquorre aou a kittaa eta hóraro no England
The little boy makes a noise	Tamitee e tootoo
The little boys make a noise	Na tamitee e tootoo
The girl makes a noise	Koteedo e tootoo
The girls make a noise	Na koteedo e tootoo
The children make a noise	E tama e tootoo
Put down my raiment	Tooko a ke durro takoo kakkahow

English.	*New Zealand.*
Why dost thou stand up?	Aána a koe ta wakkateeka ekedunga?
Sit down	Eahora pa kedárro
I know the language of England well	Kamatou aou eta koraro no England kapi
Thou art laughing at me	Akátha mi éna a koe ke aou
What do we laugh at?	Aaha taoo akátha?
What art thou laughing at?	Aaha a koe akátha?
I am laughing at thee.	Akátha attoo éna aou ke a koe
What man gave that fish-hook to thee?	Nawhi ta tungata e homi tara máttou ke akoe
Friend! come let us barter for thread	Emera! iremi taooa koyoko millo millo
There is no wet, the ground is dry	Aquorre makookoo kakittaa ta unounee
See! the mother beat the little boy	Na! ta madua whyeenee e tókke tókke ta tamitee
Art thou well? Yes	Kaoura a koe? Eana
Art thou ill? Yes	Amatte éna a koe? Eana
Let us go above to eat fern-root	Kaire taooa kedunga kia-rohoei
Friend! is it strong to you? Yes	Emera! kakeoua ea koe? Ai
Friend! let us pound fern-root	Emera! poue arohe ma taooa
No, I will not pound it	Kioure, aquorre raou a poue
Friend! Good is the koo-mara of New Zealand	Emera! Api ta koomara no New Zealand

English.	*New Zealand.*
Come let us sit down and eat	Iremi taooa kekoue kiei
Give me some fire-wood	Homi ta ti wáhea
It is good to read the language of New Zealand	Kapi ta karakea a koraro no New Zealand
It is good to write the language of New Zealand	Kapi ta tue tue a koraro no New Zealand
I go to see the house	Kaire aou kakitta e ta warree
That will do, return, it is too far off	Kate, kate, yookemi, katowítte
Come hither, thou art cold	Iremi, kamatte a koe ta makkadede
Come hither and sit down and converse	Iremi kekoue a matou éna a koe
We sail in my canoe	Kahoy tatoo e to' wauga
Art thou going to sail in the boat ? Yes	Ahoy éna akoe ? Eana
I want to go to bed very much	Kamátte aou e ta eámoe
The canoe is sailing on the back of the island, by and by it will come	Kahetooa ra ta wauga, kahetooa e ta motoo, tiho ahoymi
Thou shalt not steal	Æaha koe e tahaiei
Thou shalt not kill	Aeaha koe e pattui
Thou shalt not work upon the day of the great Atua	Aquorre akoe emáhe ta ra no ta Atua Nue
Sacred is the day of the great Atua	Atappoo éna ta ra no ta Atua Nue
The great Atua made the Heaven and the Earth	Kamáhe ta Atua Nue, kamáhe ta Ranghee a ta wenua katoa

English.	*New Zealand.*
Jehovah is the name of the great Atua	Iehovah! ta ingoa no ta Atua Nue
God is the name of the great Atua	God! ta ingoa no ta Atua Nue
Lord is the name of the great Atua	Lord! ta ingoa no ta Atua Nue
Jesus Christ is the name of of the Son of the great Atua	Iesus Christ! ta ingoa no ta tamoneke no ta Atua Nue
God loved the world, he gave his Son for me	Karoha ta tungata katoa, God, eta tungata to nomi éna ta tamoneke ke ou
Great is the love of Jesus Christ for all men	Kanue ta arohá na Iesus Christ, ka nue ta aroha ke tatungata kotoa
Who is the Son of God?	Owhi ta tamoneke no God?
Jesus Christ is the Son of God	Iesus Christ ta tamoneke no God.
God hears the conversation of us men	Karúngho God, karúngho ta na koraro tatoo
Good is the word of God	Kapi ta koraro no God
God is love, he is not soon angry	Karoha mi God, kioure addide váva
Jesus Christ is love, he came to save the souls of us men	Karoha mi Iesus Christ, e ta iremi ra ke aoura na whidooano tatoo
Adam the first man, Eve the first woman	Adam ta tane matteréva, Eve ta whyeenee
Where did Adam and Eve dwell?	Kahea ta kahingha a toko-toi ta Adam ta Eve?
In Paradise	E Paradise

English.	*New Zealand.*
God is good to all men	Kapi God ke tungata kotoa tana
Behold! all men have of-fended God	Na! tungata katoa kadid-dee ta God
God is angry with bad men	Kadídde God, kena tun-gata keno
Thou art a good man to hear the word of God	Koea ta tungata pi karung-ho eta koraro na God
Thou art a bad man not to hear the word of God	Koea ta tungata keno aquorre arungho ta ko-raro no God
It is good to speak to God. It is life	Maapi ta karakea God. kaoura ea
No trade to-day, it is sa-cred; to-morrow trade	Aquorre ayoko iheenee, a tappoo éna appopo ka-yoko
Jehovah is above; his seat is in heaven	Kedunga ra ta Iehovah, ke ta Ranghee a kahingha
Devil is the name of the bad spirit	Devil ta ingoa no ta whi-dooa keno
Satan is the name of the bad spirit	Satan ta ingoa no ta whi-dooa keno
Satan is below. He dwells in darkness	Kedarro ra ta whidooa keno, ke ta po a kahingha
Behold! God said let there be light, and there was light	Na! koraro God whihokea marámma, a maramina aua no
God saw the light, a good light	Katítte ta maramma, God, a maramma pi
God called the light day, and the darkness night	Koraro God kahou ta ra, ra, káhehábe ta ra, po

English.	*New Zealand.*
The evening and morning the first day	Eattaáheáhe, eattaata, kotihi ra
God made the heavens the second day	Kamáhe God, kamáhe ta Ranghee, kadooa ra
God made the earth, the sea, the grass and trees the third day	Kamáhe God, kamáhe ta wenua, ta tie, ta taddoo taddoo a ta na rakou. Katoodoo ra
God made the sun, moon, and stars the fourth day	Kamáhe God, hamáhe ta ra, ta maràmma a na whittoo. Kawha ra.
God made the fishes, the fowls and whales the fifth day	Kamáhe God kamàhe ta na heeka, ta na manoo, ata na tora. Kadeema ra
God made the cattle and creeping things, and God made man out of the dust of the ground the sixth day	Kamàhe God, kamáhe ta na karáddee ta na narrara. Kamahe God, kamahe ta ti tungata no ta kiddeekiddee no ta ounounee, kahunnoo ra
God made sacred the seventh day	Katappoo éna ra, God; ka tappoo éna kawhittoo na ra
God said thou shalt not work upon the day of God	Koraro God. Aquorre akoe emmahe ta ra no God
A good man loves Jesus Christ much	Kanue ta aróha a tungata pi, kanue ta aroha Iesus Christ
Jesus Christ has great love for me	Kanue ta aróha Iesus Christ ke aou

English.	*New Zealand.*
A bad man am I, I have little love for Jesus Christ	Atungata keno aou, kaitte ta aroha ke Iesus Christ
The bad spirit hates all men	Kakeno ta whidooa keno ke ta tungata katoá
Jesus Christ says to all men, come to me, and have life	Koraro Iesus Christ ke ta tungata kotoa, iremi iremi, ka oura ea
Bible is the name of the Book of God	Bible ta ingoa no ta Booka Booka no God

---

NUMERALS.

English.	*New Zealand.*	*Tonga.*
One	Kotahi	Ta'ha
Two	Kadooa	Oo'a
Three	Ka-toodoo	To'loo
Four	Ka-wha	Fa
Five	Ka-deema	Níma
Six	Ka-hunnoo	O'no
Seven	Ka-whíttoo	Fi'too
Eight	Ka-wháddoo	Va'loo
Nine	Ka-hewha	Hi'va
Ten	Kanghahoodoo	Ongofoo'loo
Eleven	Kanghahoodoo mati	Ongofoo'loo ma ta'ha
Twelve	Kanghahoodoo madooa	Ongofoo'loo ma oo'a
Thirteen	Kanghahoodoo matoodoo	Ongofoo'loo ma to'loo
Fourteen	Kanghahoodoo mawha	Ongofoo'loo ma fa
Fifteen	Kanghahoodoo madeema	Ongofoo'loo ma níma
Sixteen	Kanghahoodoo mahúnnoo	Ongofoo'loo ma o'no
Seventeen	Kanghahoodoo mawhíttoo	Ongofoo'loo ma fi'too
Eighteen	Kanghahoodoo mawháddoo	Ongofoo'loo ma va'loo
Nineteen	Kanghahoodoo mahewha	Ongofoo'loo ma hi'va

English.	New Zealand.	Tonga.
Twenty	Katikow manahoodoo	Tecow (their term for score)
Forty	Kadooa tikow	
Sixty	Katoodoo tikow	
Eighty	Kawha tikow	
100	Kadema tikow	
120	Kahúnnoo tikow	
140	Kawhittoo tikow	
160	Kawháddoo tikow	
180	Kahewha tikow	
200	Kòtihi row	
400	Kadooa row	
600	Katoodoo row	
800	Kawha row	
1000	Kadeema row	
1200	Kahúnnoo row	
1400	Kawhittoo row	
1600	Kawháddoo row	
1800	Kahewha row	
2000	Kamánnoo	
4000	Kadooa mannoo, &c.	

APPENDIX.

No. I.

Extract from Collins's History of New South Wales, being an account of two New Zealanders left in Doubtless Bay, drawn up by the late Governor King.

Hoodoo-Cocoty Towamahowey is about twenty-four years of age, five feet eight inches high, of an athletic make, his features like those of an European, and very interesting. He is of the district of Teerawittee, which, by the chart of Toogee, the other New Zealander, is a district of the same name, but does not lie so far to the southward as the part of Eaheinomauwe called Teerawittee by Captain Cook; for we are certain that Toogee's residence is about the Bay of Islands, and they both agree that the distance between their dwellings is only two days' journey by land, and one day by water. That part called by Captain Cook Teerawittee is at a very considerable distance from the Bay of Islands.

Hoodoo is nearly related to Povoreek, who is the

principal chief of Teerawittee. He had two wives and one child, about whose safety he seemed very apprehensive; and almost every evening, at the close of the day, he, as well as Toogee, lamented their separation, in a sort of half crying and half singing, expressive of grief, and which was at times very affecting.

Toogee Teterrenue Warripedo is of the same age as Hoodoo, but about three inches shorter; he is stout and well made, and, like Hoodoo, of an olive complexion, with strong black hair. Both are tattooed on the hips. Toogee's features are rather handsome and interesting; his nose is aquiline, and he has good teeth. He is a native of the district of Hododoe, which is in Doubtless Bay; of which district Toogee's father is the *etangaroah*, or chief priest, and to that office the son succeeds on his father's death. Beside his father, who is a very old man, he has left a wife and child, about all of whom he is very anxious and uneasy, as well as about the chief, (Moodewy,) whom he represents as a very worthy character. Toogee has a decided preference to Hoodoo, both in disposition and manners; although the latter is not wanting in a certain degree of good-nature, but he can at times be very much of the savage. Hoodoo, like a true patriot, thinks there is no country, people, nor customs, equal to his own; on which account he is much less curious, as to what he sees about him, than his companion Toogee, who has the happy art of insinuating himself into every person's esteem. Except at times, when he is lamenting the absence of his family and friends, he is cheerful, often facetious, and very intelligent; and were it not for the different disposition of Hoodoo, the most favourable opinion might be formed of the New Zealanders in general. It is not, however, meant to be said, that if Toogee were not present, an indifferent opinion would have been formed of Hoodoo; on the contrary, the manners and disposition of the latter are far more pleasing than could have been expected to be found in a native of that country.

At the time they were taken from New Zealand, Toogee was on a visit to Hoodoo; and the mode of their capture was thus related by them. The Dædalus appeared in sight of Hoodoo's habitation in the afternoon, and was seen the next morning, but at a great distance from the main land. Although she was near two islands which are inhabited, and which Toogee in his chart calls Komootu-Kowa and Opanake, curiosity, and the hopes of getting some iron, induced Povoreek the chief, Toogee and Hoodoo, with his brother, one of his wives, and the priest, to launch their canoes. They went first to the largest of the two islands, where they were joined by Teeahworrak, the chief of the island, by Komootookowa, who is Hoodoo's father-in-law, and by the son of that chief, who governs the smaller island called Opanake. They were some time about the ship, before the canoe, in which were Toogee and Hoodoo, ventured alongside, when a number of iron tools and other articles were given into the canoe. The agent, Lieutenant Hanson, (of whose kindness they speak in the highest terms,) invited and pressed them to go on board, with which Toogee and Hoodoo were anxious to comply immediately, but were prevented by the persuasion of their countrymen. At length they went on board; and, according to their own expression, they were blinded by the curious things they saw. Lieutenant Hanson prevailed on them to go below, where they ate some meat. At this time the ship made sail. One of them saw the canoes astern; and when they perceived that the ship was leaving them, they both became frantic with grief; and broke the cabin windows, with an intention of leaping overboard, but were prevented. While those in the canoes remained within hearing, they advised Povoreek to make the best of his way home, for fear that he also should be taken.

For some time after their arrival at Norfolk Island, they were very sullen; and as anxiously avoided giving any information respecting the flax, as our people were desirous of obtaining it. The apprehension of being obliged to work at it, was afterwards found to have been a principal reason for their not complying so readily as was expected. By kind treatment, however, and indulgence in their own inclinations, they soon began to be more sociable. They were then given to understand the situation and short distance of New Zealand from Norfolk Island; and were assured that as soon as they had taught our women "*emoukaeurakake*," i. e. to work the flax, they should be sent home again. On this promise they readily consented to give all the information they possessed, and which turned out to be very little. This operation was found to be, among them, the peculiar province of the women; and as Hoodoo was a warrior, and Toogee a priest, they gave the Governor to understand, that dressing of flax never made any part of their studies.

When they began to understand each other, Toogee was not only very inquisitive respecting England, &c. (the situation of which, as well as that of New Zealand, Norfolk Island and Port Jackson, he well knew how to find by means of a coloured general chart,) but was also very communicative respecting his own country. Perceiving he was not thoroughly understood, he delineated a sketch of New Zealand with chalk on the floor of a room set apart for that purpose. From a comparison which Governor King made with Captain Cook's plan of those islands, a sufficient similitude to the form of the Northern Island was discoverable to render this attempt an object of curiosity; and Toogee was persuaded to describe his delineation on paper. This being done with a pencil, corrections and additions were occasionally made by him in the course of different conversations; and the names of districts and other remarks, were written from his information, during the six months he remained there. According to Toogee's chart and information, Eaheinomauwe, the place of his residence, and the northern island of New Zealand, is divided into eight districts, governed by their respective chiefs, and others who are subordinate to them. The largest of those districts is I'Sonduckey, the inhabitants of which are in a constant state of warfare with the other tribes, in which they are sometimes joined by the people of Moodoo-Whenua, Tettua Whoodoo, and Wangeroa; but these tribes are oftener united with those of Chokehanga, Teerawittee and Hododoe, against I'Sonduckey, the bounds of which district Governor King inclines to think is from about Captain Cook's Mount Egmont to Cape Runaway. They are not, however, without long intervals of peace; at which times they visit, and carry on a traffic for flax and the green talc stone, of which latter they make axes and ornaments. Toogee obstinately denied that the whole of the New Zealanders were cannibals: it was not without much difficulty that he could be persuaded to enter on the subject, or to pay the least attention to it; and whenever an inquiry was made, he expressed the greatest horror at the idea. A few weeks after, he was brought to own that all the inhabitants of Poenammoo, (i. e. the southern island,) and those of I'Sonduckey, ate the enemies whom they took in battle, which Hoodoo corroborated, for his father was killed and eaten by the I'Sonduckey people. " Notwithstanding the general probity of our visitors, particularly Toogee, (says Captain King,) I am inclined to think that horrible banquet is general through both islands."

Toogee described a large fresh-water river on the west side of Eaheinamouwe; but he said it was a bar river, and not navigable for larger vessels than the war canoes. The river, and the district around it, is called Chokehanga. The chief, whose name is Tokoha, lives about half way up on the north side of the river. The country he stated to be covered with pine-trees of an immense size. Captain King says that he made Toogee observe, that Captain Cook did not on his voyage notice any river on the west side, although he coasted along very near the shore. On this Toogee asked with much earnestness, if Captain Cook had seen an island covered with birds: Gannet island being pointed out, he immediately fixed Albatross Point as the situation of the river, which Captain Cook's account seems to favour, who says, " On the north side of this point (Albatross) the shore forms a bay, in which there appears to be anchorage and shelter for shipping." Governor King on this subject remarks as follows :—"The probable situation of this river (if there be one) being thus far ascertained, leads me to suppose that the district of I'Sonduckey extends from Cape Runaway on the east side, to Cape Egmont on the west; and is bounded by Cook's Strait on the south side, which is nearly one-half of the northern island. Of the river Thames I could not obtain any satisfactory account; but I have great reason to suppose that the river he has marked in the district of Wangeroa is the Thames. Toogee's residence appears to be on the north side of the Bay of Islands, in the district called by him Hododoe, which he says, contains about a thousand fighting men, and is subject to the following chiefs; i. e. Tewytewye, Wytoah, Moodewye, Waway, Tomocomoco, Pockaroo, and Tee-koora, the latter of whom is the principal chief's son."

The following are Governor King's remarks upon taking these people to their country :

" Having rounded the north cape of New Zealand on the 12th of November, 1793, the fourth day after leaving Norfolk, we saw a number of houses, and a small hippah, on an island which lies off the north cape, and called by Toogee Modee-Mootoo. Soon after, we opened a very considerable hippah, or fortified place, situated on a high round hill, just within the Cape, whence six large canoes were seen coming toward the ship. As soon as they came within hail, Toogee was known by those in the canoes, which were soon increased to seven, with upwards of twenty men in each. They came alongside without any intreaty; and those who came on board were much rejoiced to meet with Toogee, whose first and earnest inquiries were after his

family and chief.   On those heads he received the most
satisfactory intelligence from a woman who, as he informed us, was a near relation of his mother. His father
and chief were still inconsolable for his loss; the latter
(whom Toogee always mentioned in the most respectful
manner) had been, about a fortnight past, on a visit to
the chief of the hippah above-mentioned, where he remained four days; and Tewytewye, the principal chief
of Toogee's district, was daily expected.   With this information he was much pleased.   It was remarked that
although there were upward of a hundred New Zealanders on board and alongside, yet Toogee confined
his caresses and conversation to his mother, relation, and
one or two chiefs, who were distinguished by the marks
(amoko) on their faces, and by the respectful behaviour
which was shewn them by the emokis (i. e. the working men) who paddled the canoes, and who, at times,
were beaten most unmercifully by the chiefs.   To those
who, by Toogee's account, were epodis, (subaltern
chiefs,) and well known to him, I gave some chisels,
hand-axes, and other articles equally acceptable.   A
traffic soon commenced.   Pieces of old iron hoop were
given in exchange for abundance of manufactured flax,
cloth, pattoo-pattoos, spears, talc ornaments, paddles,
fish-hooks and lines.   At seven in the evening they left
us; and we made sail, with a light breeze at west, intending to run for the Bay of Islands, (which we understood was Toogee's residence,) and from which we
were twenty-four leagues distant.   At nine o'clock, a
canoe with four men, came alongside, who jumped on
board without any fear.   The master of the Britannia
being desirous to obtain their canoe, the bargain was

soon concluded, with Toogee's assistance, much to the satisfaction of the proprietors, who did not discover the least reluctance at sleeping on board, and being carried to a distance from their homes. Our new guests very satisfactorily corroborated all the circumstances that Toogee had heard before. After supper, Toogee and Hoodoo asked the strangers for the news of their country since they had been taken away. This was complied with by the four strangers, who began a song, in which each of them took a part, sometimes using fierce and savage gestures; and at other times, sinking their voices, according to the different passages or events that they were relating. Hoodoo, who was paying great attention to the subject of their song, suddenly burst into tears—occasioned by an account which they were giving, of the I'Sonduckey tribe having made an irruption on Teerawittee, (Hoodoo's district,) and killed the chief's son with thirty warriors. He was too much affected to hear more; but retired into a corner of the cabin, where he gave vent to his grief, which was only interrupted by his threats of revenge.

" Owing to calm weather, little progress was made during the night. At day-light on the 13th, a number of canoes were seen coming from the hippah; in the largest of which was thirty-six men and a chief, who was standing up, making signals with great earnestness. On his coming alongside, Toogee recognized the chief to be Kotokoke, who is the etiketica, or principal chief of the hippah whence the boats had come the preceding evening. The old chief, who appeared to be about seventy years of age, had not a visible feature, the whole of his face being tattooed with spiral lines. At his coming on board he embraced Toogee with great affection. Toogee then introduced me to him; and after the ceremony of 'ehongi,' (i. e. joining noses,) he took off his kackahow, or mantle, and put it on my shoulders. In return, I gave him a mantle made of green baize, and decorated with broad arrows. Soon after seven, other canoes, with upwards of twenty men and women in each, came alongside. At Toogee's desire, the poop was 'etaboo,' i. e. all access to it by any others than the old chief forbidden. Not long before Kotokoke came on board, I asked Toogee and Hoodoo, if they would return to Norfolk Island, or land at Moodee-Whenua, in case the calm continued, or the wind came from the southward, of which there was some appearance. Toogee was much averse to either. His reason for not returning to Norfolk was the natural wish to see his family and chief; nor did he like the idea of being landed at Moodoo-Whenua, as notwithstanding what he had heard respecting the good understanding there was between his district and that of Moodoo-Whenua, the information might turn out to be not strictly true.— Nothing more was said about it; and it was my intention to land them nearer to their homes, if it could be done in the course of the day, although it was then a perfect calm. Soon after the chief came on board, they told me with tears of joy, that they wished to go with Kotokoke, who had fully confirmed all they had heard before; and had promised to take them the next morning to Toogee's residence, where they would arrive by night. To wait the event of the calm, or the wind coming from the northward, might have detained the ship some days longer. Could I have reached in four days from Norfolk Island the place where Toogee lived, I certainly should have landed him there; but that not being the case, (as this was the fifth day,) I did not consider myself justifiable in detaining the ship longer than was absolutely necessary to land them in a place of safety, and from which they might get to their homes. Notwithstanding the information Toogee had received, and the confidence he had placed in the chief, I felt much anxiety about our two friends; and expressed to Toogee my apprehensions that what he had heard might be an invention of Kotokoke's and his people to get them and their effects into their power. I added, that as the ship could not be detained longer, I would rather take them back than leave them in the hands of suspicious people. To this Toogee replied, with an honest confidence, that 'etiketica no henerecka,' i. e. a chief never deceives. I then took the chief into the cabin, and explained to him, assisted by Toogee, (who was present with Hoodoo,) how much I was interested in their getting to Hododoe; and added, that in two or three moons I should return to Hododoe, and if I found Toogee and Hoodoo were safe arrived, with their effects, I would return to Moodoo-Whenua, and make him some very considerable presents, in addition to those which I should now give him and his people, for their trouble in conducting our two friends to their residence. I had so much reason to be convinced of the old man's sincerity, that I considered it injurious to threaten him with punishment for failing in his engagement. The only answer Kotokoke made was, by putting both his hands to the sides of my head, (making me perform the same ceremony,) and joining our noses, in which position we remained three minutes, the old chief muttering what I did not understand. After this, he went through the same ceremony with our two friends, which ended with a dance, when the two latter joined noses with me, and said, that Kotokoke was now become their father, and would in person conduct them to Hododoe. While I was preparing what I meant to give them, Toogee (who I am now convinced was a priest) had made a circle of the New Zealanders round him, in the centre of which was the old chief, and recounted what he had seen during his absence. At many passages they gave a shout of admiration. On his telling them that it was only three days' sail from Norfolk to Moodoo-Whenua, whether his veracity was doubted, or that he was not contented with the assertion alone, I cannot tell; but with much presence of mind he run upon the poop, and brought a cabbage which he informed them was cut five days ago in my garden. This convincing proof produced a general shout of surprise.

"Every thing being now arranged and ready for their departure, our two friends requested that Kotokoke might see the soldiers exercise and fire. To this I could have no objection, as the request came from them; but I took that opportunity of explaining to the chief, (with Toogee's help,) that he might see, by our treatment of him and his two countrymen, that it was our wish and intention to be good neighbours and friends with all Eaheinomauwe; that these weapons were never used but when we were injured, which I hoped would never happen; and that no other consideration than the satisfying of his curiosity could induce me to shew what those instruments were intended for.

" About one hundred and fifty of the New Zealanders were seated on the larboard side of the deck; and the detachment paraded on the opposite side.—After going through the manual, and firing three volleys, two great guns were fired, one loaded with a single ball, and the other with grape-shot, which surprised them greatly, as I made the chief observe the distance at which the shot fell from the ship. The wind had now the appearance of coming from the southward; and as that wind throws a great surf on the shore, they were anxious to get away. Toogee and Hoodoo took an affectionate leave of every person on board, and made me remember my promise of visiting them again, when they would return to Norfolk Island with their families. The venerable chief, after having taken great pains to pronounce my name, and made me well acquainted with his, got into his canoe and left us. On putting off from the ship, they were saluted with three cheers, which they returned as well as they could, by Toogee's directions. It was now seven in the morning of the 13th; at nine, a breeze came from the north, with which we stood to the eastward. After a passage of five days from New Zealand, (having had light winds,) and ten days' absence from Norfolk Island, I landed at three o'clock in the afternoon of the 18th.

" The little intercourse that I had with the New Zealanders (as I was only eighteen hours off that island, twelve of which were in the night) does not enable me to say much respecting them, or to form any decisive opinion of them; as much of their friendly behaviour in this slight interview might be owing to our connexion with Toogee and Hoodoo, and their being with us.—

These two worthy savages (if the term may be allowed)
will, I am confident, ever retain the most grateful re-
membrance of the kindnesses they received on Norfolk
Island; and if the greater part of their countrymen
have but a small portion of the amiable disposition of
Toogee and Hoodoo, they certainly are a people between whom and the English colonists a good understanding may, with common prudence and precaution,
be cultivated."

The Fancy, a vessel from Port Jackson, in about
two years after this visit of Governor King's, anchored
in Doubtless Bay, which the master describes as a very
dangerous place for a vessel to go into, and still worse
to lie at, as it is open to the easterly winds. On their
coming to an anchor, which was not till late in the
evening, (in December, 1795,) several canoes came
round the vessel; but did not venture alongside, until
Toogee was inquired for, when the New Zealanders
exclaimed, "Miti Governor King! Miti Toogee!
Miti Hoodoo!" Some went on board, and others put
in to shore, returning soon after with Toogee and his
wife. He informed Captain Dell that he had one pig
remaining alive, and some peas growing; but what became of the rest of his stock he did not say.

No. II.

Extract from Turnbull's Voyage Round the World, between the years 1801 and 1804.

Conceiving that it may not be altogether uninteresting to our readers, and as it in some degree falls within the order of our work, we shall in this place take some notice of the active and friendly intercourse that has of late years taken place between the colonists at Port Jackson and the neighbouring country of New Zealand; an intercourse that promised the most beneficial and important consequences, namely, the gradual civilization of a whole people, but by a melancholy fatality, over which humanity mourns, through the indiscretion of an individual, was rendered wholly abortive.

In our account of the settlement of New South Wales, we stated that the whale and seal fishery on that coast has of late years been a very profitable branch of enterprise both to the colonists and the whaling trade from Europe. We also stated that, at the time of the Government of Spain being forced into a union with France, the whalers were impelled by necessity to try the coast of New South Wales. Their first efforts so far rewarded their industry, that their number have been ever since upon an annual increase, so that this harvest, which at first proved so productive, after a time began to fail them. Necessity, however, being the mother of invention, some of them tried a new field, on the coast of New Zealand, where they were very successful.

Notwithstanding the ferocious character that had been assigned to the natives, some of our countrymen, after a time, ventured with great caution on shore, where they found them vigilantly on the alert, but at the same time without any disposition to offer hostilities, unless provoked to it by previous injury. From small beginnings, this intercourse ripened into an active and friendly communication, and almost every captain that landed had reason to be satisfied with his reception. When any of these captains touched or arrived at Port Jackson, the Government of that Colony was anxious to obtain from them every information relative to the Zealanders. They almost unanimously declared, that much might be effected by fair means; adding, that a chief of great power and authority resided near the Bay of Islands, and appeared to be a man who was at the same time sensible of the mutual advantages of friendly intercourse, and had the requisite qualities upon which to commence it. From the concurrent testimony of so many respectable characters, a considerable quantity of breeding stock of all kinds, and of every thing that might be of use to a people endeavouring after civilization, was sent upon various occasions. After a continuance for some time of this friendly intercourse, the chief expressed a desire, that he and five of his sons should pay a visit to his generous patrons; a request which was very readily complied with by a Captain Stewart, who, as he was not going immediately to Port Jackson, landed him at Norfolk Island. We shall relate the circumstances of his arrival and stay at Port Jackson, in the words of the Sydney Gazette, the official paper of that Colony.

" Tippahee having expressed a desire to visit his Excellency, Captain Stewart conveyed him, with five of his sons, to Norfolk Island, where they received every attention from the Commandant and inhabitants; and after remaining there some time, they were received on board his Majesty's ship Buffalo, to be conveyed to Port Jackson. On their arrival, Tippahee was introduced by Captain Houstin to his Excellency and the officers at the Government-house, where he continued to reside during his stay in the Colony.

" He appears to be about fifty years of age, five feet eleven inches and a half high, and of an athletic form. His countenance is expressive and commanding, though much disfigured by being completely tattooed.

" Shortly after his arrival, a number of the natives assembled in the vicinity of Sydney, for the interment of Carrawaye, (whose death was occasioned by a spear-wound in the knee, which ended in a mortification,) who the night before was conveyed here in a shell composed of strips of bark; and the funeral obsequies being over, a war spectacle ensued, when an intended sacrifice to vengeance, (known by the name of Blewit,) was singled out to answer for the desperate wound by him inflicted upon young Baker. The animosity of his assailants was uncommonly remarkable; their party was far the more powerful, and, confident of their superiority, took every advantage of their numbers. The flight of spears was seldom less than six, and managed with a precision that seemed to promise certain fatality. After 170 had been thus thrown, ten of the most powerful stationed themselves so as nearly to encircle the culprit, and front and rear darted their weapons at the same instant. His activity and strong presence of mind increased with the danger: five he dexterously caught with his feeble target, and the others he miraculously managed to parry off. One of his friends, enraged at the proceedings, threw a spear, and received ten in return. Blewit turned one of his assailant's spears, and passed it through the body of old Whitaker: the affray then became general, but terminated without further mischief.

"Tippahee, who with several of his sons was present, regarded their warfare with contempt; he frequently discovered much impatience at the length of intervals between the flights, and by signs exhorted them to dispatch; he considered the heelaman, or shield, an unnecessary appendage, as the hand was sufficient to turn aside and alter the direction of any number of spears. He nevertheless highly praised the woomera, or throwing stick, as, from its elasticity, he acknowledged the weapon to receive much additional velocity. He was visibly chagrined when he saw the old man wounded through the body, and would certainly have executed vengeance upon its author, had he not been restrained by the solicitations of the spectators. The natives formed some extravagant notions of this stranger: they dreaded to approach him, and as much as possible avoided him; but whether from a deference to his rank, presumed from the very great attention shewn him, or from superstitious apprehensions excited by his appearance, is undeterminable; though the latter is by far

the more probable conjecture. One of his sons conversing familiarly with a large group of the natives on the
use of the spear, his remarks were generally acquiesced
with. He requested the loan of one of their weapons,
which was immediately presented, but as soon as he took
it in his hand, they all fled, men, women and children,
and could not by all his friendly assurances be prevailed
upon to return until he had laid it aside.

" It cannot be supposed that Tippahee's high relish
for civilization, would find an agreeable object for contemplation in the manners of a naked race, who have
for so many years disregarded its advantages; nor can it
be imagined that the implacable arraignment of a fellow-creature for an offence which custom compelled
him to commit, as was here the case, would in anywise
accord with his sentiments of justice."

The character of Tippahee is thus further described
by a very respectable colonist, who saw him often, and
seems to have observed him with a very discriminating
intelligence.

" Tippahee," says this observer, " appears to be a
man of superior understanding ; he was very inquisitive,
and examined with great attention the various manufac-
tures that were carrying on by the settlers. He was
particularly struck with the art of spinning pack-
thread and cord, and with weaving, and expressed his
deep concern that these arts were not known in his
country. He made very shrewd and just remarks on the
laws and police of the Colony, and appeared very desirous to take back with him some artizans, who might
introduce amongst his people the advantages of civilized life. From a single potatoe left with him some

years since, he is said to have filled the country with that useful root, the value of which he had the sagacity to appreciate. He personally inspected its culture, preserved the cuts, and took methods for the general planting of them throughout his district. He is now enabled to supply European vessels with that important article of food."

The chief and his sons continued here for some time. Upon their departure, in order to cultivate so promising an opening, the Governor fitted up a colonial vessel with every accommodation, and, adding a great number of appropriate presents, sent them honourably home. On the passage, however, the chief was taken sick, and a young man belonging to the vessel was ordered to wait upon him. So pleased was he with the attention of this young man, that he particularly requested the captain of the vessel to leave him with him. The captain knowing the Governor's intentions to indulge him in every thing to the very utmost of his wishes, readily consented. The young man himself was equally well inclined to accept the invitation, and thus, to all human appearance, an intercourse was opened, which promised the most important results.

The young man lived constantly under the roof of his benefactor, and having acquired a knowledge of the language, the chief gave him his daughter in marriage, and he became his factor and interpreter between all the shipping that touched there. While every thing was thus proceeding to the content of the chief, to that of the young man, and to the interest of that of the two countries, a most melancholy vicissitude was at hand,—one of those events which almost make an

Englishman ashamed of acknowledging, that the perpetrator belonged to his country; a country not only the most distinguished in the civilized world, but which, for its high honour and national probity, most amply deserves to be so.

In order that we may relate this lamentable adventure fairly, and without any suspicion of personal bias, we shall give it in the words in which it appeared in the Calcutta Journals.

" We have to relate in substance," says the writer, " the following afflicting narrative, of which the parties are, an Englishman of the name of Bruce, a princess of New Zealand, the daughter of Tippahee, and a captain of the name of Dalrymple.

" George Bruce, son of John Bruce, foreman and clerk to Mr. Wood, distiller at Limehouse, was born in the parish of Ratcliffe Highway, in 1779. In 1789 he entered on board the Royal Admiral East Indiaman, Captain Bond, as boatswain's boy. Sailed from England for New South Wales, and arrived at Port Jackson in 1790; where, with the consent of Captain Bond, he quitted the ship, and remained at New South Wales.

" At Port Jackson Bruce entered into the colonial naval service, and was employed for several years under Lieutenants Robins, Flinders and others, in exploring the coasts, surveying harbours, head-lands, rocks, &c. During this time, Bruce experienced various adventures, which do not come within the design of this narrative. After being thus employed for several years in vessels of survey, he was turned over to the Lady Nelson, Captain Simmons, a vessel fitted up for the express purpose of conveying Tippahee, king of

New Zealand, from a visit which he made to the Government of Port Jackson, to his own country. The king embarked, and the Lady Nelson sailed on her destination. During the passage Tippahee was taken dangerously ill, and Bruce was appointed to attend him; he acquitted himself so highly to the king's satisfaction, that he was honoured with his special favour; and, on their arrival, the king requested that he should be allowed to remain with him at New Zealand, to which Captain Simmons consented, and Bruce was received into the family of Tippahee.

" Bruce spent his first months in New Zealand in exploring the country, and in acquiring a knowledge of the language, manners and customs of the people. He found the country healthy and pleasant, full of romantic scenery, agreeably diversified by hills and dales, and covered with wood. The people were hospitable, frank and open; though rude and ignorant, yet worshipping neither images nor idols, nor ought that is the work of human hands; acknowledging one Omnipotent Supreme Being.

" As the king proposed to place the young Englishman at the head of his army, it was a previously necessary step that he should be tattooed, as, without having undergone that ceremony, he could not be regarded as a warrior. The case was urgent, and admitted of no alternative. He therefore submitted resolutely to this painful operation; and his countenance presents a master specimen of the art of tattooing.

This pre-requisite being performed, Bruce was recognized as a warrior of the first rank, naturalized as a New Zealander, received into the bosom of the king's family, and honoured with the hand of the princess Aelockoe, the youngest daughter of Tippahee, a maiden of fifteen or sixteen years of age, whose native beauty had probably been great, but which has been so much improved by the fashionable embellishments of art, that all the softer charms of nature, all the sweetness of expression, are lost in the bolder traits of tattooing.

" Bruce now became the chief member of the king's family, and was vested with the government of the island. Six or eight months after his marriage, the ships Inspector, the Ferret, a South Sea whaler, and several other English vessels, touched at New Zealand for supplies, and all of them found the beneficial influence of having a countryman and friend at the head of affairs in that island. They were liberally supplied with fish, vegetables, &c. &c.

" Our Englishman and his wife were now contented and happy, in the full enjoyment of domestic comfort, with no wants that were ungratified, blessed with health and perfect independence. Bruce looked forward with satisfaction to the progress of civilization, which he expected to introduce among the people, with whom by a singular destiny, he seemed doomed to remain during his life. While enjoying these hopes, the ship General Wellesley, about twelve or fourteen months ago, touched at a point of New Zealand, where Bruce and his wife then chanced to be. This was at some distance from the king's place of residence. Captain Dalrymple applied to Bruce to assist him in procuring a cargo of spars and benjamin, and requested specimens of the principal articles of produce of the island, all which was cheerfully done.

Captain Dalrymple then proposed to Bruce, to accompany him to the North Cape, distant about twenty-five or thirty leagues, where it was reported that gold-dust could be procured, and Captain Dalrymple conceived that Bruce might prove useful to him in the search for the gold-dust. With great reluctance, and after many entreaties, Bruce consented to accompany Captain Dalrymple, under the most solemn assurances of being safely brought back and landed at the Bay of Islands. He accordingly embarked with his wife on board the General Wellesley, representing, at the same time, to Captain Dalrymple, the dangerous consequences of taking the king's daughter from the island; but that fear was quieted by the solemn and repeated assurances of Captain Dalrymple, that he would, at every hazard, reland them at the Bay of Islands, the place from which they embarked. Being at length all on board, the Wellesley sailed for the North Cape, where they soon arrived and landed. Finding that they had been entirely misinformed as to the gold-dust, the Wellesley made sail, in order to return to New Zealand; but the wind becoming foul, and continuing so for forty-eight hours, they were driven from the island. On the third day the wind became more favourable, but Captain Dalrymple did not attempt to regain the island, but stood on for India. Bruce now gently remonstrated, and reminded him of his promises; to which Captain Dalrymple replied, ' that he had something else to think of, than to detain the ship, by returning with a valuable cargo to the island. Besides, he had another and a better island in view for him.'

" On reaching the Fegee or Sandal Wood Islands,

Captain Dalrymple asked Bruce, if he chose to go on shore, and remain there, when he declined, on account of the barbarous and sanguinary disposition of their inhabitants. Captain Dalrymple desired that he would choose for himself; and then took from him several little presents which he himself and his officers had given to him at New Zealand: these now were given to the natives of the islands, in the boats then alongside the vessel.

" Leaving the Fegee Islands, they steered towards Sooloo, visiting two or three islands on their passage; but the limits of this narrative do not admit of giving any account of the occurrences at those places, though they are not devoid of interest. After remaining four or five days at Sooloo, they sailed for Malacca, where they arrived in December last.

" At Malacca, Captain Dalrymple and Bruce went ashore. The latter was anxious to see the Governor or commanding officer, to state his grievances; but as it was late in the evening when he landed, he could not see him till the following morning, by which time Captain Dalrymple had weighed from Malacca roads, leaving Bruce on shore, and carrying off his wife on board the Wellesley to Penang.

" Bruce acquainted the commanding officer at Malacca with his case, and expressed his wish to regain his wife, and to return with her to New Zealand. The commanding officer endeavoured to console him; desired that he would patiently wait at Malacca, for a short time, as some ships might probably touch there, on their passage from Bengal to New South Wales, by which he would procure a passage for himself and his wife;

and that, in the mean time, he would write to Penang, desiring that his wife should be returned to her husband at Malacca.   After waiting for three or four weeks, accounts were received of Captain Dalrymple's arrival at Penang, upon which Bruce obtained the commanding officer's permission, and left Malacca in the Scourge gun-brig, for Penang, where upon his arrival he found that his wife had been bartered away to Captain Ross. On waiting upon the Governor of Penang, he was asked what satisfaction he required for the ill treatment he had experienced; Bruce answered, that all he wanted was to have his wife restored, and to get a passage, if possible, to New Zealand.   Through the interference of the Governor, his wife was restored to him.   With her he returned to Malacca, in hope of the promised passage to New South Wales; but as there was no appearance of the expected ships for that port, he was now promised a passage for himself and his wife to England, in one of the homeward-bound Indiamen from China.   By getting to England, he hoped from thence to find a passage to New South Wales; but the China ships only anchored in Malacca roads for a few hours during the night, so that he had no opportunity of proceeding by any of the ships of that fleet.   He then entreated the commanding officer to get him a passage in the Sir Edward Pellew to Penang, where he hoped to overtake the Indiamen.   A passage for himself and his wife was accordingly provided on board the Pellew; and, on his arrival at Penang, he found the Indiamen remaining still there; but he could not be accommodated with a passage to Europe, without the payment of 400 dollars.   Not having that sum, and without the means

to raise it, he came on with the Sir Edward Pellew to
Bengal, where he and his wife, the affectionate companion of his distress, have been most hospitably received,
and where their hardships and sufferings will be soothed
and forgotten in the kindness that awaits them. Opportunities will probably occur, in the course of a few
months, of a passage to New South Wales, from whence
they will find no difficulty in regaining New Zealand."

No. III.

Memoirs of Duaterra, a New Zealand Chief, as given by Mr. Marsden in a letter addressed to the Reverend J. Pratt, Secretary to the Church Missionary Society.

Parramatta, 28th October, 1815.

DEAR SIR,

I mentioned in my public letter to the Society, forwarded by the Sydney Packet in June last, that Duaterra was dangerously ill at the time I left New Zealand in February, and was very apprehensive he would not recover. I was much concerned to hear from Mr. Kendall's last communication, that Duaterra died about four days after the Active sailed. As this young chief has been one of the principal instruments, in the hands of a wise and gracious God, in preparing a way for the introduction of the arts of civilization and the knowledge of Christianity into his native country, the following short narrative of his life, since I became acquainted with him, nearly ten years ago, may not be uninteresting to the Society.

In 1805, the Argo whaler, commanded by a Mr. Baden, put into the Bay of Islands for refreshments; on this vessel leaving the harbour, Duaterra embarked on board of her with two of his countrymen. The Argo remained upon the coast for about five months, and then returned into the Bay. On the vessel's final departure from New Zealand for Port Jackson, Duaterra went in her, and arrived in Sydney Cove; after the vessel was ready for sea again, she went to fish on the coast of New Holland, where she remained about six months, and afterwards put into Port Jackson. During this cruize, Duaterra acted in the capacity of a common sailor, and was attached to one of the whale-boats. When the Argo lay in Sydney Cove, Duaterra was discharged from her, but received no reward for his services during the twelve months he had been on board. On his leaving the Argo, he entered on board the Albion whaler, then in the Cove, commanded by Captain Richardson, and was six months on the fishery in that vessel off the coast of New Zealand. When she put into the Bay of Islands, Duaterra left her, and returned to his friends. Here Captain Richardson behaved very kind to him, and paid him his wages in various European articles, for his services on board the Albion. Duaterra remained in New Zealand six months, when the Santa Anna whaler anchored in the Bay of Islands, on her way to Bounty Island, whither she was bound for seal-skins. Duaterra embarked on board this vessel, commanded by a Mr. Moody. After she had taken in her supplies from New Zealand, she proceeded on her voyage, and arrived at Bounty Island in safety, when Duaterra with one of his countrymen, two Otaheitans and ten Europeans, were put on shore to kill seals; and afterwards the vessel sailed to New Zealand to procure potatoes, and to Norfolk Island for pork, leaving the fourteen men they had landed with very little water, salt provisions, or bread. When the Santa Anna arrived off Norfolk Island, the master went on shore, and the vessel was blown off, and did not make the land for one month. About five months after leaving Bounty Island, the King George arrived, commanded by Mr. Chase. Previous to the arrival of this vessel, the sealing party had been greatly distressed, for more than three months, for want of water and provisions. There was no water on the island, nor had they any bread or meat, excepting seals and sea-fowl. Duaterra often spoke of the extreme sufferings which he and the party with him endured from hunger and thirst, as no water could be obtained, except when a shower of rain happened to fall. Two Europeans and one Otaheitan died from hardship. In a few weeks after the arrival of the King George, the Santa Anna returned, and the sealing party, during her absence, had procured 8000 skins. After taking the skins on board, the vessel sailed for England; and Duaterra having long entertained an ardent desire to see King George, embarked on board as a common sailor, with the hope of gratifying his wish. The Santa Anna arrived in the river Thames about July 1809. Duaterra now requested that the Captain would indulge him with a sight of the King, which was the only object that had induced him to leave his native country. When he made inquiries by what means he could get a sight of the King, he was sometimes told that he could not find the house, and at other times, that nobody was permitted to see King George. This distressed him exceedingly, and he saw little of London, being seldom permitted to go on shore. In about fifteen days, he told me the vessel had discharged her cargo, when the captain told him, that he should put him on board the Ann, which had been taken up by Government to convey convicts to New South Wales. The Ann had already dropped down to Gravesend, and Duaterra asked the master of the Santa Anna for some wages and clothing, but he refused to give him any, telling him that the owners at Port Jackson would pay him in two muskets, for his services, on his arrival there, but these he never received. About this time, Duaterra, from hardships and disappointments, was seized with a dangerous illness. Thus friendless, poor and sick, as he was, he was sent down to Gravesend, and put on board the Ann. At this time he had been fifteen days in the river, from the first arrival of the Santa Anna, and had never been permitted to spend one night on shore. The master of the Ann, Mr. Charles Clark, afterwards informed me, that when Duaterra was brought on board the Ann, he was so naked and miserable, that he refused to receive him, unless the master of the Santa Anna would supply him with a suit of slops, observing at the same time, that he was very sick. I was then in London, but did not know that Duaterra had arrived in the Santa Anna. Shortly after Duaterra embarked at Gravesend, the Ann sailed for Portsmouth; I had been ordered by Government to return to New South Wales by this vessel, and joined her in a few days after she had come round to Spithead. When I embarked, Duaterra was confined below by sickness, so that I did not see him, or know he was there for some time.   On my first observing him, he was on the forecastle, wrapped up in an old great coat, very sick and weak, had a very violent cough, and discharged considerable quantities of blood from his mouth.   His mind was very much dejected, and he appeared as if a few days would terminate his existence. I inquired of the master where he had met with him, and also of Duaterra what had brought him to England, and how he came to be so wretched and miserable.   He told me the hardships and wrongs he had experienced on board the Santa Anna were exceedingly great, and that the English sailors had beaten him very much, which was the cause of his spitting blood; that the master had defrauded him of all his wages, and prevented his seeing the King.   I should have been very happy if there had been time to have called the master of the Santa Anna to account for his conduct, but it was too late; I endeavoured to sooth his afflictions, and assured him that he should be protected from insults, and that his wants should be supplied.

By the kindness of the surgeon and master, and by proper nourishment administered to him, he began in a great measure to recover both his strength and spirits, and got quite well, some time before we arrived at Rio de Janeiro.   He was ever after truly grateful for the attention that was shewn to him.   As soon as he was able, he did his duty as a common sailor on board the Ann, till she arrived at Port Jackson, in February 1810, in which capacity he was considered equal to most of the men on board.   The master behaved very kind to him.   He left the Ann, and accompanied me to Parra-matta, and resided with me till the November following, during which time he applied himself to agriculture. In October the Frederick whaler arrived from England, and was bound to fish on the coast of New Zealand. Duaterra having been now long absent from his friends, and wishing to return, requested I would procure him a passage on board the Frederick to New Zealand. At that time one of Tippahee's sons, a near relation of Duaterra's, was living with me, and also two other New Zealanders. They all wished to return home ; I applied to the master of the Frederick for a passage for them ; he agreed to take them, upon condition that they should assist him to procure his cargo of oil, while the vessel was on the coast of New Zealand, and that when he finally left the coast he would land them in the Bay of Islands. They were four very fine young men, had been a good deal at sea, and were a valuable acquisition to the master; I therefore agreed with him to take them upon his own conditions, on his promising to be kind to them.

On the Frederick's leaving Port Jackson in November, they all embarked in hopes of soon seeing their country and their friends. After the Frederick arrived off the North Cape, Duaterra went on shore two days to procure supplies of pork and potatoes, as he was well known there, and had many friends among the natives. As soon as the vessel had procured the necessary refreshments she proceeded on her cruize, and in about six months or a little more was ready to depart, having got in all her cargo. Duaterra finding that it was the master's intention to sail for England, requested that himself and his three companions might be put on shore

agreeably to the master's engagement with me, previously to their sailing from Port Jackson. At this
time the Frederick was at the mouth of the Bay of
Islands, where all their friends resided; Duaterra had
got every thing ready to put into the boat, expecting
immediately they would be sent on shore. When he
urged the master to land them, he replied, he would by
and by, so soon as he had caught another whale, and
the vessel bore away from the harbour. Duaterra was
now greatly distressed, as he was anxious to see his wife
and friends, having been absent about three years, and
earnestly requested the captain to land him on any part
of the coast of New Zealand; he did not care where it
was, if he would only put him on shore he would find
his way home. This the master refused to do, and told
him that it was his intention to go to Norfolk Island, and
thence proceed to England, and then he would land
them as he passed New Zealand on his way.

On the Frederick's arriving off Norfolk Island, Duaterra and his three countrymen were sent on shore for
water for the vessel, and were all nearly drowned in the
surf, having been washed under some hollow rocks; and
was in so much danger of loosing his life, that he
emphatically observed to me, that upon reaching the
surface " his heart was full of water." At Norfolk
Island it is generally extremely dangerous for a boat to
land on account of the surf. When the Frederick was
wooded and watered, and the master had no further
occasion for Duaterra and his three companions, he
then told them that he should not touch again at New
Zealand, but sail direct for England; Duaterra became
greatly distressed again, and reminded the captain how

he had violated his promise, and used him very ill in refusing to put him on shore when the vessel left the Bay of Islands, where he was then within two miles of his own place, and also refused to land him at the North Cape when he passed that land, and was now about to leave him at Norfolk Island, and his companions in a destitute situation where they had no friends, after all the assistance they had rendered him in procuring his cargo. However, nothing that Duaterra could say had any effect upon the master's mind, as he went on board his vessel, leaving them to provide for themselves. Duaterra further stated that the master afterwards returned on shore, and took Tippahee's son by force on board again, though he wept much, and intreated the master to let him remain with Duaterra. No tidings have been heard of this young man since he left Norfolk Island; the Frederick then sailed for England, and was taken on her passage home by an American, after a severe action in which the master was mortally wounded and the chief-mate killed. Some time after the Frederick sailed from Norfolk, the Ann whaler, commanded by Mr. Gwynn, touched there for refreshments, after procuring which she was to proceed to Port Jackson. Duaterra immediately applied to the master for a passage, who very humanely complied with his request.

On the Ann's arrival at Port Jackson, the master informed me, that he found Duaterra at Norfolk in a very distressed state, almost naked, as the master of the Frederick had left him and his companions without clothing or provisions. Mr. Gwynn further stated, that Duaterra's share of the oil that had been procured by the Frederick, and also that of his companions, would have amounted to 100*l.* each, had they accompanied the vessel to England, and she had arrived safe, and he thought they had been very much injured by the above master. Mr. Gwynn was very kind to Duaterra, and supplied him with necessary clothing and such things as he wanted, for which he was exceedingly grateful. Duaterra was very happy when he arrived once more in Parramatta, and gave me an affecting history of the distress he suffered while in sight of his own district, and not allowed to see his wife or friends, from whom he had been absent so long, and also what he felt when the Frederick finally sailed from Norfolk Island, leaving him upon that island with little hopes of returning to his native country. When he sailed from Port Jackson he was supplied with some seed-wheat, tools of agriculture, and various other useful articles. But of these he was despoiled in the voyage, and on his return to the colony had nothing left of all he had received. He continued with me at Parramatta till the Ann whaler, belonging to the house of Alexander Burnie of London, arrived from England. As this vessel was going on the coast of New Zealand, he requested I would procure him a passage on board the vessel, and he would try once more to see his friends; I accordingly applied to the master, and he agreed to take him, on condition that he would remain on board and do the duty of a sailor while the Ann was on the coast. To this Duaterra readily consented; and when the Ann left Port Jackson he embarked, taking with him some seed-wheat and tools of agriculture a second time. The vessel was five months on the coast, when Duaterra, with inexpressible joy to himself and his friends, was landed.

During the time he had lived with me, he laboured early and late to acquire useful knowledge, and particularly that of agriculture.   He was well aware of the advantages of agriculture in a national point of view, and was a good judge of the quality of land; he was very anxious that his country should reap the natural advantages which he knew it possessed, as far as it related to the cultivation of the land; and was fully convinced that the wealth and happiness of a nation depended much upon the produce of its soil.   When he was landed from the Ann, he took with him the wheat he had received at Parramatta for seed, and immediately informed his friends and the neighbouring chiefs of its value, and that the Europeans made biscuit of it, such as they had seen and eaten on board of ships.   He gave a portion of wheat to six chiefs and also to some of his own common men, and directed them all how to sow it, reserving some for himself and his uncle Shunghi, who is a very great chief, his domain extending from the east to the west side of New Zealand.   All the persons to whom Duaterra had given the seed-wheat put it into the ground and it grew well; but before it was well ripe many of them grew impatient for the produce, and as they expected to find the grain at the roots of the stems, similar to their potatoes, they examined the roots, and finding there was no wheat under the ground, they pulled it all up and burnt it, excepting Shunghi.   The chiefs ridiculed Duaterra much about the wheat, told him that because he had been a great traveller, he thought he could easily impose upon their credulity by telling them fine stories, and all he urged could not convince them that wheat would make bread.   His own and Shunghi's crops in time came to perfection, and were reaped and threshed; and though the natives were much astonished to find that the grain was produced at the top and not at the bottom of the stem, yet they could not be persuaded that bread could be made of it. About this time the Jefferson whaler put into the Bay of Islands, commanded by Mr. Thomas Barnes. Duaterra being anxious to remove the prejudices of the chiefs against his wheat, and to prove the truth of his former assertions that it would make biscuit, requested the master of the Jefferson to lend him a pepper or coffee mill, in order, if possible, to grind some of his wheat into flour, that he might make a cake, but the mill was too small and he could not succeed. By the arrival of a vessel at Sydney from New Zealand, he sent me word that he had got home at last, and had sown his wheat, which was growing well, but he had not thought of a mill. He requested me to send him some hoes and other tools of agriculture, which I determined to do by the first opportunity. A short time after, the Queen Charlotte belonging to Port Jackson cleared out for the Pearl Islands. As this vessel would have to pass the North Cape of New Zealand, 1 thought there was a probability of her touching at the Bay of Islands, and therefore put some hoes and other tools of agricul-ture on board, with a few bags of seed-wheat, and requested the master, Mr. William Shelley, to deliver them to Duaterra, should the Queen Charlotte touch at the Bay of Islands. Unfortunately the Queen Char-lotte passed New Zealand without touching any where, and was afterwards taken by the natives of Otaheite; and while the vessel was in their possession, all the wheat I had put on board, as well as some other things, were either stolen or destroyed. When I received this information, I was much concerned that Duaterra should be so disappointed from time to time in his benevolent exertions to forward the improvement and civilization of his countrymen, and was fully convinced that nothing could be done effectually for New Zealand, without a vessel for the express purpose of keeping up a communication between that island and Port Jackson.

When Mr. Kendall arrived in the Earl Spencer, who had been sent out under the patronage of your Society, I soon after determined either to take up a vessel or purchase one for the service of New Zealand, and to attempt to establish a settlement, which had been resolved upon by the Society in 1808, and for which purpose Messrs. Hall and King accompanied me on my return to New South Wales. I attempted to hire a vessel, but could not get one to go to New Zealand for less than 600*l.* which sum I considered too great for one single voyage. The brig Active at this time arrived from the Derwent, and the owner proposed to sell her; I therefore purchased her. As many dreadful massacres had been committed at New Zealand both by the natives and Europeans at different times, (the whole crew of the Boyd having been cut off not long before, and the vessel burnt,) I did not think it prudent to send the families of the settlers over in the first instance, but rather wished to go myself, if I could obtain permission from the Governor, and take with me Mr. Hall and Mr. Kendall. As I knew many of the natives, I had reason to suppose that I should have sufficient influence with them to forward my views, if I could only go myself; I could then fully explain to **Dua**-terra and the other chiefs, the great object the Society had in view in sending Europeans to reside amongst them.   After I had purchased the vessel, I waited upon His Excellency Governor Macquarie, and acquainted him with my intention, and explained to His Excellency, that the Society wished to form a settlement there, and requested permission to visit New Zealand.   The Governor did not judge it prudent to give his permission for my going at that time, but told me that if I sent the Active and she returned safe, he would then give me leave to accompany the settlers and their families when the vessel returned a second time, and then I might see them properly fixed. With this answer I was satisfied, having no doubt but the Active would return in safety, under the circumstances in which she was going to visit that island. I therefore ordered the vessel to be got ready for sea, and Messrs. Hall and Kendall to proceed to the Bay of Islands, where the natives whom I knew resided. When the Active sailed, I sent a message to Duaterra to inform him for what purpose I had sent over Messrs. Kendall and Hall, and invited him to return with them to Port Jackson, and bring along with him two or three chiefs. I sent him a steel mill to grind his wheat, a sieve and some wheat for seed, with a few other presents. On the arrival of the Active, the settlers were very kindly received by Duaterra and all the other chiefs, and every attention was paid to them for the six weeks they remained there.   Duaterra was much rejoiced to receive the steel mill.   He soon set to work and ground some wheat before his countrymen, who danced and shouted for joy when they saw the meal. He told me that he made a cake, and baked it in a frying pan, and gave it to the people to eat, which fully satisfied them of the truth he had told them before, that wheat would make bread. The chiefs now begged some more seed, which they sowed, and there can be little doubt but that they will soon appreciate the value of wheat. I saw some growing in January last exceedingly strong and fine; the grain was very full and bright when reaped, which leads me to believe the climate and soil of New Zealand will be very congenial to the production of that grain. Previous to the arrival of the Active, Duaterra had determined to visit Port Jackson in the first vessel that sailed from New Zealand for the colony, in order to procure a mill, hoes, and some other articles he stood in need of. He greatly rejoiced when the Active entered the Bay, as he hoped to get a passage in her; but on receiving the mill I sent with the seed-wheat, &c. he altered his mind, and said he would now apply himself to agriculture for two years, from his having the means of carrying on his cultivation and grinding wheat. His uncle Shunghi had at this time a great desire to visit Port Jackson, and as he is a very powerful chief, and hadn o friend in Port Jackson who could speak both the English and New Zealand languages, Duaterra determined to accompany him. He told me his wives, friends and people, earnestly requested him to stay with them. He endeavoured to persuade them that he would return in four moons, but this they disbelieved entirely, from an idea that the Active would never return more. The priest told him his head wife would die if he left her before his return.

This very woman hung herself the day after Duaterra died, on account of her tender love and affection for him. He told the priest he had often returned before, and should soon return again. Accordingly, he took his leave, with his uncle and a few more friends, and embarked for New South Wales, and safely arrived in about a month once more at Parramatta. During his stay at my house, I often saw him very thoughtful, and asked him what was the cause of his uneasiness. He would reply, "I fear my head wife is either dead or very sick." What the priest told him relative to his wife dying in his absence, evidently made a strong impression on his mind, though he had been about three years in my family before, and acted with great propriety all the time, and upon all occasions was willing to receive religious instruction. Yet the superstitious notions of their religion, which he had imbibed from his infancy at New Zealand, were deeply rooted in his mind; he had great confidence in what the priest asserted, and in the effect of their prayers. I refer you to my public letter of the account I there gave of Duaterra's attention when I arrived in the Active at the Bay of Islands; and also to Mr. Kendall's letter, transmitted by this conveyance, of what took place before, and at the closing scene of Duaterra's life and after. His death has been a subject of much pain and regret to me, and appears a very dark and mysterious dispensation. For the last ten years of Duaterra's life, he had suffered every danger, privation and hardship that human nature could bear. On my arrival with him at New Zealand with the rest of the settlers, he appeared now to have accomplished the grand object of all his toils, an object which was the constant subject of his conversation, namely, the means of civilizing his countrymen. He thus observed to me, with much triumph and joy, " I have now intro-" duced the cultivation of wheat into New Zealand; " New Zealand will become a great country in two " years more; I shall be able to export wheat to Port " Jackson, to exchange for hoes, axes, spades, tea, " sugar," &c. Under this impression, he made arrangements with his people for a very extensive cultivation, and formed his plan for building a new town with regular streets, after the European mode, on a beautiful situation which commanded a view of the mouth of the harbour and adjacent country. I accompanied him to the spot. We examined the ground fixed upon for the town, and the situation whefe the church was· to stand, and the streets were to have been all marked out before the Active sailed for Port Jackson. At the very time when these arrangements were to have been executed, he was stretched upon his dying bed. I could not but view him as he lay languishing beneath his affliction with wonder and astonishment, and could scarcely bring myself to believe that the Divine Goodness would remove from the earth a man whose life appeared of such infinite importance to his country, which was just emerging from barbarism and gross darkness and superstition. No doubt he had done his work, and finished his appointed course! though I fondly imagined he had only just begun his race. He was a man of clear comprehension, quick perception, and of a sound judgment, and a mind void of fear; at the same time he was mild, affable and pleasing in his manners. His body was strong and robust, and promised a long and useful life. At the time of his death, he was in the prime and vigour of manhood, extremely active and industrious. I judge his age to be about twenty-eight years. He was seized with a bowel complaint and as toppage in his breast, attended with difficulty of breathing and a high fever, about four days before his dissolution. In reflecting on this mysterious and awful event, I am led to exclaim, with the Apostle to the Gentiles, " Oh the heights and the depths of the wisdom and knowledge of God, how unsearchable are his judgments, and his ways past finding out !"

I have now, Sir, related a few of those changes and vicissitudes in the life of Duaterra, which either came under my own immediate observation, or were communicated to me by himself. From the whole of this little history, you and the Society will be able to form some idea of the national character of these people. I do not believe that there is in any part of the world, or ever was, a nation in a state of nature superior to the inhabitants of New Zealand in mental endowment and bodily strength, nor any who would in a shorter period render themselves worthy of being numbered with civilized nations, provided they were favoured with the ordinary means of instruction in those arts by which men are gradually refined and polished. I trust that the Society will prove their benefactors, and furnish them with the necessary means for their advancement in civilization; and in due time deliver them, through the divine favour, from the horrors and miseries of heathen darkness and bondage; and, Sir, as these people are literally without hope and without God in the world, that they will be led by your Association, through the medium of divine knowledge, to him that was born King of the Jews, as the star led the Eastern Magi. With every devout wish and ardent prayer that the glory of the Lord may be revealed to all these poor benighted heathens, and that they may see the salvation of God, and the work of the Lord prosper in your hands,

I have the honour to be,

Dear Sir,

Your very obedient humble servant,

S. MARSDEN.

To the Rev. J. Pratt.

FINIS.

Hughes and Baynes, Printers,
Maiden-Lane, Covent-Garden, London.

ERRATA.

VOL. I.

Page   5, line 24, for *coasts*, read *coast.*
    49, —— 22, for *arekee*, read *areekee.*
    56, —— 7 and 10, for *which*, read *who.*
   121, —— 25, for *in the Bay of Islands*, read *in the har-
         bour of Port Jackson.*
   138, —— 10, dele *other.*
   139, —— 20, for *packaka*, read *packahá.*
   215, —— 15, for *crimes*, read *crime.*
   308, —— 11, for *were*, read *was.*
   310, —— 23, for *of*, read *in.*

VOL. II.

Page 82, line 11, for *and made free*, read *and be made free.*

9 781108 008358